To Jan 11/27/06
Love, Nancy

Published by
Dispatch·Argus·Leader

Moline Dispatch Publishing Company, L.L.C.

Copyright 2006, all rights reserved.
First Edition

Printed by
Morris Press Cookbooks

ISBN 0-9761162-6-X

acknowledgements

Project Staff

Gerald J. Taylor • Publisher
Liz Meegan • Project Director
Sally E. Trulson • Book Production
Dale Attwood • Creative Director
Kermit T. Stevenson, III • Cover & Book Design
Heather A. McBride • Page Layout & Editor
Leslie Dupree • Editor
Spencer Rabe • Editor
Terry Herbig • Liz Meegan Cover Photograph
John Greenwood • Liz Meegan Introduction Photograph
Sara Adams • Recipe Processing
Brandy Welvaert • Recipe Processing

Special Thanks

All individuals who made contributions to this cookbook by submitting recipes, thoughts and memories over these many years.

table of contents

dining out favorites 5
　　make them at home

appetizers 49
　　teasing your palate

soups & salads 57
　　a great start or a simple meal

breads & rolls 73
　　make your home a bakery

main dishes 103
　　the center of attention

side dishes 139
　　making your meal complete

desserts 169
　　save the best for last

cookies & candies 245
　　sweet tasty morsels

index 293
　　find your favorites

cooking tips 299
　　find helpful hints

Dear Curious Cook

recipes to remember forever **3**

introduction
The Curious Cook
Liz Meegan

For 30 wonderful years, I've been opening mail that begins "Dear Curious Cook." The three-decades-old reader-response column has been, and still is, a pleasure, a privilege and a joy to write.

Those three words — Dear Curious Cook — have been so much a part of my professional life with the Moline Dispatch Publishing Co. Little did I realize when the column first was published back in 1976, that it would have such a long and happy life.

Curious Cook's column is devoted mainly to readers' requests for lost recipes, answers to those requests and to precious memories associated with foods. The column first was published by The Dispatch. When the Small Newspaper Group created The Leader and then acquired The Rock Island Argus in 1986, readers of those publications were warmly welcomed to the Curious Cook's circle. Readers of all three publications have become a family joined together in a fascinating search for treasured recipes.

Through many years, Curious Cook and her readers have found hundreds of lost recipes, shared family memories and learned plenty from each other about the ins and outs of cooking and baking. Followers of the column form a help-each-other network, which the newspapers are proud to encourage.

Now, a "Dear Curious Cook" cookbook has evolved from years of columns. It would be impossible to include all of the recipes that readers have shared and that Curious Cook has researched. So we've made a careful selection of recipes on file and proudly present them in this volume.

A few of the recipes were submitted by restaurants, schools and hospitals. But most are homespun treasures of our faithful readers and their families. They are "Recipes to Remember Forever."

I gratefully acknowledge all who have contributed in any way to the long run of Curious Cook's column — the management of the newspapers, co-workers for sure. Without the encouragement of my late husband, William T. Meegan, Curious Cook never would have been so long lasting. And for many years, Barbara VandeWiele, long-time Helping Hand columnist, lent a "Helping Hand" in the never-ending and joyful challenges of recipe searches, researches and proof-reading the signature column of The Dispatch, The Rock Island Argus and The Leader.

"Dear Curious Cook" is dedicated to legions of readers who, with loyalty, generosity and enthusiasm for recipes, have kept the column in print — and put this cookbook in your hands to read, to use and to enjoy.

Dec. 16, 1998

Belgian Village Pumpkin Nut Waffles

Curious Cook recently received this plea from an Alexis reader:

"When we lived in Moline, my husband and I would go to the Belgian Village for breakfast occasionally. About five years ago we enjoyed their pumpkin waffles. The waitress told us they only made them in the fall of the year.

"When we inquired about them the following year, we were told they no longer made them.

"I have searched numerous cookbooks for the recipe but cannot find one. If you have this recipe, I would be so grateful if you would publish it. If you don't have one, maybe your readers would send you one.

"They are so good, and I am hungry for them. Thank you for your help." — *M.A.S. of Alexis*

Curious Cook has good news: the official Belgian Village recipe, compliments of Loretta Ceurvorst, the First Lady of The Belgian Village Inn. The Pumpkin Nut Waffles no longer are served at the Belgian Village Inn, and Mrs. Ceurvorst, a good neighbor of Curious Cook, graciously released the waffle recipe to Curious Cook and her readers. Thank you, Loretta.

- 2 cups flour
- 1 tablespoon baking powder
- ¾ teaspoon pumpkin pie spice (See note)
- ¼ teaspoon salt
- 1/3 cup sugar (reserve 1 tablespoon to mix with egg whites)
- 3 egg yolks
- 1¾ cups milk
- ½ cup vegetable oil
- ½ cup canned pumpkin
- 3 egg whites
- ½ cup chopped pecans

Preheat waffle iron. Thoroughly stir together dry ingredients.

Beat egg yolks. Stir in milk, oil and pumpkin. Stir into dry ingredients.

Beat egg whites until soft peaks form; then add 1 tablespoon sugar. Beat until stiff but not dry. Fold into batter. Fold in nuts.

Pour batter onto hot waffle iron and bake. Repeat with remaining batter. Makes 6 cups waffle batter.

Note: "Instead of pumpkin pie spice, I used 1 teaspoon cinnamon, ½ teaspoon allspice, ¼ teaspoon nutmeg, ½ teaspoon ginger. Better flavor than commercial spice." — ***Loretta Ceurvorst of Moline***

Nov. 27, 1996

Canned Beef-Biscuit Pinwheels (From UTHS)

J.H. of Colona recently implored Curious Cook to help find a recipe for Pinwheels, a meat dish which was served a number of years ago in the student cafeteria at United Township High School, East Moline.

J.H.'s husband and friends described Pinwheels as a meat, possibly shredded pork, rolled in a biscuit-like dough, much like a jelly-roll, sliced, baked and served with gravy.

J.H. admitted she tried to improvise but had no luck!

Well, the very next morning, Curious Cook received a telephone call from E.J. of East Moline. E.J. says that a Mrs. Hicks was cafeteria manager at U.T.H.S. for years, and that there really is not a recipe — except for a large number of servings.

E.J. described Mrs. Hicks as "the best cook" and said she did have her directions for Canned Beef-Biscuit Pinwheels. She promised to share those directions.

E.J. also said it's possible that Mrs. Hicks took leftover beef and cut it up in small pieces for the filling. She probably rolled out a dough and spread the beef pieces on the dough. She put a lot of meat on it, E.J. said. Then Mrs. Hicks rolled up the dough, sliced it, baked it and then served the Pinwheels with gravy.

E.J. kept her promise to send Mrs. Hicks' quantity recipe to Curious Cook. It's called Canned Beef-Biscuit Pinwheels and here 'tis:

BISCUITS:
- 8 cups flour
- 3-1/3 teaspoons baking powder
- 2 teaspoons salt
- 1½ cups shortening
- 2-2/3 cups milk

FILLING:
- 2 No. 2½-size cans Beef and Gravy
- ½ cup grated cheese
- 1/3 cup onions fried in 2 tablespoons oil

Roll out dough; spread with filling. Roll up like a jelly-roll. Cut in 1½-inch slices and place slices on a greased baking sheet. Bake at 425 degrees for 20 to 25 minutes. Serve with gravy or mushroom sauce. "We increase this 20 times at cafeteria." — *E.J. of East Moline*

Nov. 8, 1995

Carrots Supreme (Lutheran Hospital)

"Once again I bring out my recipe book to fill requests found in the Oct. 18 Argus. P.D. of Colona is looking for carrot recipes. This one is wonderful and it comes from the Lutheran Hospital cafeteria."

- 1½ pounds carrots, peeled and sliced
- ½ cup chopped onion
- 2 ribs celery, chopped
- 1 can (10¾ ounces) cream of mushroom soup
- 1 can (2 ounces) mushrooms, drained
- 1/3 cup margarine
- 6 ounces American cheese, grated
- 1 cup bread crumbs

Partially cook vegetables; drain well. Saute onions and celery in margarine. Add soup, cheese, mushrooms, and one half of the bread crumbs; mix well and fold in carrots. Place mixture in a greased 2-quart glass baking dish and sprinkle with remaining bread crumbs. Bake, uncovered, at 350 degrees for 30 minutes. Serves 8.

— *V.M. of Rock Island*

Aug. 6, 1997

Cherry Coke Salad from Ranch Supper Club

This recipe is from J.M. of Princeton, Iowa, who writes: "While working at the old Ranch Supper Club, I used to make a Cherry Coke Salad. Don't know if this is the exact one J.G. of Rock Island has in mind, but it is as follows:"

- 1 can cherry pie filling
- ½ cup sugar
- 1¼ cups water
- 1 large package (6 ounces) cherry gelatin
- 12 ounces Coca-Cola
- Whipped topping

Combine cherry pie filling, sugar and water and cook until sugar dissolves. Add the cherry gelatin; mix well. Cool. Add the Coca-Cola and chill until set. Top with whipped topping.

— *J.M. of Princeton, Iowa*

Cranoccoli Salad (Oh Nuts)

Feb. 26, 1997

L.S.M. of Aledo sent this plea to Curious Cook.

"I'm looking for a recipe for a salad using dried cranberries and broccoli.

"I got the recipe at Oh Nuts, but someone took their only copy. The salad was truly delicious and I hope you can help me. I've lost my copy, too. Please help. Thanks."

Curious Cook immediately contacted Mary Jo Maloney, owner of the Oh Nuts, a specialty food store in Rock Valley Plaza, Rock Island. Mrs. Maloney checked for us and says she was fortunate to locate the recipe, but locate it she did! We thank her and here's the recipe:

- 1 head of broccoli, cut into VERY small pieces
- ½ cup sunflower seeds
- 1 cup dried cranberries
- ½ cup raisins
- ½ cup diced celery, diced in small pieces
- 1 small red onion, diced
- 1 pound bacon, fried, drained and crumbled

DRESSING:
- 1 cup mayonnaise
- ½ cup sugar
- 1 tablespoon cider vinegar

 Combine broccoli pieces, sunflower seeds, dried cranberries, raisins, diced celery and onion and crumbled bacon; mix gently.

 Pour dressing over salad and refrigerate at least 1 hour prior to serving.

Cleo Pompa's Enchiladas

Feb. 2, 1994

A.D. of East Moline has supplied us with the recipe for Mrs. Pompa's enchiladas to answer a recent request from R.S. of Bettendorf for directions for Mexican Enchiladas.

"I hope this is the recipe R.S. is looking for," writes A.D . "It's my favorite enchilada recipe but, being a busy 90s woman, I use the LaVictoria canned enchilada sauce instead of making it."

This recipe for Mrs. Pompa's Enchiladas previously was featured in Curious Cook, but the clipping is undated. But here's the recipe:

24 white or flour tortillas	**Tomato juice**
Chorizo sausage	**Salt and pepper, to taste**
Potatoes	**Shortening Crisco oil, lard, etc.**
Onion, as desired	**Lettuce**
Cheese, as desired	**Tomatoes**
Peas, optional	**Additional grated cheese**
Chile ancho peppers, dried	

FOR CHILE ANCHO SAUCE: Remove seeds from ¼ pound dried peppers. Rinse. Cover with water and boil for 20 to 25 minutes. Puree in blender. Pour into medium-size saucepan. Add about 2 cups tomato juice, and salt to taste. Set aside.

FILLING: Boil 8 to 10 medium potatoes. When cooked and cooled, dice. Fry 1 pound chorizo sausage in small amount of shortening. Add onion to sausage, and cook until onion is tender. Grate cheese; drain peas. In large pan, mix together potatoes, chorizo, onion, cheese and peas. Mix thoroughly. Salt and pepper to taste. Set aside.

Bring chile ancho sauce to a boil. Pour ¾ cup of hot shortening into chile mixture. Simmer this mixture for 10 to 15 minutes, stirring frequently. While chile sauce is cooking, grease cookie sheet. Have a flat plate ready for tortillas.

With tongs, dip tortillas, one at a time, into the chile mixture, just long enough to color. Stack on plate. Continue this until 10 tortillas have been dipped and stacked on plate.

Place approximately 1 large mixing spoon of the potato mixture in the center of each dipped tortilla. Roll tortilla around potato mixture and place in a single layer on greased cookie sheet. Continue this until all the tortillas have been dipped and filled.

Enchiladas may be layered on cookie sheet if a sheet of greased aluminum foil is used between layers. When cookie sheet is full, cover and seal edges with a large sheet of foil.

Heat in oven at 350 degrees for 25 to 30 minutes. Serve on a bed of lettuce and sliced tomatoes and top with additional grated cheese.

Note: Enchiladas may be prepared a day ahead, refrigerated and heated just before serving.   — *A.D. of East Moline*

Crisp Duck a la Five

Feb. 4, 2004

A reader recently enjoyed the Crisp Duck appetizer at Five, the sophisticated restaurant in downtown Moline, and asked for help obtaining the recipe so that he can prepare a similar dish at home.

Chef Dominic Rivera of Five graciously accepted the compliment by sharing his duck directions with Curious Cook and readers.

To begin, T.S. of Silvis writes: "My girlfriend and I ate at Five and had the Crisp Duck. That had to be one of the tastiest dishes I've ever had. I'm looking for a recipe that is comparable to the one they have at the restaurant.

"The sauce was sweet and syrupy, and it had an odd (but good) taste, almost like a cotton-candy flavor," T.S. continues.

"It came with cheese on the side. The crisp part was some kind of bread at the bottom of the stack.

"The duck was served in bite-sized pieces stacked on top of each other (think of the game Jenga if that helps). I would like to attempt this at home."
— *T.S. of Moline*

Curious Cook's note: Well, dear cooks, T.S. and others now may enjoy a dinner of duck a la Five, compliments of Chef Rivera, who opened Five last May.

We called Chef Rivera on the chance that he would share the duck recipe, given our reader's enthusiasm for his dinner at Five. Judging from the accurate description by T.S., he paid attention to the composition/presentation of the dish while enjoying his meal!

Here's the way Chef Rivera prepares the duck dish for diners (see facing page):

"Take the duck breast and score on the skin side. You score to render the skin." (To score, make shallow cuts, in a diamond pattern, on the skin of the duck. This will permit duck fat to drain off.)

Chef Rivera continues: "Cook duck breast in a dry pan over low to medium flame, skin side down, for about 3½ minutes."

"Flip the duck breast over to other side and continue to cook for about another 3 minutes, to medium rare. Use a dry pan and all that duck skin will render fat."

"Remove duck breast from pan and let rest for about 3 minutes to relax; should be medium rare. Slice thinly."

"For the sauce: Take any type of raspberry liquor (Chambord, for example) and reduce it to a syrupy consistency. It will come to a syrupy consistency (in reduction).

"Add grapes. I use red grapes, for a crunch factor. Add 1 teaspoon of butter, whisking the butter into the sauce. That's the finished sauce."

Pressed for amounts, Chef Rivera suggested cooks might choose to start with about ½ cup raspberry liquor and reduce by one-third. Remember: a syrupy consistency.

The entree calls for brioche bread. "Toast brioche bread," Chef Rivera says, "toast with toaster."

Now for the goat cheese: "We use fried goat cheese. Take goat cheese and just like chicken, roll in it flour first, egg wash and then bread crumbs. Fry it in oil until light brown."

To serve the dish: "Toasted brioche bread goes on the bottom, then the thinly sliced duck breast and then the sauce over duck, dripping all over everything, and the goat cheese goes on the side."
   — *Chef Dominic Rivera, Five restaurant, downtown Moline*

Enchiladas

Feb. 2, 1994

B.D. of LeClaire very kindly submitted the following recipe for Enchiladas to answer the recent request.

"This recipe looks difficult, but really is not if you go slowly and follow directions closely," she advises.

- ½ of a large can Crisco
- 1 large can tomatoes
- 2 dozen tortillas, flour or corn
- Yellow cheese
- Onion
- Chili powder
- 1 package frozen french fries, (2 to 3 cups chopped)
- 1 can peas, optional
- 2 pounds ground beef
- 1 pound chorizo (delicatessen, any store)
- Cumin
- Hot sauce, if desired (see recipe below)

In a blender, puree the can of tomatoes and pour into a flat pan or bowl. Add approximately 2 tablespoons chili powder to taste. Melt approximately ½ of a large can of Crisco into a large frying pan. This will not be re-usable.

Grate cheese, chop onion, cut frozen fries into small pieces. You may use raw potatoes after dicing and frying them. Fry chorizo, ground beef and onion together. When done, add the frozen fries or your own fried potatoes to meat. Here you may add the can of peas, if desired. Use about 1 teaspoon cumin for bringing out flavor, and chili powder, if desired.

Construction of enchiladas: Arrange the flat pan of tomatoes, the large frying pan of hot Crisco, the large frying pan of meat and potatoes, one flat cookie sheet, one long cake pan, and one pair of tongs. Take tortilla and dip it into the pan of tomatoes; put it into hot Crisco, turn and remove to cookie sheet. Fry about 6 to 8 tortillas, as they will be too hot to fill when removed from frying pan. The grease will turn dark and some tomatoes will be left in the grease, which adds flavor.

After frying about 6 to 8 tortillas, fill with meat mixture, cheese and onion. Roll tortilla around meat, cheese and onion and place in a cake pan if preparing in advance or serve immediately. Hot sauce may be added when serving if desired. Enchiladas may be prepared ahead by covering cake pan with foil and putting in oven at 350 degrees for approximately 20 minutes.

HOT SAUCE:

- 1 small can tomatoes
- ½ onion, chopped
- 2 cloves garlic
- Salt, to taste
- 6 jalapeno peppers — or more for extra hot!

Put all ingredients in blender and blend. — *B.D. of LeClaire, Iowa*

Jan. 29, 1997
Genesis Medical Center Creamy Cabbage Soup

Curious Cook is so pleased that Steve Zurkamer, manager, Food and Nutrition Services for Geneseo Medical Center, Davenport, has answered a recent request for the medical center's Creamy Cabbage Soup. He writes:

"We noticed the letter in your column from D.G. of Dixon, Iowa, regarding our Creamy Cabbage Soup and thought you and she would like to have the recipe from the source.

"This recipe was actually adapted from an old Campbell's Soup cookbook and we expanded it to our quantity needs. The original recipe has long since vanished so we have reduced ours to a manageable 15 servings at home.

"Incidentally, we are now serving this soup occasionally on both East and West campuses!" he adds.

We thank you, Mr. Zurkamer, for taking time from your busy schedule and sharing this recipe. Here 'tis:

CABBAGE SOUP

7 cups cabbage, cut in 1-inch cubes

2 cups chopped onion

4 ounces margarine

15 slices bacon, fried crisp, drained, crumbled

2 cups cream of mushroom soup

2 cups milk

Saute cabbage and onion in margarine until tender. Add bacon. Mix soup and milk together until smooth. Add cabbage-onion-bacon mixture to soup. Heat and serve. — *Genesis Medical Center, Davenport*

Glenn Moore's Shrimp Salad

Feb. 18, 2003

C.C. can tell readers how to make an at-home version of the delicious shrimp salad which was popular years ago at Glenn Moore's restaurant, corner of 15th Street and 7th Avenue in downtown Moline.

In a recent column, D.F. of East Moline "wondered if anyone would have the recipe for the shrimp salad and dressing" that was served at Mr. Moore's place.

In his e-mail, D.F., who said he liked to lunch at the restaurant, accurately described Glenn Moore's as a "popular place back then and lots of people loved the shrimp salad."

Indeed it was and indeed they did!

Now, with a sincere thank you to Lucia Moore of Davenport, Glenn Moore's daughter-in-law, Curious Cook can publish the coveted recipe.

Interestingly, C.R.G. of Silvis, a former employee of the restaurant, also responded with the salad directions. His recipe basically is the same as the one given to us by Mrs. Moore.

Lucia Moore told Curious Cook that the entire time her father-in-law was in business, he would not reveal the salad recipe.

But then one evening when the family was out for dinner, she asked him for it. Lo and behold, and apparently to her surprise, he gave it to her!

"It turned out to be so easy," Mrs. Moore recalls.

"It's funny because so many cookbooks that came out in the 1950s and 1960s all had what they proclaimed was the 'authentic' recipe for the shrimp salad and none were even close.

"Anyway, here it is (Glenn Moore's Shrimp Salad):

"Use leaf lettuce or Romaine; cut up about ¾ cup celery and add to greens.

"The dressing is: half Kraft (or Hellmann's) Real Mayonnaise and half seafood sauce. I make mine with ½ cup ketchup, 1 full tablespoon horseradish and 1 teaspoon lemon juice," she explains.

"Mix the greens and celery with the shrimp (use fresh, never canned) and then with the dressing.

"Now the guessing is over."

— *Lucia Moore,*
of Davenport,
Glenn's daughter-in-law

Glenn Moore's Shrimp Salad

March 5, 2003

Memories. That's the theme of this week's column. We'll continue our discussion of Glenn Moore's shrimp salad.

In last week's column, Curious Cook featured the "official" recipe for Glenn Moore's very famous shrimp salad, courtesy of Mr. Moore's daughter-in-law, Lucia Moore of Davenport.

We also included another "recipe," a nearly identical version, which Curious Cook received from a former employee of the popular restaurant. Years ago Glenn Moore's Tap was located in downtown Moline and it was a mighty popular spot.

Now, Curious Cook opens her mail and finds another contribution about the salad from still another former employee who remembers the salad-making at the restaurant. All the contributors agree on the salad!

The secret, of course, to the deliciousness of this shrimp salad is in the dressing. Which, of course, is no longer a secret!

L.C. of Moline kindly sent the following information to Curious Cook.

"A gal I know, D.M. of Moline, worked at Glenn Moore's years ago. Here's her version of shrimp salad."

D.M. of Moline has written: "In the late '40s, I worked at Glenn Moore's Tap. As I watched them make the shrimp salad, which was regular tossed salad with shrimp chopped up in it, the dressing was even amounts of salad dressing and cocktail sauce.

"As I remember, they made the cocktail sauce with ketchup, horse-radish and Worcestershire sauce." — *L.C. of Moline*

Glenn Moore's Shrimp Salad

February 18, 2003

And here's the way C.R.G. of Silvis remembers Moore's shrimp salad:

"I worked as the night cook at Glenn Moore's and my mother was the salad lady who made the shrimp salad, which also was popular at night (in the late '50s)," C.R.G. explains. He continues:

"The salad was made of fresh, cut-up shrimp mixed with chopped lettuce. The dressing was very simple: one part mayonnaise and one part cocktail sauce, which was either made by DelMonte or Heinz at the time.

"The above was mixed and put on a large lettuce leaf."

— *C.R.G. of Silvis*

Hoffman School Cherry Squares

Nov. 30, 1994

H.H. of East Moline very kindly shares with us a recipe she treasures, a home version of the Cherry Squares served at United Township High School years ago. H.H. explains:

"Sometime this fall you had a request from a reader for Cherry Squares like the ones served at Hoffman School. Cherry Squares were served when I taught in the '50s and '60s at United Township High School. They were my favorite cafeteria dessert.

"Mary Winert was in charge of the cafeteria and was kind enough to cut the institutional recipe down for my use at home. Hope this is the one your reader is looking for."

We thank H.H. for sharing this favorite recipe. Here 'tis.

3 cups flour
1½ teaspoons salt
1 cup sugar

2/3 cup butter
5 cups drained cherries; reserve liquid

Sift flour, salt and sugar. Crumble in butter until it resembles cornmeal. Pat half of this mixture into bottom of 9x13 baking pan and pat firmly. Put cherries over this and add remaining crumb mixture. Bake in 375 oven for 40 minutes.

SAUCE:
4 cups cherry juice; add water if needed

2 cups sugar
Pinch of almond extract

Bring to a boil and thicken with ½ cup cornstarch which you make into a paste before you add it to the boiling sauce. Cook until thickened. Serve sauce on squares. — *H.H. of East Moline*

Illini's Celery Seed Dressing

April 10, 1996

Sharon Deyo, who's the production coordinator, dietary department, at Illini Hospital, Silvis, kindly shares a favorite recipe to answer a recent request. She writes:

"In response to L.E. of Bettendorf who is looking for a Honey Celery Seed Dressing recipe, I have one we use at Illini Hospital that's a huge hit with our CEO and Board of Directors.

"I think it's close to what L.E. is looking for."

- ½ **cup sugar**
- ¾ **teaspoon dry mustard**
- ¾ **teaspoon paprika**
- ½ **teaspoon celery seed**
- ¼ **teaspoon salt**
- ¼ **cup honey**
- ¼ **cup vinegar**
- 2 **teaspoons lemon juice**
- ¾ **cup vegetable oil**

Blend ingredients together with wire whip or electric mixer until thick. Stores well in the refrigerator. Makes 8 two-ounce servings.

— *Sharon Deyo, Illini Hospital, Silvis*

John Deere Junior High French Pastry

April 17, 2002

Curious Cook was absolutely positive the recipe for John Deere Junior High School Angel Pie would show up. We were not disappointed!

N.W. of Orion and G. of Moline both saved newspaper clippings from years ago and kindly share the recipe/information, and memories, with us.

G. of Moline sent this note along with the recipe:

"Enclosed please find a recipe for John Deere Junior High School French Pastry from Grace Verpaele. I cut this out of the Dispatch quite some time ago.

"I love to read your column and someone was looking for an Angel Dessert from John Deere Junior High. This could be the one? I don't know.

"Anyway, if this is it ... great. I grew up living next door to Grace and went to JD Junior High School so this is a memory to keep."

And the following came from N.W. of Orion:

"I had saved the following from The Daily Dispatch, 11 April 1979. It was submitted by Grace Verpaele, manager of the cafeteria at John Deere Junior High School.

"The article says the original recipe was for 300 servings. Mrs. Verpaele took the recipe home and adapted it for family-size servings.

"The dessert was popular with the school children. The ingredients became too expensive and the dessert was discontinued from the school menu.

"I attended John Deere Junior High in the 1950s and don't remember the desserts then. I was a brown-bagger coming from a large family and buying your lunch in the cafeteria was an occasional luxury.

"I have been clipping recipes from your column for years obviously and probably will never get them all tried.

"It is always fun to find an oldie that someone is looking for."

Here's the recipe — the "oldie" — for John Deere Junior High School French Pastry. (See facing page.)

BUTTER CRUST:
1 and 2/3 cups flour
2 tablespoons granulated sugar
2/3 cup butter
¾ tablespoon water

Combine flour and sugar. Cut in butter. Add water. Mix with a fork. Roll out on lightly floured board, making two crusts to fit two 9-x-9-inch pans. Prick crusts and bake about 15 minutes at 400 degrees. WATCH VERY CAREFULLY.

VANILLA FILLING:
¾ cup sugar
½ cup cornstarch
Pinch of salt
1½ quarts milk, scalded
3 eggs, well beaten
¼ cup butter
1 teaspoon vanilla

Combine sugar, cornstarch and salt. Slowly add the milk. Cook in double boiler until thick. Then add a little of this mixture to the three well-beaten eggs. Then add to the thickened pudding, stirring continuously. Cook 1 minute.

Remove from heat. Add butter and vanilla to hot mixture. Cool pudding mixture.

Using one crust in a 9-x-9-inch pan, pour filling over top. Then place other crust over filling. Chill.

To serve, cut in pieces, spoon thickened fruit strawberries on top, and add a dollop of whipped cream. Makes 9 servings.

Notes: The recipe originally was submitted by Grace Verpaele of Moline, manager of the cafeteria, and was published in The Dispatch April 11, 1979.

The original article also pointed out that when Mrs. Verpaele made the French Pastry at home, "she found she had generous portions of the pudding filling, enough for extra helpings for her husband.

"If you have more than enough pudding to your liking for the filling, just pour it into sauce dishes or berry bowls and have yourself a treat."

She also advised that it's important to use 9-x-9-inch pans for the crust.
— *The Dispatch, 1979*

Dec. 3, 2003

Irv French's Clam Bisque Soup (El Rancho 1976)

Curious Cook always is so pleased when readers share treasured recipes of the past.

Curious Cook received the El Rancho Clam Chowder recipe from E.G. of Bettendorf in response to a request published in September from J.C. of Bettendorf.

J.C. wanted a clam chowder recipe "from either the El Rancho or Town and Country (when it was in Bettendorf)."

Not only does E.G. share the clam chowder recipe, but she also tells us how she happens to have that recipe and how very much she likes the chowder.

E.G. writes:

"The recipe was given to my husband by Irv French on Christmas Eve along with a gallon of the bisque," remembers E.G. about the El Rancho Clam Bisque Soup circa 1976.

"Quantities were given for the first four ingredients only. We have experimented and are very pleased with the recipe as I have it written," she explains.

"I'm sure this is the recipe your inquirer was looking for. I hope others enjoy it as much as we do."

- 4 small cans clam chowder meat
- 1 pound butter
- 1 cup flour (scant)
- 1 quart milk
- ½ green pepper
- 1 cup celery
- ½ cup onion
- 1 cup carrots
- 1 teaspoon salt
- ½ teaspoon pepper
- ½ teaspoon celery salt

In small saucepan, with just enough water to cover, cook vegetables until tender.

In 4-quart pan, melt butter, add flour, cook until bubbly. Add seasonings. Remove from heat and stir in water and vegetables.

Return to heat. Add milk gradually. Bring to a boil, boil 1 minute. Add clams and clam liquor. Heat 10 minutes or desired serving temperature.

Serves 10 to 12.

— *E.G. of Bettendorf*

Lee's Fried Fish

Jan. 19, 2000

G.G. may have moved to Minnesota, but his culinary heart remains in the Quad-Cities. He writes:

"I'm a Quad-City boy transplanted to Minnesota. I still subscribe to The Dispatch and read your column all the time. As you get older, you start getting memories from your past (sometimes easier than things more recent, like breakfast).

"Since both businesses I'm going to ask about have long been out of business, maybe there are some ex-employees who don't have to worry about proprietary issues.

"The first is Lee's Place. We would go there almost every Friday to get fish dinners. What is their recipe for cooking the fish, and more importantly, what is the recipe for their coleslaw? I have never been able to match either." — *G.G. of Richfield, Minn.*

G.G.'s first request is easy for Curious Cook. My professional colleague, Lisa Mohr, is a member of the Mohr family which owned and operated the popular Lee's Place in Rock Island for more than 40 years. She easily answers G.G.'s request.

In her own words, here are Lisa's recollections for the fried fish and the coleslaw.

"I spent most Thursday nights of my childhood helping my mother prepare coleslaw — up to 20 gallons at a time — and most Friday nights during junior high standing in the kitchen in the back of the bar actually frying the fish while my mother waited on tables.

"The secret of the fish at Lee's was every piece was hand-dipped just before it was fried. We used fresh ocean perch that was cut to size and thoroughly washed and dried. Each piece was first rolled in seasoned flour, then soaked a few minutes in milk, then rolled in fine yellow cornmeal that was shaken free of excess before setting in the frying basket.

"Unless you have a deep fryer at home, the fish you pan fry in your own kitchen will not taste exactly the same as deep frying. But it'll be close. I use a good quality canola oil and use about half an inch of oil in the pan. On medium high heat, fry fish until brown on each side. If you are frying large quantities, you'll need to change the oil (the cornmeal in the pan will start to burn and alter the flavor).

"There is no real recipe for the coleslaw — we did it all by taste. Two things made the coleslaw at Lee's taste unique — radishes and the amount of sugar. We used a fair amount of shredded radishes in with the onion and shredded cabbage that gave it a fresh peppery taste. We also got the unique taste by balancing the amount of salt and sugar — if it tasted too sweet, we added salt, if it was too salty, sugar was added. More sugar than you really want to know about is used for our coleslaw.

"For one average head of cabbage, shredded, add one small, finely minced onion and a pound of trimmed and shredded radishes. Add a cup to 1½ cups of Hellmann's, about 1 tablespoon of salt and ½ cup of sugar. Mix well and allow to set for an hour or so. Taste it and no doubt you'll add more sugar." — *Lisa Mohr of Rock Island*

Liver Pate (The Shamrock)

Aug. 3, 2005

The secret's out! Jerry Guinn of East Moline and the Guinn family have decided to release the family's up-until-now-protected recipe for the Shamrock restaurant's ever-so-popular Liver Pate!

S.N.G. of East Moline recently requested "the recipe for the Liver Pate served at the Shamrock restaurant in Cordova in the '60s, '70s, '80s. They always served it. It was just one of the best."

Recently, responding to the request, two well-know local caterers kindly shared their favorite recipes for Chicken Liver Pate, and we are grateful to them. Then, Jerry Guinn wrote Curious Cook:

"A good Shamrock customer requested the Liver Pate recipe several weeks ago. It has been a protected recipe of ours for years, but at this time we are glad to share with her and the rest of your readers. Jerry Guinn, on behalf of The Shamrock, of Cordova, and the Guinn family."

So, dear cooks, here follows the quantity-size recipe the Guinn family used at The Shamrock:

8 pounds ground beef	4 tablespoons salt
4 pounds chicken livers	4 ounces hot sauce
6 large onions, cut up	Chicken bouillon
8 tablespoons celery salt	Cornflake crumbs
2 tablespoons garlic powder	Kitchen Bouquet
6 tablespoons white or black pepper	

Mix ground beef, chicken livers, onions, celery salt, garlic powder, pepper, salt and hot sauce in a roasting pan; then add chicken bouillon. Mixture should be fairly moist. Roast in oven at 300 to 350 degrees until well done and tender. Stir a couple of times while roasting.

When done, put into a mixer and whip to a smooth consistency. It might be necessary to add more chicken bouillon. When done mixing, add cornflake crumbs to tighten to consistency desired. Then add Kitchen Bouquet for color desired.

Note: "We believe this recipe could be quartered without difficulty. However, we have never tried it."

— *Jerry Guinn,
for The Shamrock, Cordova*

Liver Pate (Diane DeBord)

"This is my favorite pate recipe, and it's very similar to the one served at The Shamrock," says Diane DeBord, a well-known Moline caterer.

- **1 pound chicken livers**
- **½ cup chopped onions**
- **2 tablespoons butter**
- **¼ cup sherry**
- **½ teaspoon salt**
- **¼ teaspoon pepper**
- **¼ teaspoon dried thyme**
- **¼ teaspoon minced garlic**
- **1 package (3 ounces) cream cheese, softened**
- **¼ cup butter, softened**
- **3 hard-cooked eggs, chopped (optional)**

Sauté chicken livers and onion in the 2 tablespoons of butter until done. In a food processor (or blender), blend mixture until smooth.

In a small saucepan, reduce sherry to one-half. Add to mixture. Add remaining ingredients except eggs and blend well. Press into an oiled mold and chill until firm.

Optional: Fold in chopped eggs before molding, if desired. Serve pate with cocktail breads or toast points. — *Diane DeBord of Moline*

Mile High Strawberry Pie

March 31, 2004

Our readers have raved about their Mile High Strawberry Pies, and we've published several of their recipes recently to answer a request.

A.B. of Milan wanted to prepare a Mile High Strawberry Pie like "we once had at the old Town & Country Restaurant in the '60s and '70s.

"It was as light as a feather and very good and refreshing," she added descriptively.

Curious Cook received and published a number of Strawberry Pie recipes that cooks reported to be very good, but not necessarily the T&C pie requested by A.B.

And they aren't!

The gentleman who perfected recipes for pie specialties of those Town & Country restaurants tells Curious Cook that, so sorry, but our readers' recipes aren't at all like his!

Curious Cook received a note from Al Klass, who wants to set the record straight on readers' recipes for Mile High Strawberry Pie.

Mr. Klass writes:

"As the operator of the Town & Country restaurants in the '60s and '70s, I am the person who perfected the recipes for my pies, listed on the menus as Al's Mile High Pie.

"The flavors produced were lemon, strawberry, pineapple and peanut butter.

"The recipes sent to you are no way near to the recipes used by myself. Sorry to disappoint your readers," he adds.

Mr. Klass politely declined to release his recipe, telling Curious Cook it's a "proprietary secret."

And so, dear cooks, enjoy the Strawberry Pie recipes if you will, but know that the requested Town & Country specialty remains top secret.

Mile High Strawberry Pie

April 28, 2004

There's a new development in the culinary mystery of Mile High Strawberry Pie a la Al Klass.

Curious Cook has received two additional recipes, very similar, for Town and Country Mile High Pie, as requested several weeks ago by H.B. of Milan.

Faithful readers of this column will remember that Al Klass, operator of the Town & Country restaurants in the '60s and '70s, is the person who perfected the recipes for the pies, which were restaurant specialties.

Mr. Klass told Curious Cook that recently published readers' favorites "are no way near the the recipe used by myself." He added that he was sorry to disappoint readers.

Now two readers have submitted pie recipes unlike the others. These recipes include Milnot and gelatin in the ingredients.

So Curious Cook once again conferred with Mr. Klass, who says, yes, he did use Milnot in his pies, but did not use Jell-O or any gelatin.

Indeed, Mr. Klass' own pie recipe continues to be top secret. But here's a Mile High Pie version readers might wish to try for themselves.

V.D. of Rock Island writes:

"I have made this pie (strawberry) many times and have had the recipe for many years. It is so high and very good and pretty.

"I hope this is what everyone is looking for." V.D. adds.

Another Rock Island cook sent a similar pie recipe, but V.D.'s recipe is more specific.

1 can Milnot
1/3 cup water
1/3 cup sugar

1½ packages or 5 ounces any flavor gelatin
Graham cracker crust
Whipped topping

Punch two holes in the top of the Milnot can and put the can in a pan of water. Do not cover the can with water. "I put about ¾ up on the can."

Bring to a boil, carefully remove from heat, and then let the can cool in pan. Refrigerate the Milnot can overnight.

Bring water and sugar to a boil. Add any flavor gelatin. Stir and let cool. It will be syrupy.

Beat Milnot until stiff and stands in peaks. Slowly add gelatin mixture to Milnot.

"Use a large bowl because it makes a lot. I fold it in. Pile mixture in graham-cracker crust. It will be high."

Ice with prepared whipped topping. Keep refrigerated.

— *V.D. of Rock Island*

MHS Honey Dijon Salad Dressing

Feb. 6, 2002

Foods students and their teacher at Moline High School contributed the following recipe for Honey Dijon Salad Dressing to answer the recent request of J.N.

K.A. e-mailed Curious Cook: "The reader's request for Honey Dijon Salad Dressing was timely.

"The Foods II classes at Moline High School are preparing basic French dressings so the recipe was handy to send.

"Students have a choice of several dressings to prepare and serve with lettuce and homemade croutons, but the Honey Dijon was chosen by most."

1/3 cup salad oil   **2 tablespoons Dijon mustard**
1/3 cup vinegar   **1 tablespoon minced onion**
¼ cup honey

Mix all ingredients in blender, food processor or shake in covered jar. Makes about 1 cup.

Hint: "Measure the oil in a liquid measuring cup first; measure honey in same cup without wiping out, and honey slides right out! Hardly any scraping."   — *Moline High School's Foods II classes*

Moline High Angel Pie

April 17, 2002

"The following recipe is from The Daily Dispatch, 12 May 1982. It was submitted by Clara Todd, manager of the cafeteria at Moline High School.

"The school's recipe was for 15 to 18 pies and she adjusted the ingredients for a single pie."

2 cups milk
1 cup granulated sugar
5 tablespoons cornstarch
¼ teaspoon salt

2 teaspoons vanilla
3 egg whites, beaten
1 baked 9-inch pie shell
Whipped cream

Heat the milk. Mix together sugar, cornstarch and salt. Add to hot milk stirring until well mixed. Continue cooking until mixture is thick and clear. Add vanilla.

Beat egg whites stiff but not dry. Slowly add egg whites to the hot pudding.

Pour into baked 9-inch pie shell. Cool well. Serve with whipped cream.

Variations: Well-drained crushed pineapple may be added to angel pudding.

Prepare a chocolate pudding. Pour pudding into two baked shells, then divide the angel filling between the two shells for a black bottom pie.   — *N.W. of Orion*

Nun's Fudge (ICA)

June 21, 2000

"I attended the old Immaculate Conception Academy, located at 8th and Main streets in Davenport," writes D.I. of Davenport to begin her candy request.

"Since I always knew how to cook from a very early age, I did not take home economics while attending. Needless to say, there was always one regret with that.

"The nun who taught the class had a fantastic recipe for fudge drops. The girls said it was no-fail. But it always went great at bake sales, etc.

"She (the sister) simply dropped the fudge in bite-size pieces on wax paper. It was ever so creamy.

"Needless to say, I was never able to get the secret to this fudge. Someting about my not taking the class!

"Would anyone who took home economics between 1946 and 1950 at the Immaculate Conception Academy still have the recipe?

"Would love to relive my youth for a while. Thanks." — *D.I. of Davenport*

Well, D.I., you'll be happy to learn that Curious Cook has in her files from July 21, 1993, a recipe for Nun's Fudge that closely matches the description you've given! (See below.)

In the summer of 1993, M.M.B. of Bettendorf requested from Curious Cook a recipe that M.M.B. recalled from her years at Immaculate Conception Academy.

At that time, Sister Elizabeth Sprung of the Sisters of Charity of the Blessed Virgin Mary kindly answered the request and sent the following fudge recipe to Curious Cook. Surely this must be the recipe that D.I. remembers!

Sister Elizabeth Sprung died in February 1998. When she answered M.M.B.'s request, Sister was at Assumption High School in Davenport. But she wrote that she was one of the sisters who made the fudge at Immaculate Conception Academy.

July 21, 1993

Curious Cook was absolutely positive that she would hear from one of the Sisters who made the "Nun Fudge" years ago at Immaculate Conception Academy in Davenport. The Sisters always are helpful so we knew we would hear from the candy-maker if she still lives and teaches in this area. And we did!

M.M.B. of Bettendorf requested this recipe, which she fondly recalled from her days at the Academy where the Sisters of Charity of the Blessed Virgin Mary taught for many, many years. The academy was closed in the '50s when Assumption High School opened.

Sister E.S., now of the Assumption Convent in Davenport, wrote to Curious Cook: "I read Curious Cook's column with the request for Nun's Fudge. I was one of the Sisters at ICA who made the fudge."

Sister adds that she taught at the Academy in the 1950s. On the next page is her recipe.

Nun's Fudge (ICA)

July 21, 1993

2 cups white granulated sugar
¼ cup cocoa
1 cup evaporated milk, not sweetened condensed, milk
1 tablespoon white Karo syrup
1 tablespoon butter
1 to 1½ cups chopped nuts, optional
1 teaspoon vanilla

Mix together in a saucepan the sugar, cocoa, milk, syrup and butter. Cook to the soft-ball stage, stirring constantly so it won't stick. "I use a candy thermometer," Sister explained.

Butter a flat cake pan, 9x13-inches or 13x15-inches.

Beat any kind of chopped nuts — 1 cup or 1½ cups — or none at all — into the fudge mixture. Add vanilla.

Pour hot fudge into the pan and beat with a spoon until it loses its gloss. Then work fast to drop it by teaspoons on wax paper or spread it out in the same pan to harden. Cut into squares.

"I use the flat pan to beat it in because I no longer have a marble slab. It works just as well," Sister advised. — *Sister Elizabeth Sprung, B.V.M.*

Aug. 2, 2000

The mystery of the marble slab for Nun's Fudge has been solved!

In June, Curious Cook published the recipe for fudge which one of the Sisters of Charity instructed students to prepare years ago in home economics class at Immaculate Conception Academy in Davenport. The late Sister Elizabeth Sprung, B.V.M., was one of the Sisters of Charity who made the fudge at the ICA. In the summer of 1993, she shared her recipe with Curious Cook.

When Sister Sprung sent us the recipe back in 1993, she explained that she now used a flat pan to beat the candy "because I no longer have a marble slab." Why no marble slab?

Well, writes M.L.A.H., who lives in Sun City, Ariz., it's because the marble slabs on which ICA home-ec students poured fudge were part of the windows at that beautiful academy!

After her brother, L.A. of Davenport, sent her a clipping of Curious Cook's article, M.L.A.H. shared this information with her brother. He, in turn, kindly shares it with Curious Cook and readers. M.L.A.H. wrote:

"I remember vividly that the nuns would pick the student of home-ec who could make the fudge without it turning to sugar before you got it dropped, and I was one of the few that could do it.

"They had marble slabs along the windows in home ec, and you poured the fudge out of the pan onto the buttered marble slab, and then you worked it with a spatula just until it got a certain glazy look about it.

"At that moment, you stopped the spatula work and took a teaspoon and very quickly dropped it from the teaspoon onto wax paper. It made really pretty candy fudge." Such happy memories!

Plantation Dressing

Feb. 16, 1983

It's amazing how many versions The Curious Cook has received of "authentic" Plantation Dressing. The dressing certainly must be the most popular — the all-time favorite — of restaurant "house dressings" in the Quad-Cities area. I'm sure the request brings back many happy memories for readers who so much enjoyed dining at The Plantation in Moline.

I'm going to share the letters and notes I received from area cooks who sent in recipes for the dressing. I think you'll enjoy reading them and will identify with them. Some of the directions of the "authentic" recipes differ, so I shall include the variations. There seem to be quite a few "real things." And too, some recipes were more complete than others because they include exact sizes for bottles.

As you probably already know, Quad-Citians simply loved that garlicy house dressing at The Plantation. I do not know whether or not owners Al Johnson, Dave Koenig and Gary Huysman and general manager Wes Lllewellyn plan to feature the dressing when they open W.L. Velie's this spring. I would like to suggest they do so. No, I urge them to put the Plantation Dressing on the menu.

Remodeling in The Plantation, the old W.L. Velie mansion, began in January, and Quad-Citians are awaiting announcement of reopening date. The new name reflects the history of the magnificent mansion, which was built by W.L. Velie, on 7th St. near Black Hawk Road. Velie, a Moliner, designed and manufactured the famous Velie automobile and later the Monocoup airplane.

If there's any doubt in your mind about the popularity of The Plantation through many years, or its house dressing, read on.

We'll start with an interesting letter from Mrs. H.H. of Coal Valley. She captures the feeling the public has about Plantation house dressing.

"I'm positive I have the original Plantation Dressing (or a reasonable facsimile). I moved to the Quad-Cities as a bride in 1940 and shortly thereafter started working at the Rock Island Arsenal.

"Whenever an occasion warranted the 'girls' in our office going out to eat for a special treat, The Plantation was the 'in' place at that time, and the main reason for going there was the salad dressing. Even the most fastidious couldn't resist the garlic dressing, and we all left the place with the worst garlic breath. But it was worth it.

"Then one day, someone brought the recipe to the office and very surreptitiously passed it around for us to copy — with the reminder that it had been 'sneaked' out, etc. (At that time, you could buy the bottled dressing from The Plantation.)

"But with all that clandestine operation, it had to be THE ONE. Because I had eaten so much of it, when I started making my own, I could account for every ingredient.

"I'm sure the eggs, A-1 sauce, ketchup, mustard, garlic oil or garlic salt are the result of people altering or adding to the recipe. (This is bound to happen over the years, especially when people try to remember ingredients or guess at them.)

"Not only was I sure of it because of the taste, but I knew the people well enough who passed the recipe around that I believed them when they said it was the 'real' one.

"After all these years, it doesn't matter who divulged a supposedly secret recipe, but I felt at the time that I was the proud possessor of THE RECIPE for the famous Plantation house dressing. And I still feel the same about it after over 30 years.

"It is one of my most treasured recipes, not only because it is so good, but it represents an era in the history of The Plantation that now is just a memory.

"I'm sure this is the recipe Mrs. D.E.E. of Moline is looking for."

1 pint Hellmann's mayonnaise
1 cup Kraft French Dressing (thin dressing)
2 teaspoons anchovy paste, optional
2 buds garlic, grated
1 can Parmesan cheese
Melba toast

Toss lettuce with dressing. Mix ingredients, adding melba toast last.

Note: "Use nothing but Hellmann's and Kraft French dressing (the thin dressing). Be sure to use the Kraft thin dressing. NO SUBSTITUTIONS." — *Mrs. H.H. of Coal Valley*

Plantation Salad Dressing

Feb. 16, 1983

M.H. of Moline has a recipe that includes garlic powder.

- 1 pint real mayonnaise
- 1 small bottle homogenized French dressing — orange
- 2 teaspoons garlic powder
- 1 small can of Parmesan cheese
- 2 teaspoons anchovy paste

 Mix well and store in a covered jar in refrigerator. *— M.H. of Moline*

Plantation Salad Dressing

Feb. 16, 1983

"Growing up, we ate at The Plantation most Sundays. If this isn't the 'original,' I doubt one can tell the difference," points out V.E. of Moline.

- 1 pint Hellmann's mayonnaise
- 1 cup Kraft French dressing (clear orange)
- 2 teaspoons anchovy paste
- 1 can (3 ounces) Parmesan cheese
- 2 cloves garlic, minced or slightly more

 Mix all ingredients in blender. Refrigerate. *— V.E. of Moline*

Plantation Salad Dressing

Feb. 16, 1983

"This is the real dressing from The Plantation," writes B.G. of Moline. "I used to buy it in Rock Island at Bogart's years ago. He sold all the Plantation things."

- 1 quart Hellmann's mayonnaise
- 1 pint Kraft (yellow) French dressing
- Large can of grated cheese (Romano or Parmesan)
- 1 tablespoon anchovy paste
- 1 clove garlic, crushed

 Combine all ingredients but DO NOT COOK. Refrigerate. "This is really good." *— B.G. of Moline*

Plantation Salad Dressing

Feb. 16, 1983

"In reply to your request the other night, I have enclosed the recipe I have had for a number of years for Plantation Salad Dressing," writes A.D. of Moline. Here's A.D.'s version, which calls for garlic powder.

- 1 pint Hellmann's mayonnaise
- 1 cup Kraft French Dressing (1 pint)
- 2 teaspoons anchovy paste
- 1 small can Parmesan cheese
- ¼ teaspoon garlic powder

 Mix all ingredients with rotary beater and refrigerate. *— A.D. of Moline*

Plantation Salad Dressing

Feb. 16, 1983

"For Mrs. D.E.E. of Moline — hope you enjoy as much as my family and friends do," writes Mrs. M.E.R. of Moline. Her recipe differs from the others and calls for Mrs. Clark's Italian salad dressing!"

- 1 quart Hellmann's mayonnaise
- 1 bottle Mrs. Clark's Italian dressing
- 4 garlic cloves, crushed
- 1 tablespoon anchovy paste
- ¾ cup ketchup
- 4 ounces grated Parmesan cheese

Mix all ingredients in blender or with beater on medium speed in large mixer bowl. Makes almost 2 quarts and keeps refrigerated indefinitely if tightly covered. — *Mrs. M.E.R. of Moline*

Plantation Salad Dressing

Feb. 16, 1983

"I saw in your recipe column Wednesday — Feb. 2 — that someone was requesting the recipe for The Plantation Salad Dressing. This is supposed to be the real thing given to me by a friend who worked there years ago," writes W.L.K. of Silvis. "I enjoy your recipes."

- 1 pint Kraft mayonnaise
- 1 small bottle Kraft French dressing
- 3 tablespoons anchovy paste
- 1 small can Parmesan cheese
- 2 buds of garlic or more, if so desired (crushed)

Mix anchovy paste until smooth and add other ingredients. Mix well. Refrigerate. Include melba toast in salad. — *W.L.K. of Silvis*

Plantation Salad Dressing

Feb. 16, 1983

S.G. of East Moline says she worked at The Plantation Club for a short time. Here's her version, which includes onion!

- 1 pint mayonnaise (Hellmann's)
- 1 bottle Kraft orange French dressing, small size
- 2 teaspoons anchovy paste
- 2 cloves garlic, crushed through a press
- ½ medium-size onion, chopped
- 1 small can grated Parmesan cheese

Combine all ingredients; well with a blender. Store in glass jar — keeps. Refrigerate. — *S.G. of East Moline*

Mongolian Beef (Yen Ching)

March 29, 1995

Curious Cook has received a very interesting letter and a recipe on "yellowed paper" from P.M.G. of Walcott, Iowa, regarding the recent request for a recipe for Mongolian Beef like the dish served at Yen Ching's. P.M.G. writes:

"Here is the recipe for Mongolian Beef B.B. wanted from Yen Ching's. This is from said restaurant which I obtained from the owners back when they first opened in the '70s. Enjoy.

"As you can see, the paper is old. I can no longer use this recipe because of the sugar content. I am a diabetic. I do marinate beef chuck in soy sauce, 6 squirts, and Italian dressing."

1 chicken (1 pound) or 1 pound beef, cut both into thin strips 3 inches long

MARINADE:
2 tablespoons cornstarch
1¼ cups water
1/3 cup Kikkoman soy sauce
1/3 cup Karo syrup dark or light
¼ to ½ teaspoon crushed dried red pepper

SAUCE:
2 tablespoons corn oil
2 gloves garlic, minced
2 tablespoons corn oil
2 cups broccoli flowerets and sliced stems about 1½ pounds
2 onions, cut in thin wedges
1 carrot, cut into 2-inch julienne strips
Hot, cooked rice

Marinate chicken or beef all day or overnight. Can use cheap cuts of beef.

For marinade: Mix 2 tablespoons cornstarch in 1¼ cups water until smooth. Stir in soy sauce, dark or light corn syrup. Add crushed dried red pepper.

For meat and sauce: Heat 2 tablespoons corn oil over medium heat. Add skinned chicken strips or beef strips. For chicken strips, stir fry 2 to 3 minutes. For beef strips, stir fry 1 to 2 minutes. Add minced garlic; remove mixture from skillet.

Add 2 tablespoons corn oil to skillet; add 2 cups broccoli flowerets and sliced stems. Note: Peel broccoli, cut stems diagonally. Always peel broccoli, 2 cups is about 1½ pounds.

Cut 2 onions in thin wedges and cut 1 carrot into 2-inch julienne strips. Add and stir fry 2 minutes or until vegetables are tender crisp.

Return meat and rest of sauce mixture to skillet. Stirring constantly, bring to boil over medium heat; boil 1 minute. Serve over rice.

Note: "Use canola oil lowest fat."   — *P.M.G. of Walcott*

Pippins

April 27, 1994

T.D. of Davenport implored Curious Cook to find information/a recipe for pippins, which T.D. had enjoyed so very much last October while on the Spoon River Scenic Drive. The pippins, said T.D., are a dough-like confection, flat like a pancake, deep fried, rolled in cinnamon and sugar and served with a fruit topping. T.D. and her friends had eaten, and enjoyed, the pippins last fall in London Mills.

To say that T.D. raved about pippins would be an understatement. Since the tour, she had been doing some research in old cookbooks but came up short. So she turned to Curious Cook.

Finding the person who made and sold these pippins at a booth in London Mills on the Spoon River Drive turned out to be quite a challenge for Curious Cook. But with the help of Joan Johnson, Lewistown, publicity director for the scenic drive, we finally were able to reach Beulah Meadows of Abingdon.

Pippins, it seems, are one of Mrs. Meadows' culinary specialties although she prepares other baked goods, including crumpets and scones. However, she's best known for the pippins.

Mrs. Meadows told Curious Cook that pippins are made from a yeast dough. "They're fried real fast in hot soybean oil, dusted with granulated sugar and topped with fruit," she says.

Mrs. Meadows says she wanted to do a period food — pippins are of the Renaissance era — and were sold on street corners in England.

With a chuckle, she recalls that she spent a winter on research in the library. "I found a recipe at the library under old-world foods. It told about the practice of being sold on the street corners and that they were originally apple."

No recipe, but guidance, T.D. really wanted a recipe. Mrs. Meadows says she has a recipe, which she does not release. But she did offer help.

"I'll tell you something that does work," she says. "Frozen bread dough."

She explains that any good white bread dough recipe will work.

"I use a regular bread dough recipe, but on the Spoon River Drive, I used frozen bread dough," she says. She advises that it works just fine.

"Let it rise and then form into thin pieces of dough about the size of your hand. Drop in hot oil. You want to make sure it will float." She says you can use a skillet but she has a specially-made iron pan because she might fry 15 at a time.

"Then when it browns, you flip it over to brown on both sides. Lift out of the hot oil and dust with granulated sugar. Put on the topping."

Mrs. Meadows says any kind of topping may be used, but cherry and blueberry are the most popular. A prepared fruit pie filling also may be used.

— *Beulah Meadows of Abington*

Scones

May 11, 1994

Our mail leaves no doubt that the recent request for basic directions for making scones generated a great deal of interest among professional and non-professional cooks/bakers.

We've received quite a number of scone recipes, including the following one (see next page) from the pros at a bakery in Bettendorf.

Curious Cook very much enjoyed this letter from Edwin Welch, baker and owner, and Cindy Stromberg, baker, at the D.C. Deli and Bakery in Duck Creek Plaza. They give us some professional tips for scone-bakers and a couple of recipes.

Curious Cook is so pleased to share their advice with readers:

"You will find attached to this letter an easy recipe for scones, which we have used at the D.C. Deli and Bakery at Duck Creek Plaza. Scones can be tricky to make, and like the dough for muffins, can become extremely hard if overworked.

"Scones should be eaten within the first few hours after coming out of the oven to retain the fresh, flavorful taste. Additionally, spoiling may occur, as the product contains no preservatives.

"Traditionally, the scones are served by the British with clotted cream. This mixture is a bowl of settled, heavy milk or cream that has been heated and cooled. The crusty top is scraped off and used as 'clotted cream' to top the scones.

"We, Welch and Stromberg, have included an easier topping called Devonshire Easy Cream. Butter and jam are also tasty alternatives to the cream topping."

— *Edwin Welch,*
baker/owner,
Cindy Stromberg, baker,
D.C. Deli & Bakery,
Duck Creek Plaza, Bettendorf

1½ cups sifted flour
¼ cup sugar
1½ teaspoons baking powder
¼ cup butter or margarine — cold

1/3 cup raisins or chocolate chips
1 egg, lightly beaten
2 tablespoons milk or buttermilk

Heat oven to 400 degrees. Mix dry ingredients together. Cut up butter and add to dry mix. Using two forks or a pastry cutter, cut in cold butter until it resembles coarse meal. Add raisins or chocolate chips and combine. Last, add egg and milk.

Turn onto floured board and form into circles or use cookie cutter. Brush tops with egg wash if desired.

Bake at 400 degrees until golden brown on top, about 12 to 15 minutes.   — *D.C. Deli & Bakery, Duck Creek Plaza, Bettendorf.*

Devonshire Easy Cream

3 ounces cream cheese, softened
½ cup heavy whipping cream

¼ teaspoon vanilla
1 to 2 tablespoons powdered sugar

Mix all ingredients together well and top scones.
— *D.C. Deli & Bakery, Duck Creek Plaza, Bettendorf*

Popcorn Charlie's Popcorn Salad

July 10, 1996

Curious Cook heard from Popcorn Charlie, who called about the Popcorn Salad recipe from his store in Davenport. Popcorn Charlie obviously specializes in popcorn recipes and he offers the following recipe to answer the recent request.

1 cup finely chopped celery
½ cup finely chopped green onion
½ cup sliced water chestnuts
1 cup shredded Cheddar cheese

1 pound fried, crumbled bacon
1 cup mayonnaise
2 teaspoons sugar
6 cups of popped small white kernel popcorn

Combine celery, onion, water chestnuts, cheese, bacon, mayonnaise and sugar; mix well. Chill. Two hours before serving, mix in 6 cups of popped small white kernel popcorn. Serve and enjoy.   — *Popcorn Charlie*

recipes to remember forever

Dec. 13, 2000
Shannon's Baked Pork Chops and Lima Beans

Curious Cook is delighted to share "recipes" from Shannon's, a popular eatery of yesteryear in downtown Davenport.

C.E.C. of Davenport answers the recent request, something's she's well-qualified to do because she was on the Shannon's staff for 33 years!

E.S. of Bettendorf recently asked if we could find directions for Shannon's specialties ... a small meatloaf with mashed potatoes inside, served with a tomato sauce, and pork chops baked with butter lima beans.

Meat pie was another favorite of E.S. and her friend of 50 years, who have happy memories of lunching together years ago at Shannon's when they worked in downtown Davenport.

In reply, C.E.C. kindly sent these directions (continued on facing page):

"In answer to E.S. of Bettendorf about Shannon's food: Seems I am always running into a former customer of Shannon's. Seems everyone had his/her favorite foods.

"For the Baked Pork Chops and Lima Beans:

"Figure 1 pound lima beans to 7 pork chops. Check lima beans and wash. Soak beans overnight. Boil until just tender, not mushy; drain and reserve broth. Use 3 quarts beans and 2 pints bean broth to long steam-table pan.

"Add 1 cup brown sugar and 2 cups ketchup and stir. Top with pork chops. Dip pork chops and turn so as to cover chops with the liquid. Salt and pepper. Should be 15 to 16 chops to pan.

"Bake not over 350 degrees until chops are done. Time depends on thickness of chops, approximately 2 hours. We covered with either lid or aluminum foil. Uncover to brown.

"**Note:** I'm not sure how many beans you will have after you cook 1 pound of beans. Also depends on how many chops you are using and if you like the extra beans.

"I have used 1½ quarts of beans and 1 pint or less of broth, ½ cup brown sugar and 1 cup of ketchup.

"I also have used: 1 quart beans, 1 to 1-1/3 cups broth, 2/3 cup ketchup and 1/3 cup brown sugar.

"I usually use less broth as I like the beans cooked down, more like they were after sitting on the steam table a while.

"Another tip: If you add salt when you cook the beans, go easy on it, as they will pick up some from when you salt and pepper the chops.

"Also, if you add a peeled whole Irish potato when you cook the beans, it will cut down on the gas. Then discard potato.

"As for the meatloaf:

"I think she is thinking of the meatloaf with Spanish sauce. It was just a slice of our meatloaf with Spanish sauce over it — served with whipped potatoes and a vegetable. The sauce was same the as we used on Swiss steak." — *C.E.C. of Davenport*

Sindt Goulash

Aug. 1, 2001

K.S.S. of Davenport has answered requests by C.L. of East Moline and G.M.H. of Moline, both of whom were searching for goulash recipes.

"The enclosed recipe was given to me as an authentic Sindt's Goulash Soup," writes K.S.S.

C.L. wants to prepare Hungarian Goulash like the soup that was served at the old Sindt Tavern in Davenport.

"Hope it's what they both are looking for," adds K.S.S.

2 quarts cold water	**2 to 3 teaspoons cinnamon**
1 pound ground beef	**1 teaspoon ground allspice**
1 large can (28 ounces) tomatoes 3½ cups	**About 2 teaspoons ground cloves, or to taste**
1½ good-size onions, chopped	**Salt and pepper, to taste**
More than ½ cup mixed spices pickling spices, tied in bag	**¼ cup or more flour, browned to thicken soup**
½ bottle ketchup (see note)	

Place 2 quarts cold water in large pot and break up the ground beef in it.

Beat tomatoes well and add to the ground beef. Add onion. Cook for 1 hour, then let mixture simmer. Put in the spice bag at the start.

While mixture is cooking, brown the flour in the oven, stirring occasionally to make sure it doesn't burn; cool before adding to the soup.

Add spices and ketchup; then cook and stir in the browned flour to thicken goulash.   — *K.S.S. of Davenport*

Note: Cooks will have to decide for themselves the amount of ketchup to use. The recipe lists only "½ bottle of ketchup," not specifying the bottle size. Just stir in ketchup and use good judgment.

Feb. 12, 2003

Thunder Bay Grille's Baked Potato Soup

Stacy Christoffersen, director of marketing for Heart of America Restaurants, kindly has provided a copy of the baked potato soup recipe to answer a recent request in Curious Cook's column.

Ms. Christoffersen writes:

"For your request from D.B. of Rock Island. Straight from Chef Tony at Thunder Bay Grille (in Davenport).

"It's our most popular soup for as long as we can remember!" she said.

Then Curious Cook received a copy of the recipe from S.G.W. of Rock Island. She also praised this soup:

"This soup is excellent," proclaims S.G.W. "Everyone I serve it to can't believe I made it from scratch. It's been the hit of many of our family gatherings.

"It also can be served in a bread bowl for a meal in itself." (S.G.W. adds that she would "like to have a recipe for cream puff pastry.")

So Curious Cook thanks the Heart of America spokesperson and S.G.W. and presents the "popular soup."

- 2½ pounds baby red potatoes, quartered
- ½ pound raw bacon, diced
- 1 jumbo yellow onion, diced
- 3 ribs celery, diced
- 1 quart milk
- 1 quart water
- ¼ cup chicken base
- 1 teaspoon salt
- 1 teaspoon black pepper
- 1½ sticks margarine
- ¾ cup flour
- ¼ cup chopped parsley
- 1 cup whipping cream
- For garnish: shredded Colby cheese, fried bacon bits and chopped green onions

Boil potatoes in water for 10 minutes; drain and set aside.

In a large heavy pot, saute bacon, onions and celery until celery is tender. Drain bacon grease; then add milk, water, chicken base, salt and pepper. Heat over medium-high heat until very hot; do not boil.

In large, heavy saucepan, melt margarine and add flour. Mix well and allow to bubble, stirring for 1 minute, to make a roux. S.G.W. adds: "If desired, a larger amount of roux can be used to make the soup thicker."

While constantly stirring soup, slowly add the flour and margarine mixture. Continue stirring soup until thick and creamy. Stir in parsley, potatoes and whipping cream until heated.

Garnish with shredded Colby cheese, fried bacon bits, chopped green onions, or all three. Serve while hot. Serves 10 to 12.

— *Stacy Christoffersen,*
director of marketing,
Heart of America restaurants
and S.G.W. of Rock Island

Toasty Rice Pudding

May 21, 1997

Our readers have very happy memories of the rice pudding served years ago at The Toasty Shop in downtown Rock Island.

Earlier this year, a reader asked if by any chance anyone had recipes for The Toasty's meatloaf and famous rice pudding.

No one seems to have the meatloaf recipe — if indeed there ever was a recipe. But the rice pudding request drew several responses and wonderful recollections, as well as the recipe to share with all of you.

The popular restaurant was owned and operated for years by three brothers, Tom, Nick and Gust Grevas. Dr. Ted Grevas of Rock Island is the son of Gust Grevas.

After the request was published, Pat Grevas, Dr. Ted's wife, searched for and found a copy of the original rice pudding recipe. She told us one of the waitresses at The Toasty gave it to Dr. Ted years ago.

Incidentally, since locating the family recipe, Mrs. Grevas has prepared the Toasty Rice Pudding as a special treat for her husband who, of course, thinks it's delicious. Surely it's a Quad-Cities classic.

Here's the recipe Mrs. Grevas found, followed by contributions from others.

Toasty Shop Rice Pudding

May 21, 1997

½ pound of Watermaid rice   Pinch of salt
1½ cups of sugar   ½ gallon of skim milk
1/8 pound of margarine

Wash rice; drain. Add all ingredients together. Bring to boil. Turn fire to low. Cook until thickened, stirring often. Pour into the dish; sprinkle with mixture of cinnamon and sugar. Cooking time — 1½ to 2 hours.   — *Toasty Shop, Rock Island (Pat Grevas of Rock Island)*

Rice Pudding

May 21, 1997

"I was reading your article from the woman from Coal Valley wanting the recipes for Meatloaf and Rice Pudding that was made at the Toasty shop in Rock Island. I have the recipe for the Rice Pudding. I have had it for over 40 years.

"I used to work there and I, too, liked the rice pudding very much. The recipe was obtained for me from a friend who got me the job. She also worked there for years and knew the cooks very well."

¼ pound long grain rice   Pinch of salt
¼ pound margarine   1 quart milk
1 cup sugar

Cover rice with water; add salt, sugar and margarine. Bring to hard boil; add milk. Turn fire low and cook about 1½ hours until thick. Stir often. Pour into pan and sprinkle with cinnamon. To serve pour cream or milk over top.   — *N.M. of New Boston*

Rice Pudding

May 21, 1997

From I.L.E. of Rock Island: "In response to the request for the recipes from the Toasty Shop restaurant, I do not have one for meatloaf, but I do have the Rice Pudding Recipe. It was given to me by a waitress at the restaurant for many years. The original recipe is as follows:"

1 pound rice
3 cups sugar
¼ pound butter
Pinch of salt
1 gallon milk

Wash rice, then cover with cold water, add sugar, butter and salt. Bring to a hard rolling boil. Add milk and simmer until quite thick. Will thicken as it cools.

Note: "I cut the recipe in half and use slightly less sugar. Instead of simmering on top of the stove, I put it in a 9x13-inch pan and cook in the oven at 270 degrees for about 2 hours — sometimes a little longer. Stir about every half hour to keep rice from 'clumping.' I have found that using a medium-grain rice rather than long grain works best.

"P.S. It was served sprinkled with cinnamon." — *I.L.E. of Rock Island*

Toasty Rice Pudding

May 21, 1997

From B.L.H. of Moline: "Here is a recipe I got few years ago from a former co-worker. Years back we made dinner a bowl of rice pudding and a cup of coffee at 'Toasty.' This comes fairly close.

"P.S. I double this recipe and I also use 2 percent milk."

½ cup rice, uncooked
½ cup sugar
1/8 pound margarine
1 quart milk
Salt, cinnamon and nutmeg, to taste

Place rice and sugar in pan. Cover with water and bring to boil. Add margarine and milk and salt and simmer 2 hours on stove or in oven. Sprinkle on the spices.

Serve warm or cold. Can be modified in time and temperature for microwave. — *B.L.H. of Moline*

Toasty's Rice Pudding

May 21, 1997

"I have the recipe you requested for The Toasty's rice pudding," A.H. of Rock Island writes. "It was given to me by a waitress who worked for years at Carter's restaurant across the street.

"I remember the big kettle of rice pudding sitting on the back burner of the stove keeping warm. When dished up they would pour on cream and it was delicious.

"This is a very large recipe, so I usually make ½ the recipe for my family, but have made all of it and shared with friends."

1 pound rice
3 cups sugar
Pinch of salt
¼ pound butter
1 gallon milk

Wash rice, then cover with cold water. Add sugar, salt and butter. Bring to a hard rolling boil; add milk and simmer until quite thick.

Will thicken after it's cooked.

— *A.H. of Rock Island*

June 22, 1994
Trinity Medical Center Chocolate Chip Cookies

"Awhile back, I had the opportunity of eating at Trinity Medical Center East former Lutheran Hospital and they had the most delicious cookies, Chocolate Chip, Oatmeal Raisin, etc. I wonder if they would be willing to share their recipes," I.O. of Moline recently implored in her letter to Curious Cook. — *I.O. of Moline*

Good news! Curious Cook talked to Michelle Bradley in the public relations department at Trinity Medical Center. Ms. Bradley in turn talked to Verna Bergstrom, director of nutrition services for Trinity Medical Center. Mrs. Bergtrom and her staff certainly went well beyond the call of duty and adapted five of the hospital's cookie recipes to more conventional proportions for home bakers. Then they tested the home-version recipes.

"Our cookies are baked fresh every day in quantities of 72 to 90 dozen per day," Mrs. Bergstrom says. She also compliments the cooks on both campuses "who not only enjoy cooking but also are very knowledgeable."

Mrs. Bergstrom and her staff at Trinity Medical Center proudly share the recipes. And we thank them.

8 ounces butter	4 cups flour
5-1/3 ounces margarine	1-2/3 teaspoons baking soda
1¼ cups brown sugar	1 teaspoon salt
1¼ cups granulated sugar	2½ cups chocolate chips
4 eggs (4 eggs = 1 cup)	1-2/3 teaspoons vanilla

Cream butter, margarine, both sugars, vanilla and eggs together until light and fluffy.

Sift flour; add baking soda and salt; mix well. Add chocolate chips and stir until only mixed. Do not overmix at this stage.

Use No. 30 dipper to portion cookies. Place on parchment lined cookie sheet about 2 inches apart. Bake in 325 degree oven for only 10 minutes. Makes 6 dozen Chocolate Chip Cookies.

Note: Put nuts in these cookies if desired.
— *Trinity Medical Center Nutrition Services*

June 22, 1994

Trinity Medical Center Double Chocolate Chip Cookies

- 8 ounces butter
- 5-1/3 ounces margarine
- 1¼ cups brown sugar
- 1¼ cups granulated sugar
- 4 eggs (4 eggs = 1 cup)
- 2/3 cup cocoa
- 4 cups flour
- 1-2/3 teaspoons baking soda
- 1 teaspoon salt
- 2½ cups chocolate chips
- 1-2/3 teaspoons vanilla

Cream butter, margarine, both sugars, vanilla and eggs together until light and fluffy.

Sift flour; add cocoa, baking soda and salt; mix well. Add chocolate chips and stir until only mixed. Do not overmix at this stage.

Use No. 30 dipper to portion cookies. Place on parchment lined cookie sheet about 2 inches apart. Bake in 325 degrees F oven for only 10 minutes. — *Trinity Medical Center Nutrition Services*

June 22, 1994

Trinity Medical Center Oatmeal Raisin Cookies

- 2/3 pound margarine (1-1/3 cups)
- 1-1/3 cups white sugar
- 1-1/3 cups brown sugar
- 3 eggs
- 1 teaspoon vanilla
- 2 cups all-purpose flour
- 1-1/3 teaspoons salt
- 1-1/3 teaspoons baking soda
- 4 cups uncooked oats
- 1-1/3 teaspoons cinnamon
- 1-1/3 cups raisins, soaked

Soak raisins in water for about 1 hour; drain well and let drip dry.

Cream margarine, both sugars, vanilla and eggs together until light and fluffy. Add flour, salt, baking soda and cinnamon; mix well. Stir in uncooked oats and raisins

Use No. 40 dipper to portion. Bake in 325 degrees F oven for 10 minutes. Makes 5 dozen Oatmeal Raisin Cookies.
— *Trinity Medical Center Nutrition Services*

June 22, 1994

Trinity Medical Center Peanut Butter Cookies

- 1¼ cups white sugar
- ¾ cup brown sugar
- 5-1/3 ounces butter
- 4 ounces margarine
- 1¼ teaspoons vanilla
- ½ cup eggs, beaten
- 1-1/8 cups peanut butter
- 2/3 pound all-purpose flour (2-2/3 cups)
- 1¼ teaspoons baking soda
- ½ teaspoon salt
- 2/3 cup granulated peanuts, optional

Cream both sugars, butter, margarine, and vanilla together. Add eggs and peanut butter; blend well.

Sift dry ingredients together and mix in with creamed mixture. Use No. 30 dipper and flatten with fork tines.

Bake in 375 degrees F oven for 8 minutes. Makes 5 dozen Peanut Butter Cookies. — *Trinity Medical Center Nutrition Services*

June 22, 1994

Trinity Medical Center Sugar Cookies

- ¾ pound shortening (12 ounces or 1½ cups)
- 13½ ounces butter
- 1½ pounds granulated sugar (3 cups)
- 1 tablespoon vanilla
- 2 eggs
- 1¾ pounds all-purpose flour (7 cups)
- 1½ teaspoons cream of tartar
- 2 teaspoons baking soda
- 1/3 teaspoon salt
- Cinnamon-sugar mixture (See below)

Cream shortening, butter and sugar together, starting on low speed, progressing to medium, then to high speed until blended. Add vanilla and eggs, mixing thoroughly.

Combine dry ingredients. Gradually add to creamed mixture. Blend well. Portion with No. 30 dipper onto paper-lined baking pans.

For sugar/cinnamon mixture, combine 1 cup sugar and 1 tablespoon cinnamon, mixing well. Sprinkle tops of cookies with cinnamon-sugar mixture.

Bake in 375 degrees F oven for 8 to 10 minutes. Cookies will be soft in center. Makes 6 dozen Sugar Cookies.
— *Trinity Medical Center Nutrition Services*

Trio Swiss Steak

Nov. 3, 1993

Many of our readers have wonderful culinary memories of eating at the Trio Restaurant in downtown Davenport and the food specialties of that restaurant, which was so popular years ago.

Last spring, Curious Cook featured an article on Mrs. Gertrude Hohenadel, one of the owners, and her recipe for the Trio Meatloaf in answer to a reader request.

Now Curious cook has received a request from S.B. of Davenport for the Trio Swiss Steak. Mrs. Hohenadel and her daughter, Sue Ann Wood, also of Davenport, have very graciously shared that recipe as well. S.B. wrote to Curious Cook.

"This past May, you printed a column on Mrs. Hohenadel, owner of the former Trio Restaurant in downtown Davenport. You published the recipe for the meatloaf at the request of one of your readers.

"I also frequented the Trio, one of my favorite places to dine. I remember the Swiss Steak that was served there — so tender you could cut it with a fork.

"Mrs. Hohenadel stated she had given out that recipe so many times and I was wondering if she would be kind enough to share it once again, as I am sure many of your readers would love to add it to their files."

Here's the recipe:

"Dip four 6-ounce size ½-inch thick top round steak in flour and brown in heavy skillet. When nicely browned, take out and place in roaster or baking dish; salt and pepper to taste.

"Chop a medium-size onion and sprinkle on steaks. Make gravy from drippings using ¼ cup flour and 2 cups water. When thickened, add 6-ounce can tomato sauce or tomato puree and pour gravy over steaks. Bake in 350-degree oven for 1 hour or until meat is tender."   — *Gertrude Hohenadel, The Trio Restaurant, Davenport*

appetizers

teasing your palate

Dear Curious Cook

Chipped Beef Cocktail Spread

Date Unknown

This recipe from the late Anne Coryn of Moline was one of the very first recipes to be published in the Curious Cook column. "A men's favorite," she said. "Substitute fresh onion for the flakes, if desired."

- 1 package smoked beef, torn or cut in small pieces
- A few dried onion flakes
- 2 small packages (3 ounces each) cream cheese, softened
- Dash of Worcestershire sauce
- Red wine, to moisten, as desired

Combine all ingredients, mixing well. Cover and chill. Serve with crackers or cocktail breads. — *Anne Coryn of Moline*

Hawaiian Meatballs

March 18, 1998

"This is a little late for P.N. of Davenport to make Hawaiian Meatballs for the holidays, but they are good any time of the year," writes K.B. of Rock Island, answering a recent request. "Here is my recipe."

MEATBALLS:
- 1½ pounds lean ground pork (may be mixed half and half with ground beef)
- ¾ cup rolled oats
- 1 can water chestnuts, drained and chopped
- 1 egg, slightly beaten
- 1 tablespoon soy sauce
- ½ teaspoon finely chopped onion
- Dash Tabasco sauce

Mix ingredients well and form into small balls. Brown and drain off fat.

SAUCE:
- 1 can (13½ ounces) crushed pineapple
- 1 cup brown sugar
- 2 tablespoons cornstarch
- 1 cup water
- 1/2 cup red wine vinegar or lemon juice
- 2 tablespoons soy sauce
- 1/3 cup chopped green pepper

Drain pineapple, reserving juice. Mix sugar and cornstarch in saucepan and gradually add liquids. Cook, stirring constantly, until thick. Add pineapple and green pepper. Pour over meatballs and simmer for 30 minutes.

Note: "This recipe also works great for a Hawaiian meatloaf. Place meat mixture in a loaf pan with sauce over top and bake at 350 degrees for 1 hour to 1 hour and 15 minutes." — *K.B. of Rock Island*

Hawaiian Meatballs

March 18, 1998

1½ pounds ground beef
2/3 cup cracker crumbs
1/3 cup minced onion
1 egg
1 teaspoon salt
¼ cup milk
1 tablespoon shortening
2 tablespoons cornstarch

½ cup brown sugar
1 can (13½ ounces) pineapple tidbits, drained reserve juice
1/3 cup vinegar
1 tablespoon soy sauce
1 can water chestnuts, drained
1/3 cup chopped green pepper

Mix first six ingredients; form into balls and brown in shortening. Pour off fat.

Mix into a pan, the cornstarch and sugar; stir in pineapple juice, vinegar and soy sauce and cook until smooth, stirring constantly until mixture thickens. Add pineapple tidbits, green pepper and water chestnuts.

Put meatballs in Pyrex pan and pour hot sauce over them. Bake at 325 degrees for 20 minutes. Serve with rice. This is a good party recipe and serves 6. — *B.D. of Cambridge*

Hot Cocoa Mix

Feb. 1, 1995

Curious Cook is absolutely amazed at the variety — and number — of recipes we received for cocoa mixes! S.L. of Davenport, who requested the recipe, will have plenty of choices. Curious Cook thanks all who responded.

1½ cups sugar, preferabley super-fine granulated
1 cup instant, nonfat, dry milk powder
1 cup non-dairy coffee creamer powder

¾ cup unsweeteneed cocoa
1 vanilla bean, split, optional added to the mix

Mix all together, sifting in cocoa, and stir to mix thoroughly. Store in cool dry place in a 1-quart jar, and screw cap on tightly.

To make a serving, place 4 to 6 teaspoons of the mix in a large cup or mug, add boiling water and stir. Adjust amounts to suit your taste.

Note: Instead of the vanilla bean, you can add ¼ teaspoon of vanilla to the cup as you mix. Makes about 4 cups of mix, or enough to make 16 one-cup servings. Of course, you can double the ingredients or more. — *N.C. of Rock Island*

Party Mix Microwave Recipe

April 16, 1997

½ cup (1 stick) margarine
1¼ teaspoons salt
4½ teaspoons Worcestershire sauce

2-2/3 cups Corn Chex cereal
2-2/3 cups Rice Chex cereal
2-2/3 cups Wheat Chex cereal
1 cup salted mixed nuts

In a 4-quart bowl or 13x9x2-inch microwave-safe dish, melt margarine on high 1 minute. Stir in seasoned salt and Worcestershire. Gradually add cereal and nuts, mixing until all pieces are coated. Microwave on high 5 to 6 minutes, stirring every 2 minutes. — *D.B. of Moline*

Party Rye Pizza

Dec. 2, 1998

This recipe was submitted for the 1998 Quad Cities Holiday Cookbook.

Although it calls for ground beef, E.C. could adapt the ingredients to her liking.

This has been a popular hors d'oeuvre for many years.

1 pound ground beef
1 large egg
1 package (2 ounces) dry onion soup
1 dash salt

1 package party rye bread
1 jar (10 ounces) pizza sauce
1 package (8 ounces) mozzarella cheese shredded

Mix ground beef, egg, dry soup mix and salt in 2-quart glass or plastic bowl.

Arrange party rye bread spaced 1 inch apart on ungreased cookie sheet. Spread ground beef mixture on bread, top with pizza sauce and sprinkle with shredded mozzarella cheese. Bake at 350 degrees for 15 minutes. — *J.K. Of Moline*

recipes to remember forever **51**

Polynesian Meatballs

March 18, 1998

MEATBALLS:
2 pounds ground beef
½ cup fine bread crumbs
2 eggs, slightly beaten
1 teaspoon salt

Combine ground meat, bread crumbs, beaten eggs and salt. Shape into small meatballs and arrange in greased shallow pan. Bake at 450 degrees for 10 minutes.

SAUCE:
2 cups water
¼ cup vinegar
¼ cup firmly packed brown sugar
2 envelopes French Onion gravy mix
2 tablespoons Worcestershire Sauce
1 can (11 ounces) mandarin oranges drained
1 can (8 ounces) sliced water chestnuts, drained
½ cup chopped green pepper
2 tablespoons pimiento
½ teaspoon ginger

Combine water, vinegar, brown sugar, contents of gravy mix envelopes, Worcestershire sauce, and ginger stirring until smooth.

Add meatballs, oranges, water chestnuts, green peppers and pimiento. Simmer, uncovered, 10 to 15 minutes, stirring occasionally. Serve over hot cooked rice. — *J.N. of Wheatland, Iowa*

Rhubarb Punch

July 31, 1996

L.P. of Davenport sent a Rhubarb Punch recipe to answer the recent request. She says that she and her guests have enjoyed this "sweet and tart" drink.

1 quart rhubarb (about 2 dozen stalks)
Water to cover
3 cups sugar
2 cups water
6 lemons, juiced
1 cup pineapple juice
1 quart ginger ale

Cut rhubarb into 1-inch pieces. Add water to cover. Cook until soft, about 10 minutes. Drain through cheesecloth bag. Juice should measure 3 quarts. Dissolve sugar in 2 cups water. Cook 10 minutes to make a syrup.

Add lemon juice, pineapple juice and rhubarb juice. Pour over chunks of ice in a punch bowl. Just before serving, add 1 quart ginger ale. Makes 1 gallon punch or 24 servings. — *L.P. of Davenport*

Rhubarb Slush

July 24, 1996

"I think that I have the Rhubarb Slush recipe that L.H. of Reynolds is looking for," writes G.K. of Moline.

"I got it recently from a fellow Federated Woman's Club member from Geneseo. It sounds like this recipe is hitting the outlying areas before the Quad-Cities."

3 cups chopped fresh or frozen rhubarb
1 cup water
1/3 cup sugar
1 cup apple juice

1 can (6 ounces) frozen pink lemonade concentrate, thawed
1 bottle (2 liter) lemon-lime soda

Combine rhubarb, water and sugar in a saucepan and bring to a boil. Reduce heat, cover and simmer for 5 minutes, until rhubarb is tender. Cool 30 minutes.

Puree ½ of the mixture at a time. Stir in apple juice and lemonade.

Freeze until firm. Bring to room temperature for 45 minutes. Add soda to serve. You also may add vodka for zest. Makes about 10 servings.
— *G.K. of Moline*

Skillet Luau Meatballs

March 18, 1998

1 pound ground beef
1 egg, beaten
¼ cup dry bread crumbs
½ teaspoon salt
¼ teaspoon ginger
¼ cup flour
3 tablespoons salad oil

1 can 20 ounces pineapple chunks
3 tablespoons brown sugar
¾ teaspoon cornstarch
¼ cup vinegar
1 teaspoon soy sauce
2 green peppers, cut into strips

Mix beef with egg, bread crumbs and seasonings; form into balls. Dredge in flour and brown in salad oil in large frying pan. Remove meatballs from pan.

Drain pineapple, reserving liquid; add water to syrup to make 1 cup. Stir into drippings.

Mix brown sugar with cornstarch, vinegar and soy sauce; add to syrup mixture. Cook stirring constantly, until sauce is thickened and clear.

Arrange meatballs, pineapple chunks and pepper strips in sauce; stir gently to coat with sauce; Cover and simmer 10 minutes or until meatballs are done and green pepper strips are tender-crisp. Serve with hot buttered noodles or rice. Serves 4.

— *J.N. of Wheatland, Iowa*

Spiced Pecans

May 3, 2000

"Per your reader's request for Spiced Pecans, I always use the recipe below using standard oven at 300 degrees for 30 minutes," writes M.G. of Rock Island.

"I line a cookie sheet with foil, then spray with Pam. Stir the nuts several times in warm oven after it is shut off, until nuts are completely dry. Store in sealed container. They're great!"

1 egg white, beaten slightly
1 tablespoon water
3 cups pecan halves
½ cup sugar

½ teaspoon salt, or to taste
1 teaspoon ground cinnamon
½ teaspoon ground cloves
½ teaspoon ground nutmeg

In small bowl, beat together egg white and water. Stir in pecans, stirring until all surfaces are moistened.

Mix together sugar, salt, cinnamon, cloves and nutmeg; sprinkle over pecans, mixing well. Spread pecans on a lightly greased or foil-lined cookie sheet and bake in pre-heated oven, 300 degrees, for 30 minutes. Stir once or twice to crisp and dry pecans evenly. Makes 3 cups.
— *M.G. of Rock Island*

Spiced Pecans

April 26, 2000

Curious Cook still has contributions to the Spiced Pecans recipes to answer the request J.D. of Davenport sent in a few months ago.

B.V.O. of Moline writes: "Though this is made in the oven and has sugar in it, I'm sending it in case the micro recipe isn't sent. They're delicious."

Curious Cook's note: "This recipe was published in the appetizers section of the 1999 Quad-Cities Holiday Cookbook" published by The Dispatch, The Rock Island Argus and The Leader.

1 pound pecan halves
1 egg white
1 teaspoon cold water
½ cup sugar

¼ teaspoon salt
½ teaspoon cinnamon
½ teaspoon nutmeg
¼ teaspoon cloves

Beat egg white and water until frothy but not stiff. Add nuts and mix until coated.

Mix sugar and spices in large bowl. Add nut mixture to that bowl. Place nuts on buttered jelly-roll pan.

Bake at 225 degrees for 1 hour, stirring every 15 minutes. Store in refrigerator in tight container.
— *B.V.O. of Moline*

Spiced Pecans

May 10, 2000

P.R. of East Moline writes about the requested Spiced Pecans:

"The one I make every year comes from Christ United Methodist Church, Charity Circle, East Moline. They used to sell pecans as a moneymaker and included this recipe," P.R. reports. Here 'tis:

1 egg white
3 tablespoons water
1 teaspoon cinnamon
¼ teaspoon salt
½ cup sugar
1 pound pecans

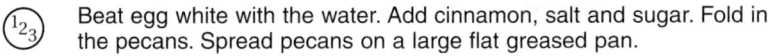

Beat egg white with the water. Add cinnamon, salt and sugar. Fold in the pecans. Spread pecans on a large flat greased pan.

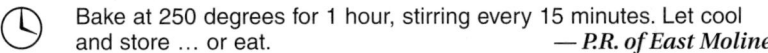

Bake at 250 degrees for 1 hour, stirring every 15 minutes. Let cool and store … or eat.

— *P.R. of East Moline*

Sweet & Sour Pineapple Meatballs

Dec. 17, 1997

"This might be the recipe that P.N. of Davenport is looking for," writes V.C. of Geneseo. "It's one of my favorite appetizer recipes that I make often."

"You can use your favorite meat or ham-loaf recipe to make the meatballs."

1½ pounds lean ground beef
1 cup tomato juice
¾ cup raw quick-cooking oats
1 egg

¼ cup chopped onion
½ teaspoon salt
¼ teaspoon black pepper

Mix all ingredients and form into small balls. Place in shallow baking dish and bake at 375 degrees for about 15 to 20 minutes.

SAUCE:
1 tablespoon oil
¼ teaspoon salt
1 medium onion, chopped
1 medium green or red pepper, chopped ("I use some of each.")
½ cup ketchup

2 tablespoons vinegar
1½ teaspoons cornstarch
1 can (8 ounces) pineapple chunks reserve syrup
2 tablespoons sherry wine, optional
Green onions, optional

Heat oil in skillet; add salt, onions and green pepper and cook until tender. Combine ketchup and vinegar and stir into onion-pepper mixture.

Make a paste with cornstarch and reserved pineapple syrup. Add to vegetable mixture. Cook, stirring, for 3 to 5 minutes or until mixture thickens.

Stir in pineapple chunks and sherry wine, if used. Mix in the meatballs and heat through. Place in serving dish and garnish with green onions.

Note: "I like to serve ham balls with this sauce also. Just substitute ground ham for the ground beef." — *V.C. of Geneseo*

soups & salads

a great start or a simple meal

Dear Curious Cook

Baked Potato Soup

March 31, 1999

To answer the recent request for a recipe for Baked Potato Soup, J.G. of Rock Island sends this well-tested soup recipe, which differs significantly from one previously published.

"Basically I make a thick white sauce and add the potatoes, onions and turkey bacon. Rather easy. It is a nice change from regular potato soup although I make it about the same way!"

2 large baking potatoes, baked
1/3 cup margarine
1/3 cup flour
¾ cup skim milk

2 green onions, chopped
3 to 4 slices bacon, chopped
1 to 2 ounces grated cheese, for topping
Sour cream, as desired

Cut and chop the baked potatoes, using half the peel. Melt margarine in pan; stir in flour until smooth. Add milk gradually, stirring until thickened. Add potatoes, onion and bacon.

For topping, add grated cheese before serving. Sour cream also may be added to bowl of soup before the grated cheese.

— *J.G., Rock Island*

Broccoli Salad

July 17, 2002

From J.B. of Bettendorf: "This is in response to a request by L.V.H. of Moline for a recipe for a Ramen Noodle Salad. I have one that sounds like the one that is described. Here it is."

1-pound package broccoli slaw
4 scallions, chopped small
1 cup sunflower seeds
½ cup slivered almonds
¾ cup vegetable oil

½ cup vinegar
½ cup sugar
Noodles from 2 packages chicken-flavored Ramen soup

In large bowl, toss broccoli slaw, scallions, seeds and nuts.

In small bowl, mix oil, vinegar and sugar and pour over slaw.

Break noodles into pieces and add to salad. Toss well and chill 2 hours before serving.
— *J.B. of Bettendorf*

B.T.L. Soup

Aug. 23, 1995

1 pound bacon, cut in small pieces
1 cup chopped onion
2 cups chopped celery
½ cup all-purpose flour
2 cans (16 ounces) each stewed tomatoes, cut up
1 can (48 ounces) spicy V-8 vegetable juice
4 cups beef stock or 4 bouillon cubes dissolved in 4 cups water
2 tablespoons sugar
1 tablespoon oregano
4 cups finely chopped romaine lettuce

Brown bacon pieces; remove from pan and set aside. Reserve ½ cup of drippings. Sauté onion and celery in drippings until tender.

Mix in flour. Add tomatoes, vegetable juice, beef stock, sugar, oregano and reserved bacon.

If soup mixture is not thick enough, add additional flour (¼ cup) with a little water. Consistency should be that of a thin sauce. Simmer for 25 to 30 minutes.

Add lettuce to soup in pot and serve immediately OR top individual bowls with lettuce when serving. Makes 15 to 20 servings.

— D.J.B. of Moline

Cherry Cola Salad

July 30, 1997

"Here is the recipe for Cherry Cola Salad that J.G. of Rock Island requested. It is exceptionally good," writes M.K. of Rock Island.

1 can (1 pound) bing cherries
1 can (1 pound) crushed pineapple
1 large package (6 ounces) cherry or black cherry flavored gelatin
1 can or bottle (12 ounces) Cola beverage
1 cup canned or package of blanched, slivered almonds (pecans can be used)

Drain cherries and pineapple. Measure syrups and add water if necessary to make 2 cups.

Heat syrups to boiling. Pour over gelatin. Stir until gelatin is dissolved. Add cola beverage; chill until consistency of unbeaten egg white.

Combine cherries, pineapple and almonds. Fold in. Spoon into 8-cup mold. Chill until firm. If desired, garnish with dairy sour cream sweetened to taste. Can be used as salad or dessert. — *M.K. of Rock Island*

Corn Chowder

April 16, 1997

- 2 cups water
- 2 chicken bouillon cubes
- 2 cups diced potatoes (see note)
- 2 or 3 carrots, diced or sliced
- 1 cup chopped celery
- 1 small onion, chopped
- 2 cans (15 ounces) each cream-style corn
- 1 can (15 ounces) whole-kernel corn, drained (See note)
- Tabasco sauce, optional

Combine water, bouillon cubes, potatoes, carrots, celery and onion; boil together for 15 to 20 minutes. Stir in cream-style and whole-kernel corn. Heat thoroughly. Add Tabasco sauce if desired.

Note: "I often have used hash-browns frozen potatoes, partially thawed. Milk may be added if desired; amount optional."

— *B.A.W. of Davenport*

Cranberry Cherry Salad

May 7, 1997

A.P.K. of Davenport included this cranberry salad recipe when she sent in her Coffee Can Bread recipe published last week.

"Am also enclosing an especially good cranberry salad but it doesn't call for sour cream as B.C. of Hampton asked for. Ate it at a potluck and liked it so much that I asked for the recipe.

Have given the recipe to others when I have taken it to suppers."

- 1 pound cranberries
- 2 cups sugar
- 1 large package cherry-flavored gelatin
- 1 can (8 ounces) crushed pineapple, drained, save juice
- 1½ cups maraschino cherries, cut-up
- ½ cup nuts, optional

Add water to pineapple juice to make 1¾ cups. Add sugar and cranberries. Cook until berries pop. Add cherry-flavored gelatin. Then add cherries and pineapple. Add nuts if desired. Put into 8x8x2-inch glass dish. Chill.

— *A.P.K. of Davenport*

Cranberry Salad

April 16, 1997

"Read in the morning paper that someone was looking for a cranberry gelatin salad recipe. I have one that was given to me 20 plus years ago," writes M.C. of Moline. "This may be the one she is looking for."

D.A.P. of Bettendorf also submitted the salad recipe.

- 2 packages (4-serving size) cherry-flavored gelatin
- 6 tablespoons sugar
- 2 cups boiling water
- 1 can (16 ounces) whole cranberry sauce
- 1 pint sour cream
- 1 can (8 ounces) crushed pineapple, drained
- ½ cup chopped pecans, optional

Dissolve gelatin and sugar in boiling water. Add cranberry sauce and place in refrigerator until partially set. Add sour cream and pineapple.

Add chopped pecans. Return to refrigerator until set or overnight.

Serves 10 to 12. — *M.C. of Moline, D.A.P. of Bettendorf*

Cranberry Salad

May 7, 1997

"This might be the recipe B.C. of Hampton is looking for," writes E.D. of Davenport. "If not, it's still a winner."

- 2 cans whole cranberry sauce
- 2 cups mini-marshmallows
- 2 unpeeled apples, diced
- 3 bananas, sliced
- 1 can (11 ounces) mandarin oranges, drained
- 1 cup coarsely chopped pecans

Mix all ingredients together and chill. Can use more or less fruit according to individual taste. — *E.D. of Davenport*

Cranberry Salad

Nov. 19, 1997

- 4 cups fresh cranberries
- 4 medium-size apples, cored and ground
- 1½ cups sugar
- 1 cup miniature marshmallows
- 1 can (20 ounces) crushed pineapple, drained
- 1 cup frozen whipped topping, thawed
- ½ cup chopped nuts

Grind cranberries and apples together. Add sugar and miniature marshmallows. Refrigerate overnight. Add drained crushed pineapple. Before serving, add whipped topping and nuts. — *D.B. of Moline*

Cranberry Salad

Nov. 19, 1997

"I hope this is the cranberry recipe C.P of Davenport is looking for. I have used this as both a salad and dessert," S.S. of Davenport tells us in her note.

- 2 cups coarsely ground cranberries
- 1 cup sugar
- 1 can (11 ounces) mandarin oranges, drained, save juice
- 1 can (8 ounces chunk) pineapple, drained, save juice
- 1 cup shredded coconut
- 1 large banana, cubed
- 2 envelopes unflavored gelatin
- 1 cup sour cream
- 1 cup whipping cream

Combine cranberries and sugar. Add oranges, pineapple, coconut and banana to cranberries. Sprinkle gelatin over ¾ cup of the combined juices to soften, over medium heat, stirring constantly to dissolve gelatin. Cool this a little and then add fruit. Fold in sour cream.

Whip cream until stiff peaks form. Fold into fruit mixture. Pour into a 2-quart mold or 13x9x2-inch pan and chill thoroughly overnight. Or may be frozen.
— *S.S. of Davenport*

Cranberry-Waldorf Gelatin Salad

June 4, 1997

"Hope this is the Cranberry Salad the lady is looking for. My family likes it anyway," writes D.R. of Bettendorf.

- 2 packages (3 ounces each) cranberry gelatin (do not use sugar-free)
- 1¾ cups boiling water
- ¾ cup cold water
- ¾ cup diced red-delicious apple
- ¾ cup diced golden-delicious apple
- ½ cup seedless green grapes, quartered
- ¼ cup chopped pecans
- Cooking spray
- ½ of an 8-ounce block fat-free cream cheese, softened
- ¾ cup low-fat sour cream
- 2 tablespoons sugar
- ¼ teaspoon vanilla

Combine gelatin and boiling water; stir until dissolved. Add cold water. Cover and chill until the consistency of unbeaten egg whites. Fold in apples, grapes and pecans. Spoon into 5-cup mold coated with spray. Chill until firm.

Beat cream cheese until smooth. Add sour cream, sugar and vanilla. Beat well.

Unmold on lettuce leaves, top with cream cheese mixture. Garnish with apple slices and chopped pecans, if desired. Makes 8 servings.
— *D.R. of Bettendorf*

Deluxe Potato Soup

March 26, 2003

Recent publication of the recipe for Thunder Bay's very popular Baked Potato Soup in Curious Cook's column prompted K.S. of Moline to share this recipe, which she highly recommends.

"This is a delicious soup, rich in vitamins, filling and very tasty," writes K.S.

"We cut out adding salt to our recipes years ago. Don't miss it one bit. Salt is in so many of our foods; spices add so much more."

"This is a 'keeper.' " she promises.

3 cups raw potatoes, diced
½ cup finely chopped celery
½ cup finely chopped onion
3 cups water
2 cups milk, scalded
2 chicken bouillon cubes, no-salt preferred

3 tablespoons unsalted butter
1 cup lite sour cream
1 tablespoon flour
½ teaspoon salt, if desired
¼ teaspoon Mrs. Dash Table Blend (see notes)

Cook potatoes, onion and celery in water until tender. Do not drain.

Mash vegetables until finely mashed. Add milk, bouillon cubes and butter. Mix sour cream with flour until smooth and add to soup.

Cook mixture while stirring constantly until thick and bouillon cubes are completely dissolved. Do not let soup boil.

Stir in salt if desired, and Mrs. Dash blend of your choice, table blend or extra spicy.

Notes: "We have started using Mrs. Dash extra spicy seasoning blend for an extra kick. If you do not wish to use Mrs. Dash mixture blends, just use 1/3 teaspoon pepper."

— *K.S. of Moline*

Frog Eye Salad

June 1, 1994

"Hope this is the recipe that H.M. of Rock Island wanted," writes M.M. of Viola. Her recipe is similar to J.B.'s, but the quantity is a little less.

½ pound Acini De Pepe
1 cup sugar
2 tablespoons flour
½ teaspoon salt
1-1/3 cups pineapple juice
3 egg yolks
2 cans (11 ounces each) mandarin oranges, drained

1 can (20 ounces) pineapple chunks, drained
1 can (20 ounces) crushed pineapple, drained
Miniature marshmallows, as desired
Coconut, as desired
Frozen whipped topping, thawed, as needed

Cook and drain Acini De Pepe; do not overcook. Combine sugar, flour, salt, pineapple juice and egg yolks in a saucepan. Cook and stir until thick. Cool slightly and add to cooked Acini De Pepe. Cover and refrigerate overnight.

Before serving, add mandarin oranges, pineapple chunks, crushed pineapple, miniature marshmallows and coconut. Fold in whipped topping.

— M.M. of Viola

Frog Eye Salad

June 1, 1994

"Here is the Frog Eye Salad. Acini De Pepe is found in the pasta section of the supermarket. It looks rather like rice, but is pasta. The recipe should be right on the box. You can't use macaroni as far as I know.

"The overall effect of this is rather like old-fashioned pearl tapioca, but it is unique.

"I got the recipe from Ma's Studio Diner in Davenport on 13th and Brady. She makes some really good homemade food and unusual recipes, and is planning a cookbook of everyone's favorites. But don't call her up; no phone. She just tells people to 'come in and eat and you'll like it!' And she's right!' " — *J.B. of Davenport*

"In the May 18 issue of The Dispatch, H.M. of Rock Island said she had lost her recipe for Frog Eye Salad. Enclosed is a copy of my recipe. Hope this will be of help to her the next time she entertains King's Daughters or any large group." — *A.J.C. of East Moline*

Here's the Frog Eye Salad recipe, more or less a composite of those submitted by area cooks.

- 1 cup sugar
- 2 tablespoons flour
- ½ teaspoon salt
- 1¾ cups pineapple juice from the canned chunks
- 2 eggs, beaten
- 1 tablespoon lemon juice
- 1 package (1 pound) Acini De Pepe macaroni, uncooked (found in pasta section)
- 3 cans (11 ounces each) mandarin oranges, drained
- 2 or 3 cans (20 ounces each) pineapple chunks, drained, juice saved
- 1 carton (8 ounces) non-dairy whipped topping, thawed
- 1 or 2 cups mini marshmallows optional
- 1 cup flaked coconut optional

Combine sugar, flour, salt; stir in pineapple juice and eggs. Cook, stirring until thick. Add lemon juice and cool to room temperature.

Cook Acini-de-Pepe according to package instructions and drain. Combine egg mixture and Acini De Pepe and refrigerate overnight in airtight container. Add remaining ingredients and mix. Cover and refrigerate until chilled, always in an airtight container.

Curious Cook's note: Most of the cooks list 25 servings for this salad. A.J.C. of East Moline advises the salad "stores well in the refrigerator up to 2 weeks. May be frozen. You may use two 20-ounce cans pineapple chunks instead of two 15-ounce cans of crushed pineapple" as called for in A.J.C.'s recipe.

— *J.B. of Davenport, D.W. of Annawan, A.J.C. of East Moline*

Honey Mustard Dressing

Feb. 6, 2002

"Hello! I am thrilled I finally have a recipe to share!," e-mails H.M. of Colona in response to J.N.'s request.

"I think it is nice and tangy with a little spice."

½ cup salad oil
¼ cup honey
3 tablespoons cider vinegar
3 tablespoons Honey Dijon mustard
3 tablespoons Boetje's mustard

In a jar with a tight-fitting lid, shake all ingredients together.

Note: "Sometime I use a little extra Boetje's because I like mine to really have a kick." — *H.M. of Colona*

Mexican Salad

April 25, 2001

From B.N. of Moline: "I hope this is the recipe C.S. of Davenport is looking for."

1 pound ground beef
¼ cup chopped onion
2 cups (1 pound) drained kidney beans
½ cup Catalina French Dressing
½ cup water
1 tablespoon chili powder
4 cups shredded lettuce
½ cup sliced green onions
1 wedge (8 ounces) Cheddar cheese, shredded

Brown meat; drain. Add onion to meat and cook until tender. Stir in beans, French dressing, water and chili powder. Simmer 15 minutes.

Combine lettuce and green onions. Add meat sauce and 1½ cups cheese and toss. Sprinkle with remaining cheese and serve with crisp tortillas. — *B.N. of Moline*

Napa Cabbage

May 22, 1996

From V.O.C. of Geneseo: "Maybe this is the recipe that M.K. of Moline is looking for. I get requests for the recipe every time I serve it."

A friend of mine used regular cabbage, grated fine, and said it worked great, too.

- 1 head Napa cabbage, cut-up
- 1 bunch green onions, cut up tops too
- 1 stick margarine
- 2 packages Ramen noodles, broken up
- ½ cup sliced almonds
- 1 ounce sesame seeds

DRESSING:
- ½ cup sugar
- ¼ cup rice vinegar
- ¾ cup oil
- 1 tablespoon soy sauce

Saute noodles, almonds and sesame seeds in margarine until lightly browned.

For dressing, bring sugar, rice vinegar, oil and soy sauce to a boil and boil 1 minute. Cool.

Mix cabbage, onions and noodle mixture. Add cooled dressing and toss.

— V.O.C. of Geneseo

Napa Cabbage Salad

July 17, 2002

Our readers always are generous about sharing their favorite recipes. They take the time, often including helpful comments, and make the effort to send them to Curious Cook.

But B.B. of Moline went beyond the call of duty, writing out her recipes left-handed because of a broken right arm!

B.B. promises that her interesting Napa Cabbage Salad "stays crisp and fresh." Here's that recipe:

- **1 cup oil**
- **8 tablespoons ginger-flavored soy sauce**
- **1 cup brown sugar**
- **½ cup white vinegar**
- **¾ stick margarine**
- **2 packages Ramen noodles (discard the seasoning)**

- **1 ounce sesame seeds**
- **3 tablespoons sunflower seeds**
- **1 package sliced almonds**
- **1 head Napa cabbage**
- **3 bunches green onions and tops, sliced**
- **1 green pepper, chopped**
- **3 or 4 carrots, shredded**

Combine oil, soy sauce, brown sugar and vinegar; bring to boil and cook for 1 minute. Cool. Store in glass jar.

Sauté the margarine, Ramen noodles, sesame seeds, sunflower seeds and almonds until "golden brown." Saute carefully and slowly because mixture burns easily. Break up noodles. Cool. Store in plastic Ziploc bag.

Slice and quarter 1 head Napa cabbage. "I like larger pieces. Not shredded," B.B. says. Add sliced green onions, green pepper and shredded carrots. Store in plastic bag in refrigerator.

Mix contents of the containers as needed. — *B.B. of Moline*

Red Cabbage with Apples

Dec. 12, 2001

"This recipe is in regard to T.J.M. of Coal Valley and the request for Hungarian Red Cabbage," writes G.V.M. of East Moline.

"I'm of German descent and we had red cabbage and this is how we prepared it."

- 1 medium-size head red cabbage
- 1 or 2 tart apples
- 2 tablespoons chicken fat or butter
- 1 medium-size onion, sliced
- 1 quart water
- ½ cup red wine vinegar
- ½ cup sugar
- ½ teaspoon salt
- ½ teaspoon pepper
- 2 cloves
- 1 bay leaf
- Juice of ½ lemon
- 2 or 3 tablespoons flour

Wash cabbage; drain; cut as for slaw.

Wash and core apples; peel and cut into small pieces.

Heat chicken fat or butter in large saucepan and saute onion and apples 3 or 4 minutes.

Add water, vinegar, sugar, salt, pepper, cloves, bay leaf and lemon juice. Stir; bring to a boil. Add cabbage. Cover and let simmer 45 minutes or until tender.

Just before serving, sprinkle flour on top to absorb liquid. Serves 4.

Note: Be sure to remove the bay leaf before serving.

— *G.V.M. of East Moline*

Red, White, Blue Layered Salad

LAYER 1:
1 large package (8-serving size) red raspberry gelatin
2 cups boiling water

Combine well and pour into a 9x13-inch pan. Refrigerate to set up.

LAYER 2:
1 envelope unflavored gelatin
½ cup cold water

Combine gelatin and water and set aside. Meanwhile, combine in medium saucepan:

1 cup half-and-half
1 cup sugar
1 teaspoon vanilla

Heat until hot and sugar is dissolved. Ingredients will coat your spoon. Beat in:

1 package (8 ounces) cream cheese, softened
¾ to 1 cup chopped nuts

Combine gelatin mixture with cooked mixture; pour over Layer 1. Refrigerate to set up.

LAYER 3:
1 small package (4-serving size) red raspberry gelatin
1 cup boiling water
1 can blueberries

Combine red raspberry gelatin and boiling water. Drain juice from can of blueberries, reserving ¾ cup. Add the ¾ cup juice to the gelatin and blend well. Pour over Layer 2. Sprinkle with the blueberries. Refrigerate.

— *M.L.G. of Moline*

Sherried Wild Rice Soup

Jan. 10, 2001

This recipe has been in our files since October 1980, when we received it and enjoyed the soup at the Newspaper Food Editors Conference.

¼ cup butter or margarine
1 medium-size onion, finely chopped
½ pound sliced mushrooms
½ cup thinly sliced celery
½ cup flour
6 cups chicken broth
2 cups cooked wild rice

½ teaspoon salt
½ teaspoon curry powder
½ teaspoon dry mustard
½ teaspoon dried chervil
¼ teaspoon white pepper
2 cups half and half
2/3 cup dry sherry
Chopped parsley or chives

In a large saucepan, melt butter over medium heat; add onion. Cook and stir about 5 minutes until golden.

Add mushrooms and celery; cook and stir 2 minutes. Mix in flour. Gradually add broth, stirring constantly 5 to 8 minutes until slightly thickened.

Stir in rice, salt, curry powder, mustard, chervil and pepper. Reduce heat to low. Stir in half and half and sherry. Bring to simmer, stirring occasionally.

Ladle hot soup into individual bowls; garnish with parsley or chives. Makes about 3 quarts.   — *From Curious Cook's files*

March 20, 2002

Swiss Cheeseburger Soup

Curious Cook received this e-mail from C.F. of Davenport. She gives us the "official" version of Swiss Cheeseburger Soup.

"I recently read your column regarding the recipes for the Cheeseburger Soup from the J.C. Penney restaurant.

"I was in management years ago and the cook, Pat, would never give out that recipe. Finally, when the restaurant was closing, we talked her into giving it to us. I still have the original sheet that we all copied.

"I know she cooked it in large batches, so I'm not sure how she was able to cut it down to this size."

Curious Cook's note: Here's the recipe shared by C.F. A similar recipe, submitted by several other cooks, was published earlier this month.

- ½ pound ground beef
- 3 ounces green pepper
- 3 ounces chopped onion
- Salt and pepper, to taste
- ½ cup unsifted flour
- 1 cup cubed Swiss cheese
- 4 cups milk
- 1 can (16 ounces) stewed tomatoes
- 5 beef boullion cubes

Brown meat, onion, green pepper — salt and pepper — until cooked. Add ½ cup flour. Add milk, slowly stirring constantly. Add tomatoes, beef bouillon cubes and Swiss cheese. Serves 6 to 8 people. "Good warmed the next day."   — *C.F. of Davenport*

April 25, 2001

Taco Salad

"This may be the Taco Salad recipe requested by C.S. of Davenport. One of our favorites," writes C.H. of Moline.

- 1 pound ground beef, cooked and drained
- 1 can (15 ounces) pinto or kidney beans, drained
- 3 green onions, chopped
- 1 to 2 cups shredded Cheddar cheese
- 1 cup mayonnaise
- 1 head lettuce, shredded
- 3 to 4 tomatoes, cut into bite-size pieces
- 1 can (6 ounces) black olives, sliced
- 1 package (6 ounces) Doritos, crushed
- ¾ teaspoon chili powder
- ½ teaspoon garlic salt

Brown and drain beef. Combine and mix remaining ingredients, except mayo, lettuce and Doritos, with beef. Toss before adding mayo and lettuce. Mixes better. Doritos on top.   — *C.H. of Moline*

Taco Salad

April 25, 2001

Well, dear cooks, our mail proves that Taco Salad surely is a favorite in the Quad-Cities area!

Curious Cook is amazed at the response to the request for that salad, not to mention the great variety in the recipes, which area cooks have treasured for years.

So, here goes, from the mailbag and e-mail:

From J.W. of Moline: "Very good!! A meal in itself. Goes with any main course. You bring none home when you take it to a party," she promises.

- **1 pound ground beef**
- **1 package taco seasoning**
- **1 head of lettuce, torn up**
- **1 onion, chopped**
- **1 large tomato, chopped**
- **8 ounces or so grated Cheddar cheese**
- **1 bag taco chips, broken up**
- **1 bottle French or Western dressing, chilled**

Fry meat and drain. Add seasoning and cook in. Set aside and cool.

Mix lettuce, onion and tomato. Add cooled meat and cheese. Just before serving, add the chips and dressing.

Note: "If your party will last for a long time, with people coming in at different times, mix just half of the lettuce mixture, half of the chips and half of the dressing. It's not near as good if the chips get stale." — *J.W. of Moline*

Applesauce Coffee Cake

Dec. 19, 2001

This recipe is from Mary Lambert of Moline, whose treasured unfrosted cake recipes were featured in a recent food section.

Mrs. Lambert writes: "J.C. of Colona asked for an Applesauce Coffee Cake. I don't know if this is what she is looking for, but it is another of my mother's recipes that is delicious. We also serve it plain — unfrosted."

½ cup shortening
2 cups granulated sugar
1 egg
1½ cups thick unsweetened applesauce
2½ cups sifted, all-purpose flour

¼ teaspoon salt
2 teaspoons soda
1 teaspoon cinnamon
½ teaspoon cloves
1 cup chopped raisins
½ cup boiling water

Cream the shortening, sugar and egg. Add applesauce. Sift together flour, salt, soda, cinnamon and cloves. Add to applesauce mixture. Add chopped raisins. Add boiling water. Pour into a greased 9x13-inch pan.

Bake at 350 degrees for 45 to 60 minutes. Test for doneness with toothpick. Serve plain, frosted or with a sauce. — *M.L. of Moline*

Bar-B-Q Biscuits

April 30, 1997

D.D. of Moline shares this biscuit recipe. "Try with hot bowls of chili and a crisp green salad," she advises.

¼ cup chili sauce
¼ cup milk
1 teaspoon snipped parsley
1 teaspoon Worcestershire sauce

½ teaspoon instant minced onion
2 cups packaged biscuit mix

In bowl, combine all ingredients except biscuit mix; let stand 5 minutes. Stir in biscuit mix to make a soft dough.

Form into a ball on floured surface; knead 5 times. Roll ½-inch thick; cut into 2-inch rounds.

Bake on ungreased baking sheet at 450 degrees for 8 to 10 minutes. Makes 10 to 12 biscuits. — *D.D. of Moline*

Bishop's Bread

July 12, 1995

"Looking for recipe for Bishop's Bread," writes Mrs. G.M. of Rock Island. "Recently I visited Riefe's Restaurant in Davenport, Iowa. They served a Bishop's Bread that was simply delicious. At some time or another, it may have been printed in your column. If at all possible, I hope it can be reprinted." — *Mrs. G.M. of Rock Island*

Curious Cook's note: Ah yes, that Bishop's Bread is wonderful. Here are two recipes that have been published previously in the 1980s in Curious Cook's column in answer to a similar requests. The home-baker will have to decide whether or not these recipes yield loaves as good as the Bishop's Bread at Riefe's!

Here goes:

BATTER:
2¾ cups sifted all-purpose flour
3 teaspoons baking powder
1 teaspoon salt
½ cup butter or margarine, softened
1 cup firmly packed light brown sugar
2 eggs
1 cup milk

Preheat oven to 375 degrees. Then lightly grease a 13x9x2-inch baking pan.

Make batter: Sift flour with baking powder and salt. In large bowl of electric mixer, at medium speed, beat butter with brown sugar and eggs, beating until mixture is very light and fluffy. At low speed, blend in milk, then the flour mixture, beating just to combine.

Turn batter into the prepared pan, spreading evenly. Make Streusel Topping.

STREUSEL TOPPING:
½ cup granulated sugar
½ cup sifted all-purpose flour
¼ cup butter or margarine
1 tablespoon cinnamon

In small bowl, combine topping ingredients; mix until crumbly. Sprinkle over batter.

Bake at 375 degrees for 25 minutes or until cake tester inserted in the center comes out clean. Let cool slightly in pan on wire rack. Serve bread warm. Makes 16 servings. — *From Curious Cook's files*

Bishop's Bread

Oct. 14, 1998

Here's the second version of the bread.

- 2½ cups all-purpose flour
- 2 cups firmly packed brown sugar
- ½ teaspoon salt
- ½ cup shortening
- 1 teaspoon baking powder
- ¾ cup sour milk
- 1 egg
- ½ teaspoon cinnamon
- Chopped nuts, raisin, extra cinnamon, optional

Mix flour, sugar, salt and shortening. Reserve ¾ cup of this mixture for top crumbs. Add remaining ingredients. Beat briskly until batter is smooth.

Pour mixture into two greased 9-inch pie plates and scatter reserved crumbs over top. Bake at 350 degrees for 25 to 30 minutes.

Note: Chopped nuts or raisins, or both, may be added to batter and extra cinnamon sprinkled on top, if desired. — *From Curious Cook's files*

Nov. 17, 1993

Bucket Bread

- 1 cup currants
- 1 cup chopped dates
- 1 cup raisins
- 2 teaspoons baking soda
- 2 cups boiling water
- ½ cup margarine
- ¼ teaspoon salt
- 1¾ cups sugar
- 2 eggs
- 4 cups flour
- 2 teaspoons vanilla
- Nuts, if desired

Pour boiling water over fruit. Add baking soda and margarine and let stand until entirely cold.

Add rest of the ingredients and mix well.

Grease and flour seven No. 303 cans (16-17 ounces size). Fill each ½ full. Bake at 350 degrees for about 45 to 50 minutes.

Slip out of cans on cooling rack. Wrap in foil to freeze.

Note: "Can use No. 2½ cans (29 ounces size) filled ¾ full and bake 1 hour."

— *C.E.S. of Davenport*

Carrot Bread

Dec. 4, 1996

2/3 cup sugar
2 eggs, beaten
½ cup oil
1 teaspoon baking soda
1½ cups flour

½ teaspoon salt
1 teaspoon baking powder
1 teaspoon cinnamon
1 cup grated carrots
½ cup raisins

Preheat oven to 350 degrees.

Beat sugar, eggs and oil together. Add dry ingredients; beat well. Stir in carrots and raisins.

Pour batter into greased 9x5-inch loaf pan. Bake at 350 degrees for about 40 minutes.

— D.C. of Bettendorf

Chocolate Zucchini Bread

Nov. 3, 1993

"R.K. of Durant requested a recipe for Chocolate Zucchini Bread, which she had lost. Last year I had submitted the enclosed recipe. I'm not sure if this is the one she used as there were several printed."

3 eggs, beaten	1 teaspoon baking soda
2 cups sugar	½ teaspoon baking powder
1 cup cooking oil	1 teaspoon salt
2 cups grated zucchini	1 teaspoon cinnamon
2 teaspoons vanilla	3 tablespoons cocoa
3 cups flour	½ cup nuts optional

Peel and grate zucchini, leaving core. Beat eggs, add oil, sugar, grated zucchini and vanilla. Sift flour, then add soda, baking powder, salt, cinnamon and cocoa. Add to batter and mix till thoroughly blended. Add nuts.

Grease and flour three 7-3/8x3-5/8 x 2¼-inch loaf pans. Bake at 325 degrees for 1 hour. Freezes well.

Note: F.A. of Bettendorf directs baking in 2 oiled and floured pans at 350 degrees for approximately 1 hour. She also lists ¼ teaspoon baking powder instead of ½ teaspoon.

J.C. of New Boston bakes her bread in two greased loaf pans at 325 degrees for 40 to 50 minutes.

— *N.S. of East Moline, J.C. of New Boston and F.A. of Bettendorf*

Chocolate Zucchini Bread

Nov. 3, 1993

M.J.A. of Davenport very kindly looked through her files and found a similar recipe for the Chocolate Zucchini Bread. M.V. of East Moline also says the bread is very good.

3 eggs	1 teaspoon cinnamon
2 cups sugar	1 teaspoon baking soda
1 cup oil	¼ teaspoon baking powder
2 cups shredded zucchini	1/3 cup cocoa
1½ teaspoons vanilla	½ cup chopped nuts
2-1/3 cups flour	

Beat eggs and sugar together. Add oil. Drain zucchini as much as possible and add to oil mixture.

Sift together the flour, cinnamon, baking soda, baking powder and cocoa; add to zucchini mixture. Add vanilla and beat well. Mix in nuts.

Pour mixture into two greased loaf pans. Bake at 325 degrees for 40 to 50 minutes. Makes 2 loaves. Freezes well.

Note: M.V.'s recipe calls for 2½ cups flour, the others for 2-1/3 cups.
— *M.V. of East Moline, M.J.A. of Davenport and M.F.J. of New Boston*

Coffee-Time Muffins

Nov. 18, 1998

"I make bite-size muffins from this recipe, also," writes K.S. of Moline of her Coffee-Time Muffins, which answer the recent request for the Cappuccino Muffins.

"Using the smallest decorative papers — sprinkle powdered sugar after muffins have come out of oven, and cooled off a bit. If you don't wait to sprinkle the powdered sugar, the heat of the muffin dissolves the powdered sugar — thus, it disappears!!

"We have used the decorative bite-size muffins for our Antique Mall open house refreshment table for quite some time now. People love the 'coffee taste' muffins."

The Moline cook also sent a recipe for Crumb Muffins (see facing page). "Both recipes are very good and so very simple to whip up," she writes. "Both recipes freeze well and store well for a number of days."

- 1¼ cups sifted flour
- 2 teaspoons baking powder
- ½ teaspoon salt
- 1/3 butter or margarine
- 1 cup firmly packed brown sugar
- 2 eggs or egg substitute equal to 2 eggs
- 1 cup cereal flakes (Grape-Nuts Flakes, Wheaties — use one that does not have sugar coating on flakes)
- 1 tablespoon cappuccino powder or granules
- ½ cup milk
- 1 teaspoon vanilla

Sift flour, baking powder and salt together. Cream butter/margarine thoroughly. Add sugar gradually, creaming well after each addition.

Add eggs/egg substitute, one at a time/or apportionable to egg measurement, beating well after each addition.

Mix in cereal. Dissolve cappuccino powder in milk until dissolved; then add vanilla. Add flour to egg mixture alternately with milk. Stir just enough to moisten flour mixture.

Grease muffin tins well, bottoms only. Spoon batter into muffin tins, filling each well only ¾ full.

Bake at 400 degrees, preheated oven, approximately 15 minutes. Make about 18 muffins using medium-size muffins wells.

— *K.B.S. of Moline*

Crumb Muffins

Nov. 18, 1998

- 1 tablespoon cappuccino powder or granules
- ½ cup milk
- 1 egg or egg substitute, slightly beaten
- 2 cups biscuit mix
- 1/3 cup sugar
- ½ chopped nuts
- ½ teaspoon vanilla
- Crumb topping (see below)

Dissolve cappuccino powder granules in milk; add egg or substitute.

Combine biscuit mix and sugar in bowl. Then add egg-milk mixture and blend well. Add nuts and vanilla.

Spoon batter into paper-lined muffin pans and sprinkle with crumb topping. Bake at 375 degrees from 25 to 30 minutes. Make 12 large muffins.

For Crumb Topping: Combine 2 tablespoons biscuit mix, 2 tablespoons sugar, 2 teaspoons cappuccino powder/granules and ¼ teaspoon each cinnamon and nutmeg into bowl. Using pastry blender or 2 knives, cut in 1 tablespoon butter or margarine to form crumbs.

Note: For added crunch, add 1/3 cup flaked coconut prior to blending crumb topping mixture. — *K.B.S. of Moline*

Coffee Can Bread

April 30, 1997

Three area cooks submitted the following version of the Coffee Can Bread recipe.

A.P.K. of Davenport writes: "I have had this recipe for 30 to 40 years and probably clipped it from a paper or magazine.

"It does call for two 1-pound coffee cans instead of a 2-pound can. Makes nice gift breads."

4 cups flour, divided	**1 teaspoon salt**
1 package active dry yeast	**½ cup ground almonds**
½ cup water	**½ cup chopped raisins**
1 cup milk	**2 eggs, slightly beaten**
½ cup butter or margarine	**2 1-pound coffee cans**
¼ cup sugar	

Mix 2 cups flour with yeast. Stir water, milk, butter, sugar and salt over low heat until butter melts; cool for about 5 minutes. Add to flour and yeast. Add remaining flour, nuts, fruit and eggs. Dough will be stiff. Knead on floured board until flour is distributed throughout.

Using a little oil, coat the inside of each coffee can. Divide dough, half in each of two 1-pound cans. Cover cans with plastic tops. Let rise in warm place 85 degrees F with dough reaches to approximately 1-inch from the top.

Remove plastic tops. Bake at 375 degrees for about 35 minutes.

— A.J.H. of Rock Island,
S.A.W. of Aledo and
A.P.K. of Davenport

Cranberry-Orange Nut Bread

Jan. 29, 2003

Several weeks ago, a reader requested a recipe for Cranberry-Orange Bread. The following recipe, which H.E.M. of Moline has had tucked in her files for years, was among those submitted to answer that request.

However, the recipe, on a newspaper clipping now yellowed with age, calls for a package of frozen cranberry-orange relish. Curious Cook could not find such a product. However, we did find a package of frozen Cranberry Orange Sauce in a 10-ounce size.

So we tested the recipe, to be certain it worked using cranberry-orange "sauce" instead of cranberry-orange "relish." The quick bread was quite a success, flavorful and appealing.

The recipe yields two loaves, which would make perfect Valentine's Day gifts.

- **1 package (10 ounces) frozen cranberry-orange relish**
- **3 cups sifted flour**
- **3 teaspoons baking powder**
- **½ teaspoon baking soda**
- **1 teaspoon salt**
- **½ teaspoon cinnamon**
- **2 tablespoons butter**
- **¾ cup sugar**
- **1 egg**
- **¾ cup evaporated milk**
- **1 tablespoon lemon juice**
- **½ cup chopped nuts**

Thaw relish. Sift dry ingredients. Cream butter and sugar. Beat in egg, then add milk, lemon juice, relish and nuts.

Stir in flour mixture until dry ingredients are barely dampened.

Bake in two small (7½x3½x2-inch) greased loaf pans at 375 degrees for about 45 minutes. Yield: Two small loaves.   *— H.E.M. of Moline*

Danish Puff

Oct. 25, 2000

This recipe for Danish Puff was published Nov. 5, 1997, in the Quad-Cities Holiday Cookbook, an annual publication of The Dispatch, The Rock Island Argus and The Leader.

- 2 sticks regular (not diet) margarine
- 2 cups flour
- 2 tablespoons very cold water
- 1 cup tap water
- 1 tablespoon vanilla
- 3 extra large eggs

Cut 1 stick of margarine into 1 cup of the flour as you would to make a pie crust until the mixture resembles coarse meal. Add cold water; stir until well blended.

Divide dough in half. Press each half into a 3- to 4-inch wide strip on each side of a 15x11-inch jelly-roll pan.

In a saucepan or in your microwave, bring 1 cup water and the remaining stick of margarine to a boil. Remove from heat and add vanilla. Stir in remaining flour. Add eggs, individually, beating well after each. Spread this mixture over the oblong dough strips.

Bake at 350 degrees for 40 to 50 minutes or until crisp and brown. Makes 2 coffeecakes, 15x4-inches each.

FROSTING:
- 2 cups confectioners' sugar
- 1 tablespoon margarine, melted
- 4 tablespoons milk or cream
- 1 teaspoon vanilla
- 2 cups coarsely chopped walnuts

Combine confectioners' sugar, margarine, milk and vanilla; mix well. Frost cooled "puffs" and sprinkle with coarsely chopped walnuts. Cut into 1-inch slices to serve. — *1997 Quad-Cities Holiday Cookbook*

Date Nut Bread

Nov. 17, 1993

Two Geneseo cooks sent nearly identical recipes for Date Nut Bread. D.H.N. of Geneseo writes: "Enclosed is a recipe for Date Nut bread. I have made this recipe for at least 40 years and still make it occasionaly. It keeps well and freezes. Hope this is the one H.C. of East Moline wanted."

M.G.C. of Geneseo writes: "This bread may be served plain or can be sliced thinly for cream cheese sandwiches.

"It is equally good served with a hot sauce or with whipped cream for a dessert. This recipe was requested by H.C. of East Moline for her granddaughter."

Then we received this note and the recipe from C.K.T. of Eldridge. "Use No. 2 cans (20 ounces) having a gold lining," she writes. "Grease well. Fill half full. Bake in a 350-degree oven about 45 minutes, depending on your oven. Recipe says 5 cans. Usually 5 or 6 or more. Very good. Given to me by my mother."

G.J. of Rock Island also sent her "favorite date or raisin Boston Brown Bread recipe. I have used this recipe since 1956. My mother before that. I am 79 years young, I hope."

Here's the recipe:

- **1 package (1 pound) dates**
- **2 teaspoons baking soda**
- **2 cups boiling water**
- **2 tablespoons shortening**
- **2 eggs, beaten**
- **2 cups sugar**
- **4 cups flour**
- **1 teaspoon salt**
- **1 or 2 teaspoons vanilla**
- **½ cup nutmeats**

Cut up dates, sprinkle soda over and cover with 2 cups boiling water. Set aside until cool.

Mix together the shortening, eggs, sugar, flour, salt and vanilla; beat thoroughly. Add to cooled date mixture and lastly add nuts. Fill four, five or six ungreased No. 2 cans (20 ounces) about half full.

Bake at 350 degrees for 30 to 50 minutes. D.H.N. says 45 to 50 minutes; M.G.C. bakes for 30 to 45 minutes. Test as for cake.

And G.J. bakes her bread at 350 degrees for 1 hour. G.J. advises: "Remove from oven. Let cans set for 15 minutes. Bread will slide out."

G.J. uses 1 cup raisins or dates.

Remove breads from cans. Wrap in wax paper or aluminum foil. Store in refrigerator. Keeps two or three weeks. Or freeze.

— *D.H.N. of Geneseo, M.G.C. of Geneseo, C.K.T. of Eldridge and G.J. of Rock Island*

Fadden for Christmas

Aug. 16, 1995

The topic of Ferden, the German or Danish dough balls, has generated more interesting contributions from Quad-Cities area Ferden devotees.

Often served as a Christmas food tradition, these dough balls are known by a variety of names. Spelling apparently varies somewhat with the cooks as the recipes are passed down from generation to generation and/or by national origin of the recipe.

Here's a note/recipe from H.G. of Milan: "Although this is a different spelling Fadden, I'm sure this is the recipe R.W. is looking for. The process takes all day but is well worth it!"

- 1 pint warm milk
- 1 package dry yeast dissolved in about ¼ cup warm water
- ½ cup sugar
- 3 eggs, beaten
- 2 tablespoons butter, melted
- 1 rounded teaspoon ground cardamom
- 1 rounded cup raisins
- 1 teaspoon salt
- 5½ cups flour, approximately

Mix all together. The dough must be thicker than German pancakes but thinner than dumplings.

The sour dough is placed in a warm place to rise and is covered with a greased lid. Let it rise almost to the lid, then stir it down as often as is needed, about every 2½ hours for a total of about 12 hours.

Fry in oil in a Fadden skillet over medium heat until golden brown. Roll in granulated sugar. The recipe makes about 60 Faddens.

— *H.H.G. of Milan*

Ferden from Mother's Mother

Aug. 9, 1995

From M.L. of Bettendorf: "Happy to enclose my recipe for Ferden handed down from my mother's mother many years ago."

She adds: "We made these as a special treat on Christmas Eve."

1 cake yeast	¾ cup sugar
2 teaspoons sugar	4 tablespoons butter, melted
Lukewarm water	3 eggs, beaten
4 cups flour	3 cups milk
1 teaspoon salt	Raisins or currants
1 teaspoon ground cinnamon	

Break 1 cake yeast into a cup filled with about ½ to ¾ cup cup lukewarm water. Add 2 teaspoons sugar and stir with a fork until yeast breaks up and mixture is foamy. Let ferment about ½ hour.

Combine flour, salt, ground cinnamon and ¾ cup sugar. Make "well" in flour mixture and add melted butter, beaten eggs and milk. Add yeast and stir. Should be a little thicker than pancake batter. Let rise until fluffy and spongy.

Heat Ferden pan until very hot and put a little shortening in each "hole." Add 3 or 4 raisins or currants to each "ladle." Fill each hole ½ full. Each Ferden pan has 6 holes. Pans still sold but called by Swedish name. They are cast-iron.

Fry for a few minutes and then turn over so makes round Ferden. Roll in sugar. — *M.L. of Bettendorf*

Ferden or Furden

Aug. 16, 1995

From S.B. of Davenport: "In answer to the request for Ferden or Furden, please find the enclosed recipe. These are traditionally served as a Christmas Eve treat in Germany."

1 pint milk	**¼ cup sugar**
4 egg yolks, save whites	**Pinch of salt**
1 package dry yeast	**3 cups flour**
½ teaspoon cardamom	**4 tablespoons butter, melted**
½ cup raisins or currants	

Mix milk, egg yolks, dry yeast, cardamom, sugar and salt. Gradually add 3 cups of flour and the melted butter along with the raisins or currants, mixing well.

Beat egg whites until soft peaks occur. Gently fold the egg whites into the batter. Drop batter by spoonfuls into heated shortening in Furden pan.

When they are brown, turn them over and brown the other side. They may be rolled in sugar when hot. Serve immediately.

Each person is given a dish of sugar to dip the hot Furden.

— *S.B. of Davenport*

Heise Weckens

March 13, 1996

"I am looking for the recipe for Heise Wecken from Walcher or BonTon bakeries Davenport," M.R. of Eldridge writes. "It's a raised 'bun' with raisins and cardamom.

"Perhaps a family member or past employee of either of the two would have it and be willing to share. My family would be very grateful.

"P.S. I have a recipe from the newspaper in the late '70s or early '80s, but it is not quite the same. Here it is for comparison."

¾ cup raisins
1 cup milk
1 tablespoon sugar
1 cake or package yeast
1½ cups flour
½ cup butter

½ cup sugar
3 eggs, beaten
½ teaspoon cardamom
¼ teaspoon salt
2 cups flour

Cook ¾ cup raisins in water to cover for 5 minutes; drain and cool. Scald and cool 1 cup milk. Dissolve 1 tablespoon sugar and 1 cake or package yeast in warm milk. Add 1½ cups flour; mix well and let rise 1 hour.

Cream ½ cup butter and ½ cup sugar. Add, gradually, 3 beaten eggs. Then add the raisins, ½ teaspoon cardamom and ¼ teaspoon salt. Add this to first mixture and beat well. Add about 2 cups flour for a soft dough. Let rise until doubled in bulk.

Spoon onto well-greased cookie sheet. Let rise until light. Bake at 350 degrees for 25 to 30 minutes, until golden brown.

Makes about 24 when dropped from a dessert spoon.

— *M.R. of Eldridge*

Grandma's Nut Roll

Oct. 27, 1999

J.L. of East Moline needs our help. She writes:

"In one of the past Holiday Cookbooks, I don't know which one, there was a recipe for Grandma's Nut Roll. Part of my recipe has been torn off and I would like very much to make these rolls again.

"The lady said her 15-year-old son said, 'This bread is awesome.' Her grandmother learned to make this from the Europeans who settled in the coal-mining town where they lived in Pennsylvania.

"Please can you help or the lady who sent the recipe to the paper. Thank you."

Curious Cook can help! A search of our electronic library brought up Grandma's Nut Roll from the Quad-Cities Holiday Cook 1997! The recipe (see facing page) was submitted by Tina Larson of Davenport. She wrote:

"This nut roll has been part of our holidays for three generations. My grandma learned to make this from the Europeans Croations, Polish and Slovaks who settled in the coal-mining town where they lived in Pennsylvania.

"This is one of the many delicious breads that were made at every holiday. After years of watching my grandma and mom make these without a recipe, I measured all the ingredients and came up with this recipe that I can pass on to my daughters.

"In the words of my 15-year-old son, 'This bread is awesome!' Enjoy."

SWEET ROLL DOUGH:
¾ cup warm water
1 tablespoon yeast
½ cup milk
½ cup sugar
2 teaspoons salt
2 eggs, beaten
½ cup butter, melted
5 cups flour
Additional melted butter, for brushing

NUT FILLING:
4 cups finely crushed walnuts
¾ cup evaporated milk
1 cup sugar
1 teaspoon vanilla

For dough: In a large bowl, mix yeast and water. Add milk, sugar, salt, beaten eggs, ½ cup melted butter and enough flour to make a smooth elastic dough. Knead 5 minutes. Let rise until double. Make nut filling.

Punch down dough; divide in half. Roll out each half into approximately a 9x13-inch rectangle. Brush lightly with melted butter and spread dough with half of nut mixture. Roll up lengthwise and pinch seams together. Repeat with the rest of the dough.

Brush with melted butter and let rise until almost double on a foil-lined 11x15-inch cookie sheet. Bake at 350 degrees for about 20 minutes or until golden brown. Slice when cool — if you can wait.
— *T.L. of Davenport*

Jan. 7, 1998

Lemon Nut Bread

Mrs. R.H.L. of Moline sent a note and recipe to Curious Cook to answer a recent request for Lemon Nut Bread.

She writes, "I always check the recipes first in Wednesday papers! I enjoy the sharing of recipes and thank you for this service.

"M.M. of Davenport asks for a Lemon Nut Bread. She might like to try this one, which is a favorite at our house.

"This is a Dispatch recipe from Mrs. H.S. of Moline many years ago," Mrs. R.H.L. points out.

1 cup granulated sugar
6 tablespoons shortening
Grated rind of 1 lemon
2 eggs
1½ cups all-purpose flour
½ teaspoon salt
1 teaspoon baking powder
½ cup milk
½ cup finely chopped nuts
¼ cup granulated sugar
Juice of 1 lemon

Cream together the 1 cup sugar and shortening. Add grated lemon rind. Beat eggs separately and add to creamed mixture.

Sift together the flour, salt and baking powder. Add alternately with milk to creamed mixture, beginning and ending with flour mixture. Stir in chopped nuts.

Pour mixture into greased 9x5x3-inch loaf pan. "I also line my pans with wax paper cut to fit." Bake at 325 degrees for 35 minutes.

In a pan, heat ¼ cup granulated sugar and juice of 1 lemon. Or substitute 2 tablespoons whole lemon juice. Slowly pour hot mixture over the bread.

Note: "For bake sales, I use two smaller loaf pans 7½x3½x2-inch for this one recipe. Bakes in about the same length of time."

— Mrs. R.H.L. of Moline

Monkey Bread

Nov. 3, 1993

C.L. of Alexis sent in a Monkey Bread recipe to answer a request and B.M. of Bettendorf sent one that's nearly identical.

2/3 cup sugar	Chopped pecans, as needed
2 or 3 tablespoons cinnamon	1½ sticks margarine
3 tubes (10 ounces) each refrigerated biscuits 10 each	1 cup brown sugar
	1 teaspoon cinnamon

 Mix together the 2/3 cup sugar and 2 or 3 tablespoons cinnamon in a bowl or plastic bag. Cut each biscuit into fourths, drop into sugar mixture to coat, one tube at a time.

Grease a Bundt pan and arrange biscuit pieces in layers with chopped pecans sprinkled between layers.

Melt the margarine, 1 cup brown sugar and 1 teaspoon cinnamon together and pour over top.

Bake at 350 degrees for 25 to 30 minutes. Unmold immediately on plate. To eat, pull apart. — *C.L of Alexis and B.M. of Bettendorf*

Orange Raisin Scones

May 18, 1994

"This is in reply to the request for 'Scones.' I understand how B.Y. would like to make her own. Mom and Grandma used to say they were rich baking powder biscuits with an egg.

"I have been making them for over 50 years. Add any kind of fruit, cheese even sauted onions or herbs for a variety for a 'Brunch.' They are best eaten freshly baked from the oven. Scones are a rather dry product best eaten with butter, honey, jam or jelly.

"The oven temperature ranges from 400 to 425 degrees, but I find my oven works better at 325 to 350 degrees."

1¾ cups flour	1 egg, beaten
3 tablespoons sugar	½ cup raisins
2½ teaspoons baking powder	4 to 6 tablespoons half-and-half or milk
2 teaspoons grated orange peel	1 egg, beaten
1/3 cup butter	

In a medium-size bowl, combine flour, sugar, baking powder and grated orange peel. Cut in 1/3 cup butter until crumbly. With fork stir in 1 beaten egg, raisins and half-and-half or milk. Stir until dough leaves side of bowl. Knead 10 times.

Roll into 9-inch circle; cut into 12 wedges. Place on ungreased cookie sheet. Brush with 1 beaten egg. Bake 400 degrees for 10 to 12 minutes. Serve with Orange Butter. Makes 12 scones.

ORANGE BUTTER:
½ cup butter, softened
2 tablespoons orange marmalade

Mix butter and orange marmalade. Serve with scones.

— *J.L.M. of Durant*

Overnight Coffee Cake

May 17, 1995

- 1 cup white sugar
- ¾ cup butter
- 2 eggs
- 1 cup sour cream
- 1 cup chopped nuts optional
- 2 cups flour
- 1 teaspoon baking soda
- 1 teaspoon baking powder
- ½ teaspoon nutmeg
- ½ cup brown sugar
- ½ teaspoon cinnamon

Cream butter, white sugar and eggs. Mix in sour cream; then add nuts.

Sift together dry ingredients — flour, baking soda, baking powder and nutmeg. Combine the dry and the creamed mixtures; mix well. Pour batter into a well-greased 9x13-inch pan.

Combine ½ cup brown sugar with ½ teaspoon cinnamon. Sprinkle with brown sugar mixture on top of batter. Cover and refrigerate overnight.

In the morning, uncover and bake at 350 degrees for 35 to 40 minutes.

— *C.W. of Bettendorf*

Overnight Coffee Cake

May 17, 1995

"I am sending a recipe for Overnight Coffee Cake for L.L.F. of Bettendorf," writes D.L.N. of Moline. "I hope this is the one she is looking for."

- 2 cups flour
- 1 teaspoon baking powder
- 1 teaspoon baking soda
- 1 teaspoon cinnamon
- ½ teaspoon salt
- 2/3 cup margarine
- 1 cup granulated sugar
- ½ cup brown sugar
- 2 eggs
- 1 cup buttermilk

TOPPING:
- ½ cup brown sugar
- ½ cup chopped nuts
- 1 teaspoon cinnamon
- 1 teaspoon nutmeg

Sift all dry ingredients for cake together. Cream margarine and sugars; add eggs and beat well.

Add dry ingredients to creamed mixture alternately with the buttermilk, starting and ending with dry ingredients. Spread batter into a well-greased 9x13-inch pan.

Mix topping ingredients together and spread on top of cake batter. Cover pan with aluminum foil or plastic wrap and refrigerate overnight.

In the morning, uncover baking pan, pre-heat the oven to 350 degrees and bake for 45 minutes. — *D.L.N. of Moline*

Overnight Coffee Cake Swirl

May 24, 1995

A.K.S. of Davenport sent us another version of the Overnight Coffee Cake. She writes:

"This is an answer to L.L.F. of Bettendorf. I don't know the origin of the recipe. It's copied on a scrap of white paper. I have no idea who, or when, it came from. It's good!"

1 cup flour	**TOPPING:**
¼ cup white sugar	**¼ cup brown sugar**
¼ cup brown sugar	**¼ cup nuts**
½ teaspoon baking soda	**½ teaspoon cinnamon**
½ teaspoon baking powder	**¼ teaspoon nutmeg**
¼ teaspoon salt	**GLAZE:**
½ teaspoon cinnamon	**½ cup powdered sugar**
½ cup buttermilk	**3 to 4 teaspoons milk**
1/3 cup shortening	**¼ teaspoon vanilla**
1 egg	

Grease and flour 9-inch round cake pan.

For cake: Combine flour, ¼ cup sugar, ¼ cup brown sugar, baking soda, baking powder, salt, cinnamon, buttermilk, shortening and egg. Blend at low speed of electric mixer until moist. Beat 3 minutes at medium speed.

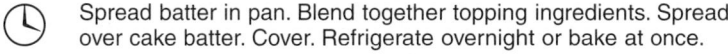

Spread batter in pan. Blend together topping ingredients. Spread over cake batter. Cover. Refrigerate overnight or bake at once.

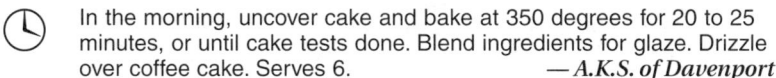

In the morning, uncover cake and bake at 350 degrees for 20 to 25 minutes, or until cake tests done. Blend ingredients for glaze. Drizzle over coffee cake. Serves 6. — *A.K.S. of Davenport*

Pop-Up Bread

Oct. 9, 2002

A gentleman from Port Byron is looking for a recipe from long ago. L.M. writes:

"Sometime between 1967-69, The Dispatch published a bread recipe, which was baked in 1-pound coffee cans," L.M. remembers.

"I worked for the State Police in Springfield in the summers and attended Illinois Wesleyan University in the fall. I made a lot of that bread for the people at work, but I lost the recipe after I went back to school.

"Is there a chance anyone would have that recipe?"

— *L.M. of Port Byron*

Good news! Curious Cook has the recipe! Curious Cook also remembers baking and enjoying the Pop-Up Bread, many years ago, as L.M. points out.

But, we wondered, where in the world is that recipe now? How many of you have asked yourselves that very question?

Well, dear cooks, the short search of a large collection of my recipes was a success. Curious Cook found a letter dated July 1978 from E.V. of East Moline.

At that time, in 1978, E.V. was answering a request for Bucket Bread. E.V. pointed out that the recipe had appeared in The Dispatch nine or 10 years prior to that date. Which, of course, puts it right where L.M. did, between 1967 and 1969.

So for L.M. and other home bakers who want an easy way to bake bread. Here's that recipe (on facing page), circa 1968.

3 to 3¼ cups enriched flour	¼ cup sugar
1 package dry yeast	1 teaspoon salt
½ cup milk	2 eggs
½ cup water	1 cup (4 ounces) grated Cheddar cheese, optional (See note)
½ cup oil	

Stir together 1½ cups flour and yeast. Heat milk, water, oil, sugar and salt over low heat only until warm, stirring to blend.

Add liquid ingredients to flour/yeast mixture and beat until smooth, about 2 minutes on medium speed of electric mixer or 300 strokes by hand. Blend in eggs, and cheese if desired.

Stir in remainder of flour to make a stiff batter. Beat until batter is smooth and elastic, about 1 minute on medium speed or 150 strokes by hand.

Divide batter into two, well-greased, 1-pound coffee cans, or one 2-pound coffee can. Cover with the plastic lids. Let rise in warm place 80-85 degrees until light and bubbly, about 1 hour. Batter should be about ¼ to ½ inch below covers. Remove lids.

Bake in preheated oven, 375 degrees, for 30 to 35 minutes or until done. Cool in cans 15 minutes before removing.

Note: The grated Cheddar cheese may be added to the batter for an extra special touch. — *From Curious Cook's files*

Pear-Walnut Coffee Cake

Dec. 19, 2001

I.O. of Moline sent a Pear-Walnut Coffee Cake recipe and this note:

"I'm hoping this is the recipe D.R. of East Moline is looking for. I have been helped so many times by Quad-Cities cooks, I felt I should reciprocate."

¼ cup butter
½ cup sugar
1 teaspoon vanilla
1 egg
1 cup flour
½ teaspoon baking powder
½ teaspoon baking soda
¼ teaspoon salt
½ cup sour cream
1½ cups peeled, cored, diced pears
½ cup brown sugar
¾ teaspoon cinnamon
2 tablespoons butter, softened
½ cup chopped walnuts

Cream butter and ½ cup white sugar until light and fluffy. Beat in vanilla; then egg. Beat until smooth.

Mix flour, baking powder, baking soda and salt. Add to butter mixture alternately with sour cream. Mix just to blend after each addition. Fold in pears. Spread in a greased 8-inch square pan.

Mix brown sugar, cinnamon and the softened butter until well combined. Stir in the chopped walnuts. Sprinkle the nut topping evenly over the cake.

Bake at 350 degrees for 40 to 45 minutes, or until top is well browned and a toothpick comes out clean. Cut into squares and serve warm or at room temperature.

— I.O. of Moline

Peachy Nut Bread

Oct. 16, 2002

J.J. of Coal Valley recently asked Curious Cook to help find a "wonderful" but long-lost Peach Bread recipe.

J.J. said she longs for that recipe at this time of year, when fruit quick breads seem to be so much in season.

As usual, readers have come to her rescue, and we hope one of these recipes is that wonderful Peach Bread.

"Enclosed is a recipe for a Peachy Nut Bread," writes C.L. of Geneseo. "J.J. of Coal Valley wanted a Peach Bread recipe. Hope she will like this one.

"This is very good and pretty. I have made this many times. It was given to me by a dear cousin many years ago."

2 cups flour
1 teaspoon baking powder
½ teaspoon baking soda
½ teaspoon salt
2/3 cup sugar
1/3 cup margarine
2 eggs
¼ cup buttermilk
1 cup drained, mashed canned peaches (4 large halves)
¼ cup cut maraschino cherries
½ cup chopped nuts ("Black walnuts are best.")

Mix flour, baking powder, baking soda and salt. Cream sugar and margarine; add eggs and beat well. Stir in buttermilk and peaches.

Add dry ingredients, mixing only until all dry ingredients are moistened. Fold in cherries and nuts. Do not beat.

Pour into greased 9x5x3-inch loaf pan. Bake at 350 degrees for 50 to 60 minutes.

Note: "I also have used two smaller loaf pans." — *C.L. of Geneseo*

Something Different Sweet Rolls

April 16, 2003

Judging by the response to the request for this recipe, which Curious Cook simply could not find in an exhaustive search of her files, these sweet rolls are very, very popular.

Just as we thought, the Something Different Sweet Rolls recipe was included in a Holiday Food Guide, a contribution of Loretta Minnaert of Atkinson and her daughter, Joline Sierens of Annawan. Mrs. Minnaert kindly refreshed our memory with this note (and the recipe):

"Seek and you shall find! I have the recipe requested by D.B. in The Dispatch and Rock Island Argus.

"This recipe was in the Nov. 10, 1985, Holiday Food Guide, called 'Entertaining With Taste.' In fact, my picture along with my daughter's picture, Joline Sierens of Annawan, was featured because unknown to each other, we both sent in the recipe."

Then we received a copy of that photo and the recipe from V.L.C. of East Moline.

Many other area cooks/bakers sent the recipe and rave reviews of the rolls. Curious Cook greatly appreciates each and every contribution.

1 package (18¼ ounces) yellow cake mix without pudding in mix
2 packages (¼ ounce each) dry yeast
5 cups flour
2½ cups hot water
¼ cup margarine, softened or melted
Cinnamon and sugar, amount desired
Powdered-sugar icing or frosting mix

Stir together dry cake mix, yeast, flour and hot water, mixing well.

Cover and let rise until doubled in size.

On floured surface, roll mixture into a rectangle shape. Dough may be divided in half before rolling, if desired. Spread rectangle with softened margarine.

Combine sugar and cinnamon. Sprinkle rectangle with cinnamon/sugar mixture. If dividing dough, repeat with second half of dough. Roll up, jelly-roll fashion, and cut into 1½- to 2-inch pieces. Place in two well-greased 9x13-inch pans. Cover and let rise until doubled in bulk.

Bake in 375-degree oven for 20 to 25 minutes. When cool, frost with favorite powdered-sugar icing or frosting mix. These rolls freeze well.

— *Originally from the 1985 Holiday Food Guide, "Entertaining with Taste"*

main dishes

the center of attention

Dear Curious Cook

Brunswick Stew

Dec. 10, 1997

- 1 hen (4½ pounds)
- 4 cups canned chicken broth, or use broth from cooking chicken, plus water as needed
- 1 pound onions, peeled and diced
- 1 pound red potatoes, peeled and diced
- 1 pound beef chuck, trimmed and cut into 1-inch cubes or BBQ pork, if available
- 6 slices bacon, diced
- 1 can (28 ounces) whole tomatoes, undrained and chopped
- 1 tablespoon Worcestershire sauce
- 1 teaspoon salt
- ½ teaspoon lemon pepper
- ½ teaspoon crushed red pepper
- 2 cans (15 ounces) each lima beans, drained
- 2 cans (15 ounces) each creamed corn
- Hot sauce or hot pepper vinegar, optional

Place hen in a large Dutch oven and cover with water. Bring to a boil; cover, reduce heat, and simmer for 2 hours, or until tender.

Remove hen from broth and cool. If desired, reserve broth for stew, adding water if necessary to make 4 cups.

Remove skin and bones from chicken and shred meat. Return chicken to Dutch oven; add the 4 cups broth and next nine ingredients. Bring to a boil, reduce heat, cover and simmer 30 additional minutes, stirring often. Add beans and corn; cover and simmer 30 additional minutes, stirring often. Add more broth if necessary.

Serve in bowls with hot sauce or vinegar, if desired. Yields 10 to 15 servings.

Note: "The BBQ pork has a smoked flavor that really enhances this stew."
— *L.G.F. of Davenport*

Cashew Chicken

Feb. 23, 1994

"Enclosed is my Cashew Chicken recipe," writes S.A.C. of Walcott. "It's endorsed by our five foster kids from Vietnam and Cambodia, now grown and gone.

"They loved my Chinese food, but thought it strange I could make Mexican food!"

- 2 whole chicken breasts, skinned
- 4 green onions, chopped
- 1 can bamboo shoots, drained, cut in half
- 1 cup sliced fresh mushroom
- 4 tablespoons oil
- ¼ cup cashew pieces raw from health food store
- Hot cooked rice
- Soy sauce

COOKING SAUCE:
- 1 cup water
- 2 tablespoon cornstarch
- ¼ cup soy sauce
- 1 tablespoon chicken bouillon crystals dry powder

Remove bones from chicken, freeze chicken until firm; cut into thumbnail-size pieces. Set aside.

Cut vegetables, putting onions in one small bowl, mushrooms and bamboo shoots in another. Mix cooking sauce ingredients; set aside.

In wok or fry pan, heat 1 teaspoon oil. Toss cashew pieces very briefly; they burn easily. Remove and set aside. Add rest of oil, heat, add chicken and green onions, stir-fry until chicken is opaque.

Add mushrooms and bamboo shoots, stir-fry 2 minutes more. Stir cooking sauce; pour into mixture. Cook and stir until mixture thickens, adding more water if necessary to make a medium gravy-type sauce. Remove from heat, stir in cashews.

Serve over hot cooked rice with soy sauce to pass. Serves 4.

— *A.C. of Walcott*

Chicken and Broccoli Curry

June 2, 1999

A very easy meal-in-one for guests as well as family. It can be prepared a day in advance and stored in the refrigerator. Add 15 to 30 minutes to cooking time.

- 1 can (10¾ ounces) cream of celery soup
- 1 can (10¾ ounces) cream of mushroom soup
- 1 cup mayonnaise
- ½ cup chopped onion
- 2 tablespoons curry powder
- 1 cup rice
- ½ cup dry white wine
- 2 packages (10 ounces each) frozen broccoli spears, thawed
- 1½ pounds skinless, boneless chicken breasts, cut into 2-inch cubes
- ¼ cup slivered almonds

Preheat oven to 350 degrees. In a medium-size saucepan, combine celery and mushroom soups, mayonnaise, onion and curry. Cook, stirring, over medium heat, until blended.

Pour rice into a greased 13x9x2-inch baking dish. Stir in wine and one-third of soup mixture. Arrange broccoli around outside edges of baking dish, overlapping stems to form a decorative border. Reserve several spears.

Add chicken pieces to remaining soup mixture. Pour into center of baking dish. Top with remaining broccoli spears. Garnish with slivered almonds.

Cover with foil. Bake at 350 degrees for 1 hour, until chicken is tender and done and rice is cooked. Serves 4. — *V.M.F. of Geneseo*

Chicken Broccoli Casserole

June 9, 1999

"I received this recipe from a Colorado friend," D.M. of Davenport tells us as she answers the recent request for a chicken casserole. "It is very good," she reports.

- 2 packages (10 ounces each) frozen broccoli
- 6 cooked skinless, boneless chicken breast halves
- 1 can (10¾ ounces) cream of chicken soup
- 1 cup mayonnaise
- 1 tablespoon lemon juice
- 1 tablespoon curry powder
- ½ cup bread crumbs
- Shredded Cheddar cheese

Cook broccoli crisp and drain well. Arrange in oiled 9x13 pan. Arrange chunks of cooked chicken pieces on top.

Combine chicken soup, mayonnaise, lemon juice and curry powder. Spread over top of chicken and broccoli. Top with bread crumbs and Cheddar cheese. Bake at 350 degrees for 40 minutes.

— *D.M., Davenport*

Chicken wings

March 31, 1999

J.H. of Coal Valley offered specific instructions on preparing chicken wings.

"I hate to give out my wing recipe — given out only once — since I learned it in Denver in the early '80s," J.H. writes.

"I make them in an electric frypan because it's easier to control the heat and has no spots. But then my fry pan is from my grandmother and has to be at least 25 years old. A very durable heavy aluminum mirror frypan.

"Chicken wings (cut in 3 pieces) — couple of pounds enough to fill pan — non-meaty pieces saved for stock. Brown drumette and two-bone piece in butter or margarine until brown. Do not flour or season.

"If wings are fatty and you have a lot of oil, drain but leave a couple of tablespoons for richness of sauce and also so it doesn't stick, 3 or 4 tablespoons.

"Pour over — 1 cup sherry cooking wine mixed with 1 package Good Seasons Dry Italian Zesty dressing mix. For pan of full wings, I use two packs mix and 1 bottle cooking wine — 12 to 16 ounces.

"Simmer 30 minutes. Do not boil. Turn chicken, scrape bottom to get food up and mixed with liquid.

"Open vent on lid of fry pan to evaporate liquid. Simmer until chicken is coated with candy-like glaze. Great as an appetizer or main course.

"I am sorry my directions are obtuse; but my mother, grandmother and great aunts taught me to cook, and everything in our houses were done by watching and learning, i.e. — a cup of flour was not a measuring cup but the green cup without a handle in the flour bin.

"I hope you will try this for your family and friends; they will really enjoy it.

"One pan cooked on the picnic table, a green salad and cold beers — nothing better for a summer evening. Don't forget the napkins."

— *J.H. of Coal Valley*

Chop Suey

April 17, 1996

M.K.O. of Moline shares with us her mother's Chop Suey recipe, which she says "makes a hit every time I serve it."

This is in answer to a recent request from J.V. of Atkinson. Although J.V. asked for a chop suey recipe calling for pork, be assured this is a much loved, tried-and-true recipe from M.K.O.

1 pound beef — flank steak, round steak or chuck roast, cubed
Salt and pepper, to taste
3 cups diced celery
1 cup diced onions
3 tablespoons molasses
3 tablespoons soy sauce
1 can bean sprouts OR mixed chop suey vegetables

Sear meat. Season with salt and pepper. Add water to cover and simmer for an hour, or until meat is tender. Add celery and onions. When the vegetables are tender, add the molasses and soy sauce. Lastly add the bean sprouts and heat through.

Make a flour and water paste — about ¼ cup flour to 1 cup water — and thicken mixture to a gravy consistency, as desired. Bring to boil. Serve with flaky boiled rice or Chinese noodles. — *M.K.O. of Moline*

Cousin Ed's Chicken Rosemary

Nov. 16, 1994

We've been kept busy with letters, recipes and information about making ice cream in a coffee can. The topic turned out to be quite a fascinating one. But now it's time to turn to other requests — the Chicken Rosemary, for example.

One of the first responses Curious Cook received to the chicken recipe request is from a favorite cousin in Rock Island. L.M.M. writes:

"This is your Cousin Ed's favorite chicken dish. We have it about once a month. We got the recipe from a waiter in Chicago years ago at an Italian restaurant. They called it Chicken Bassieber or Chicken Rosemary. Hope your readers will try it and enjoy it as much as we have over the years. It's delicious cold too, cut up and put into a tossed salad."

Curious Cook is just delighted to share Cousin Ed's Rosemary Chicken with our readers.

3 pounds whole or cut-up chicken

1 bottle (8 ounces) of Italian Salad dressing

Garlic salt

Rosemary leaves (2 to 3 tablespoons), crushed

3 to 4 potatoes, peeled and cubed

Place chicken pieces in a baking pan and sprinkle on Italian salad dressing. Sprinkle on garlic salt. Cover and marinate the chicken in the refrigerator for 3 to 4 hours, or overnight.

Before placing chicken and salad dressing into a pre-heated 325 degree oven, baste and sprinkle on crushed rosemary. Bake, uncovered, at 325 degrees for 1½ to 2 hours, basting every 20 minutes or so.

Peel 3 to 4 potatoes, cube and place in baking dish with chicken during the last half hour of baking. Test potatoes with fork before removing from oven to see if they are done.   — *L.M.M. of Rock Island*

Dilled Fish

May 31, 2000

L.M. of Bettendorf has a recipe to answer the recent request for Dilled Cod directions. L.M. writes:

"In answer to L.W. of Long Grove who had Dilled Cod at Jumer's:

"I love Jumer's food but have never had the cod. I have a recipe I like very much and maybe she will like it, too.

"I used sole, but cod is fine," L.M. promises.

1/3 cup chopped green onions **Salt and pepper, to taste**
1½ pounds sole or cod fillets **2 teaspoons lemon juice**
1 cup commercial sour cream (see note) **½ teaspoon crushed dillweed**

Preheat oven to 350 degrees.

In a shallow casserole, lightly greased, layer one half of the fish, one half of the onions, salt and pepper to taste; sprinkle with 1 teaspoon of lemon juice and ¼ teaspoon of the dillweed. Cover with one half of the sour cream.

Place on another layer of fish and repeat, ending with sour cream.

Cover and bake at 350 degrees for 30 minutes or until fish is cooked and bubbly. Serves 4.

Note: "Can use fat-free sour cream nicely." — *L.M. of Bettendorf*

Dilled Salmon Bake

July 10, 1996

Mrs. L.R. of Davenport answer the request for a canned salmon casserole with her recipe. She says she serves the casserole with Cucumber Dill Slice Salad "and everyone wants the recipe. A very nice meal or luncheon," she promises.

3 cups uncooked egg noodles
1 teaspoon salt
1 can (7¾ ounces) red salmon
1 can (10¾ ounces) cream of celery soup
¼ teaspoon dillweed
1 package (10 ounces) frozen mixed vegetables, thawed and drained

2/3 cup chopped onion
2/3 cup chopped celery
Potato chips or seasoned bread crumbs, for topping
1 tablespoon butter or margarine, melted

Preheat oven to 375 degrees. Cook noodles with 1 teaspoon salt according to package directions; drain and wash under cold water. Drain and flake salmon; reserve liquid. In medium-size bowl, combine liquid with soup and dillweed.

Place drained noodles in large bowl; add salmon, vegetables, onion, celery and soup mixture. Stir until well blended. Spoon into greased 2-quart casserole. Cover with crushed potato chips or ¼ cup seasoned bread crumbs and 1 tablespoon melted butter or margarine. Bake at 375 degrees for 35 to 40 minutes.   — *L.R. of Davenport*

Cucumber Dill Slice Salad

July 10, 1996

This is the salad that Mrs. L.R. of Davenport serves with her Dilled Salmon Bake casserole. "I make this salad the night before," she reports.

2 packages (3 ounces each) lemon flavored gelatin
2 teaspoons salt
2 cups boiling water
1 cup cold water

3 cups chopped cucumber, chopped not too fine
¼ cup chopped onion
2 teaspoons dillweed

Dissolve gelatin and salt in boiling water; mix well and add cold water. Chill until thickened. Fold in cucumber, onion and dillweed. Chill 4 hours. Makes 12 servings.   — *L.R. of Davenport*

Dutch Baby Pancakes

March 15, 2000

A Geneseo cook has lost a recipe and needs our help. She writes:

"Awhile ago you had a recipe in the paper for a pancake that you put in the oven. I lost it and would really like to get it again. I can't remember the exact name, but I think it was something like Baby Elephant Cake that you put in an iron skillet and baked in the oven." — *P.H. of Geneseo*

P.H. is referring to those delicious oven-baked pancakes that go by such names as Dutch Baby, Puff Pancake, Popover Pancake, Oven Pancake and High-Rise Pancake. But I've never heard of Baby Elephant Cake. Readers, have you?

Although I can't find the origin of the name Dutch Baby, let me assure you that batter for this puffy pancake is very easy to prepare and bake in an ovenproof skillet.

When finished, the spectacular "bowl" formed by the risen batter may be filled with fruit or simply sprinkled with confectioners' sugar and lemon juice and served with a high-quality maple syrup.

The following tested recipe for Dutch Baby was published in The Dispatch and The Rock Island Argus in 1992. It previously had been published in a magazine-style section of a newspaper but the clipping gave no clue of its identity or a date.

2 or 3 eggs
½ cup sifted all-purpose flour
½ teaspoon salt
½ cup milk
2 tablespoons butter or margarine, melted

1 tablespoon lemon juice, or more if desired
Confectioners' sugar
Fresh fruit
Maple syrup

In a medium-size bowl, beat eggs until frothy. Sift flour and salt together and add with milk to eggs. Beat until smooth. Stir in melted butter or margarine.

Preheat oven to 450 degrees. Pour batter into a greased 9-inch ovenproof skillet. Place skillet on bottom shelf of oven and bake at 450 degrees for 20 minutes. Reduce oven temperature to 350 degrees. Prick shell of pancake and continue to bake for 10 minutes.

Remove from oven; drizzle with lemon juice and sprinkle with confectioners' sugar. Fill "bowl" of pancake with fresh fruit of choice. Cut in wedges to serve.

Or, drizzle pancake with maple syrup, cut in wedges and serve with fresh fruit (or bacon) on the side. Makes 4 to 6 servings.

Egg Beaters version of Dutch Baby Pancake: Instead of using 2 or 3 eggs in the recipe above, I used Egg Beaters to equal the 3 eggs. And the recipe works perfectly. To make the procedure even quicker and easier, I combined all the ingredients in a blender and blended until well mixed. Then just follow directions for baking and serving.

— *The Dispatch and Rock Island Argus, July 29, 1992*

Eggplant Parmesan

Aug. 17, 1994

Curious Cook should have known that area cooks would respond enthusiastically to the requests for ways to use eggplant and zucchini.

We appreciate the time and energy cooks put into preparing and mailing their recipes to share with their fellow cooks.

For example, D.B. of Moline sent a great collection of her personal, favorite ways of preparing both eggplant and zucchini.

"We really do like the Eggplant Parmesan," she says.

Here is D.B.'s recipe.

1 large eggplant
2 or 3 eggs, beaten
Cracker crumbs
oil for frying
2 cans (15 ounces) each tomato sauce
1 medium onion, diced
1 to 2 teaspoons oregano
1 head of garlic, crushed
Salt and pepper, to taste
Grated Parmesan cheese
Mozzarella cheese

Peel and cut the eggplant into slices. Dip each slice into the egg and then the crumbs. Fry in oil on each side until golden. Drain on a paper towel and set aside.

Mix together tomato sauce, diced onion, oregano, garlic, salt and pepper. Simmer ingredients together for sauce for 15 minutes.

In a shallow, greased 9x12-inch casserole, place a layer of the eggplant, top with oregano, tomato sauce and Parmesan cheese. Repeat with another layer of all.

Bake in 350-degree oven for a total of 20 minutes. Remove from the oven, add a layer of sliced Mozzarella cheese and return to the oven for 5 minutes or until melted. Serves 6. *— D.B. of Moline*

Eggplant Parmesan

April 9, 1997

From N.W. of Hillsdale: "Enclosed is the recipe for Eggplant Parmesan that A.C.G. of East Moline requested."

- 2 cups seasoned bread crumbs
- ¼ teaspoon salt
- ¼ teaspoon black pepper
- 4 eggs, lightly beaten
- 1 large eggplant
- Vegetable or olive oil for frying
- 3½ cups spaghetti sauce, divided
- 3 cups shredded mozzarella cheese, divided
- 1 teaspoon dried basil, divided
- ¼ cup grated Parmesan cheese, divided

Combine bread crumbs, salt and pepper in a shallow dish; place the beaten eggs in another shallow dish and set both aside.

Wash the unpeeled eggplant and cut crosswise into ¼-inch thick rounds. Dip the rounds in the bread crumbs, then the egg, then again with the bread crumbs. Depending on the size of the eggplant, more bread crumbs and egg may be necessary.

Lay the rounds flat on a cookie sheet and chill for 30 minutes.

Heat about 1/8 inch of oil in a large skillet. Fry the eggplant rounds until tender and golden on both sides. Add more oil when necessary. Drain on absorbent paper towels.

Preheat the oven to 350 degrees. Coat a 9x13-inch baking dish with non-stick vegetable spray, then place ½ cup of the spaghetti sauce over the bottom of the dish.

Arrange a layer of the eggplant over the sauce, then pour 1 cup of sauce over that. Cover with a cup of mozzarella cheese, then sprinkle with basil and Parmesan cheese. Repeat with two additional layers and bake at 350 degrees for 30 to 40 minutes, or until the cheese is melted and light golden. 8 servings.   — *N.W. of Hillsdale*

Eggplant Souffle

Aug. 17, 1994

1 medium eggplant
2 tablespoons butter
2 tablespoons flour
1 cup milk
1 cup grated sharp cheese
¾ cup soft bread crumbs

2 teaspoons grated onion
2 tablespoons tomato ketchup
2 eggs, divided
1 teaspoon salt
½ teaspoon pepper
¼ teaspoon cayenne pepper

Peel the eggplant and cut into small cubes. Cook in salted water until tender. Mash after eggplant is well drained.

Make cream sauce of the flour, butter and milk. When smooth, add cheese, eggplant, seasonings, bread crumbs, onion, ketchup, beaten egg yolks. Beat egg whites until stiff peaks form. Fold stiffly beaten egg whites into eggplant mixture.

Pour into buttered casserole and place the casserole in a pan of hot water. Bake in 350 degree oven for 45 minutes. Serves 4 to 6.
— *D.B. of Moline*

Fettuccine a la Romana

April 11, 1979

½ pound Fettuccine noodles, cooked according to package directions
¼ cup butter
½ cup freshly grated Parmesan cheese

¼ cup heavy cream, heated
1/3 cup finely shredded proscuitto or ham

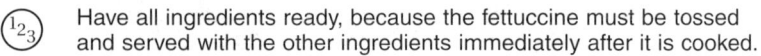

Have all ingredients ready, because the fettuccine must be tossed and served with the other ingredients immediately after it is cooked.

Cook fettuccine about 8 or 9 minutes, or according to package directions. Test for doneness. Drain. Mix well with butter. Mix noodles well with all other ingredients. Serve immediately.

Let each guest season his fettuccine with freshly grated pepper, especially if ham is substituted for proscuitto, suggests B.D. of Moline.

Note: Prosciutto is Italian smoked ham that is cut in very thin slices.
— *B.D. of Moline*

Fred Hitchcock's Goulash

Oct. 5, 1994

"I would like to share with you a recipe that has been in our family since 1918," A.C. of Geneseo tells Curious Cook and her readers.

"This was given to my mother by a neighbor when we lived in Davenport. The gentleman had a tavern, saloon, and this was served to people who came in.

"Of course, ladies couldn't go into a tavern but there was always a back door and private room. And although I was very young, I remember going in with my folks and being served this goulash, mother called it Hungarian goulash.

"My father loved it, but my husband didn't care for it so I haven't made it for myself. But I'd sure like to taste it again.

"The gentleman, Fred Hitchcock, gave mom this recipe which he cut down for her. I've always kept it, in mom's handwriting and haven't even shared it because so many people change recipes around and then it's not the same."

Here's the recipe from A.C. for Fred Hitchcock's Goulash "as mom called it," she says.

- 2 pounds beef, cut in small cubes
- 2 pounds pork, cut in small cubes
- 1 pound veal, cut in small cubes
- 2 quarts water
- A bag of mixed spices
- 5 cardamom seeds
- 1 can tomatoes, crushed
- 5 ribs celery, cut fine
- 2 medium onions, cut in small pieces
- Butter, as needed
- 1 tablespoon paprika
- 1 tablespoon salt
- Pinch of cayenne pepper
- 1 cup flour
- ½ cup sherry
- 1 tablespoon rum

Add 2 quarts of water, a bag of mixed spices and 5 cardamom seeds to the cut-up beef, pork and veal. Boil until tender.

Add 1 can crushed tomatoes and 5 ribs finely cut celery. Fry in butter the 2 medium-size, cut-up onions; add to meat mixture. Add all together then the 1 tablespoon paprika, 1 tablespoon salt and a pinch of cayenne pepper. Cook all together.

Then brown 1 cup of flour and use to thicken. At end, add ½ cup sherry and 1 tablespoon rum.

"I hope you can make sense of this, but this is the way it is written. She gave it to me when I was married at 20, but as I said he didn't like it. I can still remember it. 'It calls for a glass of beer and would be nice for a men's party.'"

— *A.C. of Geneseo*

French Toast

May 19, 1999

"This might be the recipe that L.B. of Alpha requested," writes N.J.H. of Colona. "It came from my friend D.R. in Springfield."

- 4 eggs
- 2/3 cup orange juice
- 1/3 cup milk
- ¼ cup sugar
- ¼ teaspoon nutmeg
- ½ teaspoon vanilla
- 1 loaf (8 ounces) Italian bread, cut in 1-inch slices
- 1/3 cup butter margarine, melted
- 1/3 cup chopped macadamia nuts or pecans

With wire whisk, beat together first six ingredients — eggs, orange juice, milk, sugar, nutmeg and vanilla.

Place bread in a tight-fitting casserole. ("I use a 9x13-inch pan with lid.") Pour liquid mixture over bread. Cover and refrigerate overnight, turning bread once.

In the morning, preheat oven to 400 degrees. Pour 1/3 cup melted butter or margarine on jelly-roll pan, spreading evenly.

Arrange soaked bread slices in a single layer on pan. Sprinkle with ½ cup of chopped macadamia nuts or other nuts (pecans). Bake at 400 degrees for 20 to 25 minutes, or until golden. — *N.J.H. of Colona*

French Toast Overnight

May 19, 1999

- ½ cup margarine
- 1½ cups brown sugar
- 1 teaspoon cinnamon
- 8 to 12 slices of bread to cover bottom of pan
- 8 to 9 eggs
- Pinch of salt
- 1¾ to 2 cups milk

In a 9x13-inch pan, melt margarine in oven at 350 degrees F. Combine brown sugar and cinnamon; sprinkle over melted margarine. Layer bread in bottom of pan.

Mix together eggs, pinch of salt and milk. Pour over bread slices. Cover and refrigerate overnight. Next morning, uncover and bake at 350 degrees. for 45 minutes. To serve, turn upside down on plate. — *B.C. of Port Byron*

French Toast Overnight

May 12, 1999

B.E.J. of Moline sent this e-mail: "Not sure if this is the recipe L.B. of Alpha wanted because there are no pecans, but this is very good and I'm sure pecans could be put on top."

6 cups 1-inch cubes day-old French or Italian bread
6 eggs
1½ cups milk
1 tablespoon firmly packed brown sugar
1 tablespoon vanilla
2 teaspoons cinnamon
½ teaspoon salt

Place bread cubes in greased 13x9x2-inch baking dish. In medium bowl, beat together remaining ingredients until well blended.

Pour mixture over bread and lightly toss until bread is evenly coated. Cover and refrigerate several hours or overnight.

Uncover and bake in preheated 350 degree oven until golden brown, about 50 minutes. Serve warm with confectioners' sugar and maple syrup, if desired. — *B.E.J. of Moline*

Glaze for Chicken

March 31, 1999

V.M. of Rock Island shares this recipe for Glaze for Chicken. "Couldn't be easier! Good on pork chops, too," she writes.

1 envelope Lipton onion soup mix
1 bottle (8 ounces) Wishbone Russian dressing
1 jar (12 ounces) apricot preserves

Combine soup mix, dressing and preserves; mix well. Pour over chicken pieces in baking dish.

Bake at 375 degrees for 1 hour. This quantity is sufficient for a 9x13-inch dish of wings or other chicken pieces. — *V.M. of Rock Island*

Ham baked in bread dough

March 9, 1994

"I enjoy your column very much. Now I'm looking for information on how to bake a ham in bread dough. Does it have to be a fully cooked ham or can a shank or butt of a smoked ham be used? How long and what temperature for baking?

"I've had Hy-Vee bake hams, but would like to try doing it myself. The ones Hy-Vee did were delicious nice and moist. Thank you."

— *D.A. of Davenport*

Curious Cook went right to the top. We called Robin Kline, M.S., R.D., director of consumer affairs for the National Pork Producers Council in Des Moines, who knows everything there is know about ham. Yes, she says, a fully cooked boneless ham may be baked in bread dough.

Use about an 8-pound ham, she advises, but note that the ham must be fully cooked and must be boneless. Prepare your favorite bread dough recipe and wrap the ham in the dough, sealing securely.

Bake at 350 degrees for about 1¾ hours. "That will bake your crust and make it nice and brown and will heat the ham through," Ms. Kline says.

Ms. Kline also advises that "a rich dough, like a brioche dough, works well. It's nice to make a mushroom stuffing — sauteed mushrooms — to place between the ham and the dough," she suggests.

— *National Pork Producers Council*

Ham baked in bread dough

Nov. 23, 1994

"Do you or your readers have a recipe for ham baked in bread dough? Walcher's bakery did this many years ago for the holidays. I would like to try it.

"P.S. People I have asked don't know, but would like it also. Thank you." — *B.G. of Eldridge*

Curious Cook answered a similar inquiry several months ago and fortunately the directions for baking a ham using frozen bread dough still are in our files from May 25, 1994.

I'm sure that Walcher's bakers didn't use frozen bread many years ago. But let's hope these directions help you bake a ham in dough at least somewhat similar to Walcher's way.

Jenna Jackson at Rhodes International in Salt Lake City provided these instructions, which we'll repeat for B.G. The ham must be the boneless, pre-cooked type. To bake the ham in frozen bread dough, Ms. Jackson says:

1. Buy frozen bread dough, making sure it's within code. There's a quick-lock; make sure the bread has not thawed, is not icy, nor stuck together. In other words, make sure the product is in first-class condition.

2. Allow bread to thaw in refrigerator or at room temperature. It will need to warm up to room temperature if thawed in the fridge. Get dough to the point where it's warm and bubbly, just rising a bit. You want it to be a warm, soft dough. Leaving it out on the counter is just fine. If it even rises and falls a bit, it will be OK. Just be careful about following directions.

3. At the point when the dough is warm and bubbly, just roll out the dough with a rolling pin. The ham must be a boneless, pre-cooked ham. Put ham on the dough, wrap, tuck ends underneath and secure well so the juices do not seep out. Place on greased baking pan/sheet and bake immediately. If you let the dough rise, it will form a bubble under the ham.

4. Bake at 350 degrees, until golden brown, about 20 to 25 minutes. Do not underbake; you don't want it to be doughy. "Our rolls and breads bake about 20 minutes. Because of the ham, baking time may be a little longer. Check at 20 minutes for golden brown color," Ms. Jackson advises.

5. Remove the ham from the oven; remove "ham en croute" from baking pan and place on cooling rack. Brush with butter.

Notes: Ms. Jackson also advises: "This is not a pastry dough; it's a yeast dough, which has the gluten in it. It won't taste the same as puff pastry dough, which would be light and flaky. It will taste very good. Be sure to brush butter on after baking. Also, you need to remove it from the pan immediately and put on cooling rack."

recipes to remember forever **119**

Ham baked in bread dough

April 12, 1995

Curious Cook has received a very interesting note from B.G. of Eldridge regarding baking a ham in frozen dough. B.G. also sent in a Poppy Seed Cake recipe, but her success story with the ham/dough baking procedure is fascinating.

In answer to a request about a year ago, Jenna Jackson with Rhodes International in Salt Lake City gave Curious Cook directions for baking a pre-cooked ham encased in frozen bread or roll dough.

Ms. Jackson recommended using a boneless, pre-cooked ham. However, it appears the Eldridge cook had very good luck with a bone-in, pre-cooked ham. Here's what she did:

"I was the person who wrote in about a dough-covered ham. I fixed the ham for Christmas. I had a whole ham with bone. I put brown sugar, pineapple slices and cherries on top of the ham.

"Then I covered it completely with frozen sweet roll dough — 5 rolls, 21-pound ham. I rolled out the dough flat, one roll at a time, then pinched the seams so juice would not run out.

"Bake it on a cookie sheet at 350 degrees. I put a foil tent over it, so it would not brown too fast, for about 3 to 4 hours.

"It was the best ham ever. I was so proud of it. Picture perfect. Everyone asked what the dough tasted like. I was so excited about the way it looked, I forgot to try the dough before I threw it out. Thank you for your help."

Curious Cook thanks you very much, B.G., for this follow-up report. Curious Cook called Ms. Jackson and told her about your "culinary discovery"!

March 10, 1999

Golden Lasagna

- 3 tablespoons butter
- ¼ pound mushrooms, sliced
- 1/3 cup finely chopped onion
- ½ cup diced green pepper
- 1 can low-fat cream of chicken soup
- 1/3 cup skim milk
- ¼ cup chopped pimiento
- 1 tablespoon dried basil, or to taste
- 2 cups cubed cooked chicken
- Thyme, tarragon and garlic, optional
- 8 lasagna noodles, cooked and drained
- 1 carton (16 ounces) creamed low-fat cottage cheese
- 2 cups low-fat Cheddar cheese
- ½ cup grated Parmesan cheese

Saute mushrooms, onions and green pepper in butter. Add soup, milk, pimiento, basil, chicken and optional seasonings as desired.

Place four cooked noodles in a greased 9x13-inch pan. Add one-half of the cottage cheese, then one-half of the sauce, one-half of the Cheddar cheese and one-half of the Parmesan cheese.

Put four more noodles in the pan and repeat cheeses and sauce. Bake at 350 degrees for 45 minutes. Let set for 8 minutes before serving.
— *C.D. of Davenport*

Irish Stew

June 27, 2001

M.A. of East Moline wanted a recipe for Irish Stew and Curious Cook has two such recipes to share with readers today.

First of all, Curious Cook remembered the Irish Stew prepared by Sister Mary Paulina, B.V.M. of Sacred Heart Catholic parish, Rock Island, for an ethnic dinner more than a year ago.

The occasion was one of a series of celebrations of the parish's 100th anniversary and the dinner featured foods of various nationalities represented in the parish.

So, after receiving the Lamb Stew request from M.A., we asked Sister Paulina for permission to publish her recipe.

Curious Cook promises you, dear cooks, that this stew is delicious. And Sister Paulina promises you that it is not only delicious but also easy to prepare!

6 tablespoons all-purpose flour, divided	3 cups water
1 teaspoon salt	8 extra-small or boiling onions
1/8 teaspoon pepper	3 medium-size carrots, cut into 1-inch pieces
1½ pounds lamb stew meat, cut into 1-inch cubes	2 large potatoes, peeled and cubed
2 tablespoons cooking oil	½ cup light cream
½ teaspoon dill weed	Hot biscuits

Combine 4 tablespoons flour, salt and pepper in a plastic bag. Add lamb; shake to coat.

In a 4-quart Dutch oven, heat oil; brown lamb on all sides. Add dill and water; bring to a boil. Reduce heat; cover and simmer for 1½ hours or until meat is almost tender.

Add onions, carrots and potatoes. Cover and simmer for 30 minutes or until the meat and vegetables are tender.

Combine cream and remaining flour; stir into stew. Cook and stir until boiling and slightly thickened. Serve over hot biscuits.

Yield: 6 servings. — *Sister Mary Paulina of B.V.M. Rock Island*

Irish Stew

June 27, 2001

Here's another Irish Stew recipe to answer the recent request of M.A. of East Moline.

- **6 pounds of lean lamb or beef**
- **1 tablespoon salt**
- **1 teaspoon pepper**
- **6 tablespoons vegetable oil**
- **4 onions**
- **1½ cups chopped celery**
- **1 tablespoon sugar**
- **3 to 4 cups beef broth or water**
- **3 to 4 cups sliced carrots, if desired**
- **4 pounds potatoes, cut into 2-inch cubes**
- **4 tablespoons chopped parsley**

Wash lamb or beef well. Dry and cut meat into 2-inch cubes. Sprinkle meat with salt and pepper.

Heat oil in large Dutch oven. Add meat and saute until browned. Remove meat from pan. Add onions, celery and sugar to drippings. Saute again, stirring constantly until lightly browned.

Add broth or water, carrots and potatoes. Heat to boiling. Reduce heat to low and add meat. Cover and continue to simmer until meat is tender, about 2 hours.

Skim fat from broth. Thicken with flour and water paste if necessary. Add parsley just before serving. — *M.A. of East Moline*

Italian Beef

Oct. 13, 1993

No doubt W.M.W. of Rock Island will be most pleased.

This gentleman recently requested a previously published recipe for preparing Italian beef in a slow cooker. Our readers responded in their usual generous and enthusiastic style.

Here are the slow-cooker Italian beef recipes.

- 3 pounds of beef round or beef rump roast
- Salt and pepper, to taste
- ½ cup vinegar
- 3 tablespoons Worcestershire sauce
- 1 tablespoon oregano
- 1 onion, sliced
- 4 to 5 cups water
- 3 beef bouillon cubes
- 2 packages Italian salad dressing mix
- 2 bell peppers "cut in strips and added. Makes better sandwiches."
- Hard rolls, for serving

In a kettle, mix everything together, except the beef roast and hard rolls. Bring mixture to a boil. Place roast in slow cooker and pour the sauce mixture over the roast.

Cook on low for 8 to 10 hours, or on high for 4 to 6 hours. Serve on hard rolls.
— *V.S. of Colona*

Italian Gourmet Beef

Oct. 13, 1993

- 2 to 4 pounds beef, any shape or size of pieces "Use an inexpensive roast of beef, such as blade-bone, pot roast or brisket."
- 2 or 3 green peppers, chopped
- ½ to 1 cup chopped onion
- 3 or 4 cloves of garlic, sliced
- Salt and pepper, to taste
- 1 to 2 tablespoons leaf oregano
- 1 to 2 tablespoons basil leaf
- Water, bouillon, wine, wine vinegar

Put meat, peppers, onions, garlic, herbs and seasonings in slow cooker. Add water, bouillon, wine — any combination — or just one and up to ¼ cup wine vinegar, to cover meat. Cook 8 hours or more on low.

Remove fat and bone, skim or strain out part or all of the onion, green pepper, etc.

Using two forks, string the beef into small portions, leaving in the juice.

Serve on fresh bread, French buns, sourdough bread or buns. Makes excellent hot dip sandwiches. Freezes well! Enjoy. — *L.E.G. of Moline*

Poor Man's Lobster

March 22, 2000

C.D. of Bettendorf will be pleased to learn that Quad-Cities cooks are responding to her recent request for directions for Poor Man's Lobster.

C.D. remembers a Poor Man's Lobster that her mother used to prepare and she recently asked our help finding that recipe.

"The recipe uses cod and spices, and I think you boil the cod and the end result is similar to lobster," C.D. told us in her note asking for the directions.

Curious Cook found and recently published a recipe for Poor Man's Lobster calling for monkfish or haddock. We had used the recipe years ago.

Then H.C. of East Moline sent us a yellowed newspaper clipping. H.C. writes: "I've had this recipe for Poor Man's Lobster from The Dispatch for years. I'm happy to forward the original OLD copy to you."

The clipping obviously is from one of the early Holiday Cookbooks, apparently the one that featured ethnic dishes. Here's the recipe:

Frozen haddock fillets ("Haddock works best")
1 quart water per pound of haddock fillets
1 tablespoon salt
2 tablespoons vinegar
Melted butter
Paprika
Fresh parsley, for serving
Melted butter, for serving

Cut frozen haddock fillets into pieces. The size of pieces depends on whom you are serving. For example, children will eat smaller pieces.

Use approximately 1 quart water per pound of haddock fillets.

In a large saucepan, bring water, salt and vinegar to a rolling boil. Drop frozen haddock pieces into boiling water. Bring water back to a full boil and boil for 15 minutes.

Remove haddock from water and place on a broiler pan covered with aluminum foil. The broiling firms the haddock to lobster consistency.

Brush haddock lightly with melted butter and sprinkle with paprika. Broil for 2 minutes. Remove from oven and arrange on a platter with fresh parsley. Serve with melted butter.

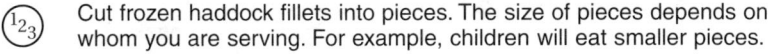

— *H.C. of East Moline*
(Holiday Cookbook, Circa 1970s)

March 8, 2000

Monkfish, haddock with lobster flavor

"I am looking for a recipe for Poorman's Lobster," writes C.D. of Bettendorf. "My mom used to make it and recently my dad asked me for the recipe.

"The recipe uses cod and spices, and I think you boil the cod and the end result is similar to lobster.

"If you can help me with this, I would be so grateful. Thank you!"
— *C.D. of Bettendorf*

Many years ago, the following directions for preparing lobster-flavored monkfish or haddock were published in The Dispatch. It's so long ago that my undated clipping is yellowed.

The "recipe" calls for using monkfish or haddock. Perhaps this is what C.D. remembers as Poor Man's Lobster.

Curious Cook does not have any directions calling for cod to taste like lobster tail. But if our readers do, I know they will share their information/recipes.

To learn if monkfish still is available, Curious Cook checked with salespersons at fish counters of two local supermarkets and with the Great Midwest Seafood Co. in Davenport.

Although none of the fish sellers had monkfish on hand, all said it could be ordered. Apparently it's just not as plentiful as it was years ago and, of course, it's more costly now.

To prepare either monkfish or haddock to taste like lobster tail, follow these easy directions from our old clipping (on facing page):

To prepare either monkfish or haddock to taste like lobster tail, follow these easy directions:

Monkfish or haddock, ½ pound per serving
Boiling water, to cover fish
2 tablespoons vinegar
1 teaspoon salt
Butter
Lemon or lime juice

In a kettle large enough to hold the fish, bring to a boil enough water to cover the fish. Stir in vinegar and salt.

Drop the fish into the boiling water, reduce heat and cook slowly about 15 minutes. Cook about 5 minutes longer if using frozen fish.

Remove fish from boiling water and place flesh side down on a broiler pan. Fish should be slashed, or cut into serving pieces, so that it does not curl.

While fish is cooking, melt butter in a pan; add lemon or lime juice, salt and pepper to taste.

Before broiling the fish, brush generously with lemon-butter mixture. Broil 3 to 5 minutes. Serve immediately with broiler pan drippings and additional hot lemon butter for dunking.

Note: The salt will keep the fish from flaking, the vinegar enhances the flavor of the fish and the broth may be saved for chowders, fish soups and sauces. — *Originally from The Dispatch*

Pork Chops

Oct. 20, 1993

Curious Cook has received "the" pork chop recipe to answer a recent request. Both C.B of Davenport and E.J. of Prophetstown responded with the recipe that follows.

C.B. of Davenport writes: "This is the beauty of your column — we can help each other! Quoted below is the recipe that I cut out of the Leader, date unknown."

"I noticed plea from O.D. of Woodhull for one of my very favorite recipes," R.C. of Moline tells Curious Cook. "It is the easiest, most delicious thing — if you want, use it for her. I have used it for years and years."

4 or 6 pork chops, lightly pounded "Very important! Tenderizes them."

¾ cup Italian salad dressing "Don't use other kind; it does not work."

1½ cups finely crushed cornflakes

Preheat oven to 375 degrees. Dip chops, after pounding them on both sides, into the salad dressing. Let them drip off a little, then roll in crushed cornflakes, covering them well.

Place pork chops on a greased baking sheet and bake at 375 degrees for 45 minutes. Do not turn. — *C.B. of Davenport*

Roast Duck a la Orange

Dec. 10, 2003

D.D. of East Moline has answered the request of R.H. of Davenport for an orange glaze for duck.

"The Orange Glaze Sauce can be used with about any type of fowl," advises D.D. "I've used it on duck and Cornish hens.

"I have had Orange Glazed Duck at The Cellar in Geneseo, which is very, very good. But I prefer my own recipe. It has a very good orange flavor."

1 duck (4 to 5 pounds)   **See following recipe for Orange Sauce. Prepare ahead.**

For duck you will need an open roasting pan with wire rack. Preheat oven to 325 degrees.

Duck may be roasted whole or cut in half. Brush skin with oil or butter. If cut in half, cook skin side up on wire rack with ½ cup of water in bottom of pan. Place on center rack of oven, cover with foil and cook for 1 hour.

Remove from oven and brush bird with prepared orange sauce. Return to oven, uncovered, and cook for 30 minutes longer. Remove from oven and repeat orange sauce step, adding more water if needed.

Return to oven, covered with foil, for 30 to 45 minutes longer or until done. Remove from oven and allow to cool for 10 minutes before carving.

Serve with small dish of warm orange sauce for each diner to dip meat. Yield: 2 servings.   — *D.D. of East Moline*

Orange Sauce (for duck)

¼ cup granulated sugar
¼ cup light brown sugar (packed)
¼ teaspoon salt
1 tablespoon cornstarch

1 tablespoon orange zest or 1 teaspoon dried orange peel
1 cup orange juice (see note)
1 tablespoon triple sec liqueur (optional — see note)

In a 1-quart saucepan, combine sugars, salt, cornstarch, orange zest and orange juice. Stirring constantly, cook on low heat until mixture boils and becomes thickened and clear.

Remove from heat and allow to cool slightly. Then strain through a sieve to remove orange zest.

Serve extra orange sauce warm in individual custard cups to allow diners to dip meat.

Note: If using triple sec, add 1 tablespoon liqueur to cup and fill with orange juice.   — *D.D. of East Moline*

Salmon Patties

Oct. 15, 2003

"Since we spend three months in Algoma, Wis., fishing for salmon, I have home-canned and frozen salmon all winter.

"We have found that a pint of our home-canned salmon equates to two cans of the deskinned, deboned, drained commercially canned salmon.

"For patties, I use 1 pint of canned salmon.

"We fillet our salmon so there are no bones or skin in our pints and it is dry packed, so home-canned has very little liquid compared to commercial. However, we drain ours as well.

"My daughter increases the bread crumbs and adds a bit of the liquid off our pints. But I like the more solid, salmon patties with less bread.

"For extra special salmon patties or nibblies for a party, I add two cans of the very tiny salad shrimp, double the other ingredients, shape in finger-food-size patties, spray and bake or fry. These salmon/shrimp patties are unbelievable.

"These are all a matter of taste, and adding a can of the small salad shrimp does make an exceptional patty with a taste and texture all its own.

"Thought some of your other readers might like this recipe. The mayonnaise acts in place of the egg binder and the ketchup gives the patties a nice rosy glow.

"We like these with a simple tartar sauce, a horseradish-based seafood sauce, creamed peas and a big salad."

1 pint of home-canned salmon, drained
8 crushed soda cracker squares (individual crackers)
¼ cup mayonnaise
¼ cup finely chopped onion
2 tablespoons ketchup
¼ cup sweet pickle relish

"I mix this all together. Drop into a bowl of half cornmeal, to coat, drop into bowl of half flour, shape into patties and fry in ½ inch of hot oil OR spray with Pam and bake on a greased cookie sheet at 350 degrees for 15 to 20 minutes, until brown and hot through.

Note: "These can also be coated with cornflake crumbs or one of the commercial coating mixes for baking."   *— B.P. of Moline*

Stuffed Eggplant

1 medium-sized eggplant
1 cup bread crumbs, divided
1 tablespoon butter
3 large scallions, chopped
2 tablespoons chopped parsley
¼ teaspoon salt
¼ teaspoon pepper
2 tablespoons grated Parmesan cheese
2 tablespoons butter, melted

Boil the eggplant until tender. Drain well. When cool enough to handle, cut in half lengthwise. Remove pulp leaving a shell ¼ inch thick. Chop the pulp and reserve.

Arrange shells in a shallow baking dish. For the stuffing, brown ½ cup bread crumbs in 1 tablespoon butter. Add the scallions, including the green tops, 2 tablespoons parsley and saute for 3 minutes. Add the eggplant pulp and sprinkle with the salt and pepper. Cover and cook for 5 minutes.

Pile this filling into the eggplant shells and sprinkle with the other ½ cup of bread crumbs mixed with 2 tablespoons Parmesan cheese and 2 tablespoons melted butter. Dot with butter.

Bake in a 350 degree oven for 20 minutes. Serves 4. — *D.B. of Moline*

Swedish Meatballs

May 5, 1999

We received this e-mail regarding meatballs from D.W: "This message is in response to your comment that you have always wanted a recipe for meatballs that cling together but almost fall apart when you cut them with a fork." This was a recent request by one of our Davenport readers.

"My mother, A.W. of Prophetstown, is first generation U.S. born of Swedish immigrant parents," D.W. continues. "The following is her recipe."

2 pounds ground beef (good chuck or round)
Dry bread crumbs (1½ to 2 slices)
1 potato, boiled and crumbled
Medium onion, chopped
2 eggs
Salt and pepper, to taste

Mix all ingredients and form into balls about the size of golf balls. Brown in oiled skillet. Add small quantity of water, cover and simmer until done. — *A.W., Prophetstown*

Swedish Pancakes

Feb. 14, 1996

Two cooks — M.L.J. and S.R.D., both of Davenport, sent the following directions for Swedish Pancakes.

"This recipe came from my grandmother, who came to the United States in 1905," writes S.R.D. "She had been a cook in Sweden and cooked for prominent Davenport/Bettendorf families. My grandchildren request Swedish Pancakes every time they come over. They roll up the pancake and have maple syrup with it."

Here's a composite of the two recipes:

1 cup flour, sifted
½ teaspoon salt
5 tablespoons sugar
2 cups milk
3 whole eggs, well beaten

Sift together the flour, salt and sugar. Add milk and eggs. After skillet/griddle becomes hot, add a small amount of cooking oil. Pour scant ¼ cup of batter onto griddle, tilting pan so batter forms a thin, even coating over medium heat. When light brown on one side, run spatula around edges and turn to cook other side. Makes 12 to 14 thin pancakes. — *M.L.J and S.R.D. of Davenport*

Swedish Pancakes

Feb. 14, 1996

Curious Cook had quite a good response to the recent request for a recipe for Swedish Pancakes. "This one I have had for years," reports R.J. of Rock Island via e-mail.

3 eggs
1 cup milk
1½ cups sifted flour
1 tablespoon sugar
½ teaspoon salt
½ cup cream
2 tablespoons butter, melted

Beat eggs until very light. "I sometimes have beaten them separately, and then fold them together." Add half the milk and fold in the flour sifted with the sugar and salt. Add cream, butter and remaining milk. Fry in usual manner on hot griddle. Serves 3 to 4.   — *R.J. of Rock Island*

Swedish Pancakes

Feb. 14, 1996

6 eggs
6 tablespoons margarine, melted
1 cup milk
1 cup cream
1 cup flour
¼ teaspoon salt
¼ cup sugar

Beat the eggs; add melted margarine, milk and cream. Add flour, salt and sugar. Mix well. Pour onto a buttered griddle. Turn when set and brown the other side.

Note: "I use 1 can (12 ounces) evaporated milk and enough water needed to make the 2 cups of liquid."   — *B.H. of Coal Valley*

Swedish Pancakes

Feb. 21, 1996

"Swedish Pancakes are a family favorite and are great for Sunday after church. They're a favorite for the grandchildren and always a first request!"

2 eggs, beaten
2 cups milk
1 tablespoon sugar
1 cup flour
¼ teaspoon salt
1 teaspoon baking powder
1 teaspoon oil

Whisk ingredients together. Pour small amount of thin batter on griddle and allow it to spread thin. Turn when it looks dry on top. Served with butter and powdered sugar sprinkled on top. Also good with lingonberries and whipped cream. Roll like a crepe.   — *N.J.L. of Orion*

Swedish Pancakes Platter

Feb. 21, 1996

From K.M. of Geneseo: "I saw the request for the enclosed recipes in the paper and wasn't sure if you'd received them yet." K.M. sent this recipe for Swedish Pancakes.

2½ cups flour
3 tablespoons sugar
½ teaspoon salt

2 eggs, beaten
1 quart milk
4 tablespoons melted butter

 Mix dry ingredients together. Add beaten eggs and milk, beat until smooth, adding milk 2 cups at a time. Add melted butter last.

"Batter bakes on a griddle or crepe pan and is thin. Brown on both sides. Served with syrup, or preserves or powdered sugar. This is originally from Ruth Bengston from Sweden." — *K.M. of Geneseo*

Tamale Pie

June 7, 2000

1 cup chopped onions
1 cup chopped peppers
1 pound ground beef
2 cups tomato sauce
1 tablespoon sugar
1 clove garlic, minced
1 teaspoon salt

1 teaspoon pepper
2 to 3 teaspoons chili powder, to suit your taste
1½ cups shredded cheese
1 can (12 ounces) whole-kernel corn, drained, optional
1 cup chopped ripe olives, optional

 Cook onions and peppers in small amount of fat. Add meat and brown lightly.

 Add remaining ingredients except cheese. Simmer until thick, about 20 to 30 minutes. Add cheese; stir until melted. Pour mixture into greased 8x8-inch greased baking dish.

CORNMEAL TOPPING:

¾ cup cornmeal
2 cups cold water

1 teaspoon salt
1 tablespoon margarine

 Stir cornmeal into cold water; cook until thick. Add margarine and salt; mix well. Spread over mixture in strips or drop by small spoonfuls. Bake at 375 degrees for 40 minutes. — *E.J.S. of Davenport*

Texas Lightning White Chili

Jan. 10, 1996

R.J. of Rock Island promptly answered a chili request: "D.L. of Davenport requested a recipe for White Chicken Chili. Enclosed is a recipe I have enjoyed for a similar chili."

- 1 teaspoon olive oil
- 1 medium onion, chopped 1½ cups
- 2 large garlic cloves, crushed
- ¾ pound boneless, skinless chicken breast
- 3 teaspoons cumin
- 1 tablespoon fresh oregano OR 2 teaspoons dried oregano
- 1 can (15½ ounces) Great Northern beans, drained and rinsed
- ¾ cup chicken stock
- 2 medium-size jalapeno peppers, seeded, chopped
- Several drops hot pepper sauce
- Salt and pepper, to taste

Sauté onions in oil for 5 minutes; do not brown. Add garlic and sauté 3 minutes. Cut chicken into thin strips. Add to pan with cumin and oregano. Saute 2 minutes. Drain and rinse beans. Add to the pan with chicken stock and jalapenos. Cook gently for 3 minutes or until the sauce begins to thicken. Add hot pepper sauce and blend in well. Add salt and pepper. Serve chili over hot cooked rice and add appropriate toppings. Serves 2. — *R.J. of Rock Island*

Tex-Mex

Dec. 4, 1996

"One of my favorite one-dish meals for L.R. of Eldridge," continues D.C. of Bettendorf.

- 1 envelope all-purpose meat marinade
- 1 can (14½ ounces) tomatoes, cut up "I use a potato masher."
- 1½ or 2 pounds beef round steak, cut in thin strips
- 1 can (4 ounces) chopped chilies
- 1 teaspoon cumin
- 1 teaspoon sugar
- 1 clove garlic, minced
- 1 can (15 ounces) refried beans or refried with sausage
- 2 cups cooked rice
- ½ cup sour cream
- ½ cup shredded Cheddar cheese
- Corn chips

In 12-inch skillet or heavy 4-quart cooking pot, combine dry meat marinade and undrained tomatoes. Stir in steak strips. Let stand 10 minutes. Stir in chilies, cumin, sugar and garlic. Bring to boil; reduce heat and simmer, uncovered, 15 minutes, stirring occasionally. Stir in beans and rice and heat through. Top with sour cream and ring with Cheddar cheese. Cover and heat a couple more minutes. Serve over corn chips. Serves 6. — *D.C. of Bettendorf*

Veal Hungarian Goulash

April 12, 2002

Curious Cook is so pleased to open her mail and find recipes and information from cooks like C.A. of Rock Island.

C.A. responded to a reader's request for a Hungarian Goulash recipe with an "authentic" version from Hungary and an interesting note as well. C.A. writes:

"In response to the request for authentic Hungarian Goulash, I'm sending these recipes obtained while living in Hungary for a year. My husband and I were on teaching assignments there.

"I'd like to point out that goulash known the world over has little in common with the traditional dish of Hungary, containing beef and potatoes cut in cubes and stewed in a thick paprika and onion sauce.

"There are several versions made with either beef, pork or veal as well as a thinner version — Goulash Soup!

"I recall tasting a version where a combination of veal, pork and beef was used. Delicious!" she adds.

Curious Cook enjoyed an informative visit with C.A. about the wonderful year she and her husband spent living and teaching in Hungary and traveling in Europe. She is very enthusiastic about this "authentic" Hungarian Goulash, a culinary reminder of the Hungarian experience.

C.A. provides directions for Veal Hungarian Goulash and Beef Hungarian Goulash (see facing page). "Pork Goulash is made in the same manner as the beef version," she points out.

BEEF VERSION:
1 large onion, finely chopped
1 tablespoon oil
1¾ pounds veal shoulder, cubed
1 teaspoon paprika
Salt, to taste
1 medium tomato, peeled and cut into small pieces
1 tablespoon tomato paste
2 large green peppers, diced
1/3 pint sour cream
1 teaspoon flour

BEEF VERSION:
2 onions, finely chopped
3 tablespoons oil
1¾ pounds beef, cubed
Pepper/salt, to taste
1 tablespoon paprika
1 medium tomato, peeled and cut into small pieces
1 tablespoon tomato paste
2 green peppers, diced
1 clove garlic, crushed

Method for veal version: Fry the finely chopped onion in oil. Add meat, which has been cut into cubes, and continue frying until brown. Remove from stove and sprinkle with paprika. Add a little water, about 1 tablespoon, and the tomato paste and bring to boil. Add green peppers and the tomato that has been skinned and diced. Add salt. Cover with lid, return to stove and simmer until done. Stir occasionally, adding a little water if necessary to avoid sticking. When the meat is done, thicken with sour cream mixed with flour and do not let mixture burn. Serve with galuska or rice.

Method for beef version: Saute the finely chopped onion in oil; add meat cubes cut into small pieces, brown well, remove from heat. Mix in paprika, salt and pepper. Add the peeled tomato cut into small pieces, and the tomato paste diluted with a little water — about 1 tablespoon water. Add the diced peppers and crushed garlic. Cover, return to heat and stew at moderate heat. Add a little water now and then if necessary. Continue stewing until tender. Serve with boiled potatoes or galuska small dumplings. — *C.A. of Rock Island*

Galuska

7 ounces (about 1¾ cups) flour
2 eggs, beaten

¼ teaspoon salt
2 tablespoons oil

Work together the flour, eggs, salt and sufficient water to produce a firm dough. Roll into "pencil form" and nip off small pieces into boiling water. Each galuska should be 1½ cm. long. Cook only a few at a time.

When the galuskas rise to the surface of the water, lift out, rinse with hot water and drain. Heat them in a little oil and serve with the goulash. — *C.A. of Rock Island*

White Pizza

Sept. 17, 1997

Curious Cook received this interesting contribution via e-mail from B.P. of Davenport.

"In your Curious Cook column of The Leader the 8-20 edition, J.G. of Rock Island requested recipes for white pizza. I have tried my best to put them into terms for your publishing purposes.

"I had a catering business for 20 years on the East coast before moving here 15 months ago and have used these recipes often. However, having been taught to cook from the age of 5, I rarely use or follow recipes.

"These recipes both can be converted into extraordinary lasagna dishes also using the same ingredients by simply adding some riccota.

"I thoroughly enjoy your column and look forward to it each week. I have gotten some great recipes from your column! Keep up the good work!

"I hope these are enjoyed!" B.P. adds.

"Start with sautéing fresh garlic cloves (be generous with the amount you use) and small amount of onion in olive oil. OR, you can use roasted garlic-flavored cooking oil — also good in your dough.

"At the end of your sauteing, add some sweet basil and oregano, other spices of your choice. If you have pesto, it can be used also in addition to the above items. After initial sauteing, allow to simmer slowly for a short time to thicken slightly as the garlic breaks down.

"Spread this mixture over your partially baked pizza dough. Then top with your favorite cheese. This one is best with at least three cheeses. (See note.) Be creative! Bake and enjoy!

"This pizza can also be easily converted to a Broccoli Pizza by simply adding chopped or small pieces of broccoli to it before adding the cheese.

Note: "I would suggest using a combination of mozzarella, mild Cheddar, Parmesan and Provolone, or a great combination pack of three or four cheeses already blended and shredded.

"Cheese seems to work best for me when I use shredded or hand-grate it myself. Cubes or chunks seem to put too much flavor in one spot."

— *B.P. of Davenport*

side dishes

making your **meal complete**

Dear Curious Cook

Aunt Mary's Potato Kugelis

Feb. 28, 2003

A recent request by B.P. of Moline certainly has filled Curious Cook's mailbox. The request for Kugelis, a Lithuanian specialty, generated a great deal of interest among our readers/cooks.

We received a considerable number of recipes, many of them with notes explaining the origin of the potato dish and how traditional it is to those of Lithuanian descent. Comparison of recipes is part of the joy of cooking, especially when the recipes reflect a heritage.

So today and next week, Curious Cook will bring you recipes/information about Kugelis. It's not surprising that the recipes are very much the same, yet they differ.

From P.B. of Bettendorf: "In reply to a request in the Feb. 14 edition of The Leader for a Potato Kugeli recipe, here is one that has been in our family for years.

"It was my Aunt Mary's specialty and we have enjoyed it over and over again."

6 to 8 large potatoes, pared and grated, drain excess liquid

¼ of a small onion, grated

3 eggs, well beaten

1 cup hot milk

6 tablespoons margarine

2½ teaspoons salt

Blend potatoes and onion; stir in beaten eggs, hot milk in which margarine has been melted, and salt.

Pour into a well-greased, 9- by 13-inch baking dish. Bake, uncovered, at 350 degrees for 1 hour and 15 minutes. Serve warm with sour cream. — *P. B. of Bettendorf*

recipes to remember forever

Feb. 28, 2003

Grandmother Anoinette's Lithuanian Kugelis

A recent request by B.P. of Moline certainly has filled Curious Cook's mailbox. The request for kugelis, a Lithuanian specialty, generated a great deal of interest among our readers/cooks. We received a considerable number of recipes, many of them with notes explaining the origin of the potato dish and how traditional it is to those of Lithuanian descent.

Comparison of recipes is part of the joy of cooking, especially when the recipes reflect a heritage. So today and next week, Curious Cook will bring you recipes/information about kugelis. It's not surprising that the recipes are very much the same, yet they differ.

"Since I thought I was the only Lithuanian-American transplanted to Iowa, I loved seeing your request for Lithuanian 'soul food' — kugelis!" writes C.E.E. of Bettendorf.

"This recipe is from my Grandmother Anoinette who made it at every family meal for 50 years. Kugelis is somewhat like a giant potato pancake and truly a staple of the Lithuanian kitchen, much like serving pasta if you're Italian.

"Warning: grated potatoes quickly turn brown when exposed to air, so the use of Fruit-Fresh or ascorbic acid keeps them white.

Note: C.E.E. adds: "Your reader's request made me crave a bit of kugelis myself. I'm making some tonight. Thank you Aciu! for your column that is a wonderful forum for Quad-Cities cooks!"

- 4 pounds russet or Idaho potatoes, peeled and grated
- ½ pound bacon, diced
- 3 tablespoons bacon fat
- 1 very large onion, diced
- 1 tablespoon Fruit-Fresh
- 4 eggs, beaten
- 1 can (5 ounces) evaporated milk
- 1½ teaspoons salt
- ½ teaspoon pepper

Preheat oven to 350 degrees. Dice cold bacon and fry in large frypan until almost crisp. Remove bacon from pan. Save 3 tablespoons bacon fat in the pan. Dice the onion; saute in the pan with 3 tablespoons bacon fat until the onion is clear; set all aside.

Dissolve 1 tablespoon Fruit-Fresh in large bowl half-filled with water. Peel and grate the potatoes. Though the traditional method is to hand grate with a metal grater, this can be really hard on your knuckles! You also can process the peeled potatoes in several small batches in your food processor until finely grated. Put each batch of processed potatoes immediately into the bowl of water with Fruit-Fresh. Potatoes exposed to the air quickly turn brown.

In small bowl, beat eggs slightly. Drain water from grated potatoes. Put a clean dishtowel on top of potatoes and squeeze out excess water. Mix beaten eggs into the potatoes; stir in onions with bacon fat, evaporated milk, salt and pepper. Do not drain bacon fat or kugelis will be too dry when cooked.

Spray a 9- by 11-inch glass baking dish with Pam. Pour in potato mix. Spray top of potatoes lightly with Pam. Bake at 350 degrees for about 45 minutes or until top is lightly brown and mixture is pulling away from sides of baking dish. Serve warm with sour cream. Serves 8 to 10.

— *C.E.E. of Bettendorf*

Kugelis

Feb. 28, 2003

From P.B. of Alpha: "This is the way my grandmother, who emigrated to Illinois, made Kugelis."

- 4 large potatoes, grated not shredded
- ½ pound bacon, cooked and crumbled
- 1 onion, minced
- 3 eggs, beaten slightly
- 3 teaspoons salt
- 1 cup sour cream
- ¼ cup half-and-half

Grate the potatoes into cold water; drain well by squeezing.

Mix with all the other ingredients. Bake in a greased 13x9-inch pan at 400 degrees for 20 minutes. Reduce oven to 350 degrees and bake 50 minutes more or until brown. Enjoy!!

Note: "The hardest part of this is the grating because the food processor blade for potatoes just doesn't do the job!" — *P. B. of Alpha*

Baked Cabbage

April 5, 2000

A.H. shares a favorite cabbage recipe. She writes:

"Am sending my recipe for Baked Cabbage. I have been making this for many years.

"It's delicious, easy to prepare and a favorite in our family."

- 1 medium-size head of cabbage
- 1 tablespoon sugar
- 2 tablespoons flour
- 1 cup cream or use 12-ounce can of evaporated milk
- Salt and pepper, to taste
- 2 or 3 strips of bacon (See note)

Shred cabbage and place in buttered casserole. Mix sugar, flour and cream. Add salt and pepper and pour over cabbage. Place bacon on top.

Cover and bake at 350 degrees for 50 minutes. Remove cover awhile before taking from oven so bacon is crisp.

Note: A.H. likes to partially cook the bacon before putting the strips on top of the casserole and she adds the bacon grease for flavor.
— *A.H. of Davenport*

Baked Carrot Soufflé

Oct. 23, 2002

"I make this Carrot Soufflé and it is good," promised B.P. of Moline as she answered the request.

"You either can make it as a semi-dessert or a savory by simply changing the spices and using either sugar with cinnamon/ginger/allspice, or softened onion with rosemary/thyme/sage."

"Because soufflés are so touchy and must be served immediately, I have found that my family likes a puffy carrot casserole that doesn't deflate if it isn't served for a few minutes. All I do is add one more cup of mashed carrots, add a teaspoon of baking powder to the egg yolks and proceed with the recipe.

"I then use a regular 2-quart baking dish. The carrots will puff, and fall somewhat like a pumpkin pie, but they are still beautiful. This makes a colorful potluck casserole and it is an interesting and unusual dish.

"The savory version is the one most people like the best. The sweet is usually mistaken for a sweet potato or pumpkin custard depending on the seasonal color of the carrots."

4 tablespoons flour

4 tablespoons margarine/ butter

Salt, to taste

1 cup sour cream

2 cups cooked, mashed carrots

4 well-beaten egg yolks

Sugar/spice mix or herb mix (See note)

4 stiffly beaten egg whites (they should hold a peak, but still be glossy)

Melt margarine and stir in flour; add salt to taste. Blend until bubbly. Remove from heat and stir in sour cream, then mashed carrots and beat by hand or low speed on mixer until smooth.

Add a small amount of this mixture to the egg yolks, stirring constantly. Then, still stirring, pour warmed egg yolk mixture into remaining egg yolks. Mix well. At this point, add either the sugar/spice mix or the herb mix. "If I make a savory, I soften the onions in the original flour/margarine." Fold gently into the egg whites and pour into a 1½-quart soufflé dish.

Bake in preheated 350-degree oven for 30 minutes or until a knife inserted comes out clean.

Note: For the sugar/spice mix, B.P. combines ½ cup sugar with 1 teaspoon cinnamon, ¼ teaspoon ginger and ¼ teaspoon allspice. She points out that individual taste preferences should prevail and the sweetness of the carrots must be taken into consideration.

For the herb mix, B.P. finely chops 1 onion and adds 1 teaspoon or less of rosemary, thyme and sage. As she advises, the seasonings are to your liking.

— *B.P. of Moline*

April 5, 2000

Carrot Casserole

Curious Cook has received two recipes for the requested Carrot Souffle. Both recipes have a Southern origin, so perhaps this dish is a specialty of good cooks down South.

First, J.K. of Aledo: "This is in response to a recipe for Carrot Souffle. I received this recipe from a friend in Chattanooga, Tenn."

1 stick margarine, melted
2 cups cut-up carrots, cooked and mashed
1 cup sugar
3 tablespoons flour
3 eggs, beaten
1 teaspoon baking powder
½ teaspoon cinnamon

Melt margarine in 8-inch Pyrex dish. Stir in remaining ingredients, mixing well.

Bake at 400 degrees for 15 minutes. Reduce heat to 350 degrees for 30 minutes or until set. Yield: 8 to 12 servings. *— J.K. of Aledo*

Copper Pennies

Oct. 18, 1995

"Enclosed is a recipe for P.D. of Colona for canned carrots. We love it, a great vegetable side dish. I've heard it is called 'copper pennies.'"

- 2 pounds cooked carrots, sliced
- ½ cup diced green pepper
- 1 medium onion, dried
- 1 can (10¾ ounces) tomato soup, undiluted
- 1 tablespoon Worcestershire sauce
- 1 tablespoon prepared mustard
- ½ cup sugar
- ½ cup cider or wine vinegar
- ¼ cup oil

Place cooked carrots in a large glass bowl, add green pepper and onions.

In a medium-size saucepan, combine tomato soup, Worcestershire sauce, mustard, sugar, vinegar and oil. Bring to a boil, add salt to taste. Pour over carrots and marinate, covered in the refrigerator, for 24 hours.

Serve cold, or reheat and serve hot. Makes 10 servings.

— *L. M. H. of unknown town*

Escalloped Cabbage

March 8, 2000

From R.G. of Morrison: "Someone asked for a recipe for Escalloped Cabbage. I cannot remember where I got the recipe, but have made it several times. It is very good and a nice change."

- 2 cups milk
- 4 tablespoons flour
- 4 tablespoons butter
- ½ teaspoon salt
- ½ cup sharp cheese
- 1 medium-size head cabbage, shredded
- Buttered cornflakes

Cook cabbage until tender crisp. Make cream sauce — with milk, flour, butter and salt — with cheese added last, until it is melted.

Drain cabbage. Put in buttered casserole. Pour cream sauce over cabbage. Top with buttered cornflakes. Bake at 350 degrees for 45 minutes.

— *R.G. of Morrison*

Escalloped Corn

March 24, 1999

"In answer to E.M. of Aledo who asked for an Escalloped Corn recipe, this is what I make," reports D.H. of Rock Island.

"It is a 'hand me down' from my mother and my sons expect it at all family celebrations. Hope it will fill the bill."

- 1 regular 4-serving size can cream-style corn
- 1 cup crushed saltine crackers
- ½ cup milk
- 1 egg
- 1 tablespoon sugar
- ½ teaspoon salt
- ¼ teaspoon pepper

Crush crackers and soak 2 to 3 minutes in the milk. Beat in the egg. Add sugar, salt, pepper and cream-style corn. Blend well.

Pour mixture into greased 8x8-inch baking dish. May use deep round pie plate or casserole. Bake at 350 degrees for 45 minutes. Serves 6 to 8. Easily doubled.

Note: "I like to drizzle a couple of tablespoons melted butter or margarine on top before putting it in the oven. Also could put a couple of crushed crackers on top, too." — *D.H. of Rock Island*

Escalloped Corn

March 24, 1999

From D.O. of East Moline: "E.M. of Aledo wanted a recipe for Escalloped Corn without a cornbread mix. This is our favorite. The cheese gives it a good flavor."

1 can (16 ounces) whole-kernel corn	2 tablespoons finely chopped onions
2 eggs, beaten	¼ teaspoon salt
1 can (16 ounces) cream-style corn	1/8 teaspoon pepper
2/3 cup evaporated milk	1¾ cups crushed soda crackers
¼ cup margarine or butter, melted	12 ounces grated Velveeta cheese

Drain whole-kernel corn and reserve ¼ cup liquid.

Combine everything except crackers and cheese, including the ¼ cup liquid. Grate the cheese over this mixture and it folds in easier. Fold in crumbs. Pour into buttered 2-quart casserole. Bake at 325 degrees for 1 hour. — *D.O. of East Moline*

Escalloped Corn

April 13, 1999

2 cans cream-style corn	2 tablespoons dried minced onion
½ cup milk	Pepper to taste
1 cup saltine cracker crumbs, divided	Margarine

Mix together the corn, milk, ¾ cup of cracker crumbs, dried onion and pepper. Place in greased 1½ quart casserole dish. Sprinkle with remaining cracker crumbs and dot with margarine. Bake at 375 degrees for 45 minutes. — *V.M. of Rock Island*

Escalloped Corn

April 14, 1999

Because of the overwhelming response to the request for escalloped corn recipes, and the enthusiasm of local cooks for their recipes, Curious Cook has more corn recipes to share this week and next. The variations are interesting.

Here's a contribution from D.D. of East Moline. His directions may be used for corn dishes for one or more people. He writes:

"Here is one that our family uses all the time because of the ease of preparation. Not only is it easy to prepare, but it tastes very good.

"The small recipe is great for people who live alone, but still like home cooking. This recipe was handed down from my father who was a very good cook."

FAMILY SIZE:
- 1 can (15 ounces) cream-style corn
- ½ teaspoon granulated sugar
- Pinch of salt
- Pinch of white pepper
- 10 soda crackers, crushed
- Paprika to sprinkle over baked scalloped corn (optional)

POTLUCK SIZE:
- 3 cans (15 ounces each) cream-style corn (see note)
- 1½ teaspoons granulated sugar
- ¼ teaspoon salt
- ¼ teaspoon white pepper
- 24 soda crackers, crushed
- Paprika to sprinkle over baked scalloped corn (optional)

Preheat oven to 350 degrees. Use 1-quart baking size for Family Size recipe, 3-quart size baking dish for potluck size recipe.

Crush 6 crackers (18 for potluck size) and mix with corn in baking dish. Add sugar, salt and pepper, mixing well. Top with 4 crushed crackers (6 for potluck size), sprinkling evenly over top of corn.

Bake at 350 degrees for 45 minutes for family size (60 to 70 minutes for potluck size). After baking, sprinkle top with paprika.

For a person living alone: Use 1 can (8 ounces) of cream-style corn, ¼ teaspoon sugar, a dash of salt and pepper. Bake in a small individual baking dish for 30 minutes.

Note: When preparing potluck size, one can of whole kernel corn may be substituted for one can of cream-style corn, if desired.

— *D.D. of East Moline*

German Potato Salad

Sept. 14, 1994

"This makes a big amount," advises N.C. of Rock Island who is sharing a recipe for German Potato Salad in response to the recent request.

"I found this recipe in the Argus Aug. 2, 1978, from Katherine Wise who cooked for 11 children!"

5 pounds potatoes
3 to 5 onions, chopped
½ pound bacon, diced
5 eggs
1 cup vinegar
½ cup white sugar
½ cup water
Salt and pepper, to taste

Boil, peel and dice approximately 5 pounds of potatoes. Add chopped onions to potatoes.

In a skillet, fry bacon. Add to potatoes and onions. Beat eggs until lemon-colored and frothy.

In the same skillet, put vinegar, white sugar and water; add beaten eggs and cook over low flame until the consistency of gravy. Pour over potatoes, onions and diced bacon.

Add salt and pepper to taste and mix well. Serve warm or chilled.

— *N.C. of Rock Island;*
originally appeared in The Argus Aug. 2, 1978,
courtesy of Katherine Wise

Ferden

Dec. 20, 2000

A.G. of Davenport e-mailed her ferden information. (Her spelling is with an "e.")

"The recipe I'm sending along tastes exactly like the yummy ones my German mother-in-law Ruby made every Christmas," writes A.G. "She might tell you hers were better but to me they are exactly the same."

"The secret to her recipe is cardamom (have to buy this specially and use so very little) so maybe this is a German tradition."

A.G. calls her recipe Ferden, which she got from Janalee Keppy.

1 package dry yeast   **¼ cup warm water**

Dissolve 1 package dry yeast into ¼ cup warm water. When dissolved, pour into VERY large bowl. Next ingredients should be at room temperature. Add:

4 eggs, beaten   **4½ cups flour**
1 teaspoon salt   **¼ teaspoon cardamom**
3 cups milk   **1 cup raisins, softened in hot water and cooled and drained**
½ cup sugar
½ cup cream half-and-half

Mix well, stirring with large spoon. Cover and let rise in warm place 1½ to 2 hours.

Fry in ferden pan, preheated with generous dollops of Crisco make each little section about half-full with the melted Crisco and ladle out a generous tablespoonful or gravy ladle of batter or less — you don't want the ferden to get too big.

The pan should be about the temperature for deep-fat frying, not too hot and not too cool. Fry until batter rises in shape of ball and use fork to carefully peek on the bottom to see if nicely browned. Then, with the fork, gently turn over and cook until the tops are nicely browned.

Place on paper towel and keep warm while you are preparing the rest. Add more Crisco for next batch.

We always had a little bowl of granulated sugar to dip the warm ferden in or sometimes used cinnamon sugar. I don't think the batter can be kept overnight but you can space out the cooking over a few hours.   — *A.G. of Davenport*

recipes to remember forever **149**

Holst Family Furden

Dec. 20, 2000

Maryn Holst of Moline was the first to respond to the request for a recipe for ferden. Or, furden, if you will. We'll go with furden.

Some 24 years ago, Curious Cook featured Ms. Holst in a food cover article about furden, which are fried dough balls rolled or dipped in sugar or sugar/cinnamon.

Mrs. Holst used then ... and still does ... a generations-old family recipe from the late Mary Nielson Holst of Moline, grandmother of Maryn's husband, Dave Holst.

Maryn Holst says of course she's still using the same recipe, "flipping the furden" for husband Dave, their two sons and now for five grandchildren!

These delicious dough balls are a treasured Christmas holiday tradition with families of German or Scandinavian descent.

The dough balls are fried in a small amount of shortening in the individual round holes or depressions of a cast-iron furden or ebleskiver pan. Fat Crisco is heated, dough is dropped into the indentations, turned or flipped and fried until browned, forming balls.

The dough balls sometimes contain raisins, sometimes not. Families can be firmly divided on this issue. After furden is fried, the dough balls are rolled or dunked in cinnamon/sugar and served warm.

1 quart of milk
¾ cup lard or butter
5 cups flour
1 dozen cardamom seeds, crushed
1 lemon rind
2 teaspoons salt

1/3 cup sugar
½ teaspoon cinnamon
1 package or cake yeast
¼ cup warm water
5 egg yolks
5 egg whites, beaten until stiff

Heat the milk and lard or butter together and set aside.

Combine the flour, crushed cardamom seeds, lemon rind, salt, sugar and cinnamon to the milk/fat mixture.

Dissolve the yeast in ¼ cup warm water and add to the flour mixture. Add the 5 egg yolks to the mixture.

Beat the egg whites until stiff; fold into mixture. Let rise for 3 hours in a warm place, protected from a draft. Cook furden in greased furden pan.

Drop 2 or 3 raisins in each furden and fry slowly, but not too slowly. Flip with a fork and when the fork comes out clean, furdens are done.
— *Maryn Holst of Moline*

Dec. 27, 2000

Jackie Tanner's Slow Cooker Stuffing

D.M.H. of Moline highly recommends this recipe for Slow Cooker Stuffing to J.H. of Coal Valley who requested the directions.

The recipe originally was submitted by Valerie Prickett of East Moline and was published in the "1999 Quad-Cities Holiday Cookbook" published by The Dispatch, The Rock Island Argus and The Leader.

D.M.H. reports she has used this recipe with great success. So, for your New Year's Day dinner, consider preparing Jackie Tanner's Slow Cooker Stuffing.

- 1 pound bulk pork sausage, browned
- 1 cup margarine
- 2 cups chopped onion
- 2 cups chopped celery
- ¼ cup chopped parsley
- 2 cans (8 ounces each) mushrooms, drained
- 12 to 13 cups prepared stuffing mix (See note)
- 2 eggs, beaten
- 3½ to 4½ cups chicken broth or turkey broth with giblets
- Optional: apples, raisins or personal favorites

Sauté onion, celery and parsley in margarine. Mix all ingredients together and place in Crockpot.

Cover and cook on high for 45 minutes. Reduce heat to low and cook for 4 to 8 hours. Stir occasionally.

Note: Seasoning for dried bread crumbs: Combine 1 teaspoon poultry seasoning, 1½ teaspoons salt, 1½ teaspoons sage, 1 teaspoon thyme, ½ teaspoon pepper, ½ teaspoon marjoram; mix well.

— *D.M.H. of Moline,*
originally printed in the 1999 Holiday Food Guide

Make Ahead Mashed Potatoes

Nov. 15, 1995

"I am looking for a recipe for Make Ahead Mashed Potatoes," writes J.H. of Bettendorf.

"The recipe appeared in a ladies magazine several years ago, and contains both sour cream and cream cheese. It could be made a day ahead and then just heated in the oven before serving." — *J.H. of Bettendorf*

Curious Cook is sure this recipe is the one you want. It's excellent and dependable. For many years it has become a holiday tradition at our house as well as at many others I am sure.

- 8 to 12 medium-size potatoes, peeled, cooked and drained
- 1 package (8 ounces) cream cheese, softened
- ¼ cup sour cream, or more as needed
- Salt and white pepper, to taste
- Melted butter
- Paprika

Cook and drain potatoes. When potatoes are ready, proceed immediately. Potatoes must be hot to be mixed smoothly.

In large bowl of electric mixer, beat together the cream cheese and sour cream. Gradually add hot potatoes, beating constantly until mixture is light and fluffy. Add additional sour cream as needed to achieve desired consistency. Season to taste with salt and white pepper.

Spoon mashed potatoes into a buttered 2-quart casserole. Brush top with melted butter, or dot with small pieces of butter. Sprinkle with paprika. Bake, uncovered, at 325 degrees for 20 to 30 minutes.

Note: This dish may be prepared ahead, covered and refrigerated or frozen. When ready to bake, remove from refrigerator, uncover and bake about 30 to 45 minutes. If frozen, thaw in refrigerator before baking.   — *From Curious Cook's files*

Make Ahead Potatoes

Nov. 29, 1995

"I have used this recipe several times for family and friends and they go back for seconds," M.N. of East Moline tells us with her recipe for Make Ahead Potatoes. It is a little different than the recipe we recently published.

- 5 pounds potatoes, cooked and drained
- 1 package (8 ounces) cream cheese, softened
- 1 cup half-and-half
- 1 teaspoon onion salt
- 1 teaspoon seasoning salt
- 1 teaspoon plain salt
- ¼ teaspoon pepper
- ½ cup butter or margarine
- Paprika

Boil and drain peeled potatoes. Whip potatoes, cream cheese, half-and-half and seasonings until smooth and creamy. Put mixture into large baking dish. At this point you may cover and refrigerate up to one week.

When ready to bake, uncover and brush with butter, sprinkle with paprika and bake for 30 minutes in 350 degree oven. If it has been refrigerated, bake for 45 minutes. — *M.N. of East Moline*

Mock Shannon's Potato Salad

March 17, 1999

"Now I'll share a recipe I adapted, which might interest some readers. I clipped and made the Shannon's Potato Salad but it was a lot of work AND needed a raw egg, which isn't very safe nowadays.

"I adapted the recipe and came up with one that is very close. I never measure, but will explain how I make it, and it's the EASIEST, fastest potato salad I make. I have several different styles I use depending on the mood I'm in."

- About 6 or 7 potatoes, to fill a 3-quart pan, boiled in jackets, cooled and peeled
- About 5 hard-cooked eggs, cooled and peeled
- About 5 green onions, cleaned
- Salt, to taste
- Hellmann's AND Miracle Whip
- Yellow mustard

Cut up the potatoes, eggs and onions including the green tops. Sprinkle with moderate amount of salt to taste. Toss lightly.

Dump in approximate equal amounts of both Hellmann's and Miracle Whip topped with a very generous squirt of yellow mustard.

Stir all together and let blend in refrigerator overnight.

— *A.G. of Davenport*

Nelda's Sausage and Rice Dressing

Nov. 15, 2000

"You know what happens when you bring a recipe into work to share?" asks C.G. in her e-mail to Curious Cook. Curious Cook had a pretty good idea!

"If you don't make a copy of it first, it can be lost forever!!!" she laments.

"Several years back in one of your holiday inserts — I'm talking late '80s, early '90s — there was a recipe for what I would call a stuffing. It was the hit of Thanksgiving for many years.

"Then my husband started taking me out on Thanksgiving, so never gave it much thought. Now that I need the thing, I'm cooking again for the holiday, I can't find it and know who I gave it to, but she has no recall of the whole episode. No hard feelings there, but I could really use your help!!

"I believe it may actually have been titled a main dish casserole or a side dish casserole, but to us it was stuffing.

"My memory is slim, but know there was sausage and wild rice in it. I believe the other ingredients may have included onion, celery, broth, croutons and mushrooms, with I'm sure a seasoning or two.

"If there is any chance for me to find this thing, let me know. If it means coming to your office and looking through the old Holiday Cookbooks myself, fine, I'll be there. Anything you can do would be greatly appreciated." — *C.G.*

Well, C.G., looking for this recipe in our collection of Holiday Cookbooks is like the proverbial "needle in the haystack."

But with the expert help of JoAnn Parmley, The Dispatch/The Rock Island Argus/Leader librarian, Curious Cook did find a recipe (on facing page) that matches the description you give of your lost recipe.

However, Nelda's Sausage and Rice Dressing by Ann Jahn of Taylor Ridge was in the 1996 edition of the Holiday Cookbook, a much later issue than mentioned in your e-mail.

1 package (6 ounces) long grain and wild rice
¼ cup margarine
1 cup chopped onion
1 cup chopped celery
1 pound sausage
1 box stuffing croutons
1 can (2 ounces) mushrooms
2 eggs, beaten
3 cups chicken broth
½ cup chopped walnuts or pecans
¼ teaspoon pepper

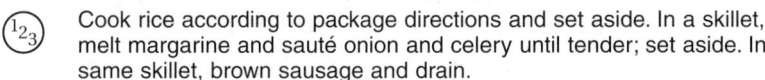

Cook rice according to package directions and set aside. In a skillet, melt margarine and sauté onion and celery until tender; set aside. In same skillet, brown sausage and drain.

In a large bowl, combine rice, onion, celery and sausage. Add remaining ingredients.

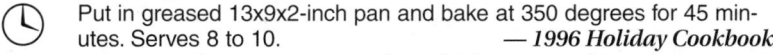

Put in greased 13x9x2-inch pan and bake at 350 degrees for 45 minutes. Serves 8 to 10. — *1996 Holiday Cookbook*

April 8, 1998

Mohl Buettle, Meal Ball (Johnny in the Sack)

H.K. of Rock Island has a family recipe to share, answering a recent request. She writes:

"When I read the request of M.D. of Orion for Meat Ball or Johnny in the Sack it didn't mean anything. But when I read how it was made, it brought back memories of my mother making this on the top of our wood-burning range years ago.

"It was a recipe brought from Germany by my grandmother. It was called Mohl Buettle. That might mean Meal Ball.

"I shall enclose the recipe and make a few additions as the original is quite brief."

1 cup sugar	**2 cups milk**
½ cup butter	**4 cups flour (might need more)**
3 eggs, slightly beaten	**1 cup raisins**

Mix all ingredients except the raisins until well mixed and very stiff. Set aside.

Take a large dish towel — not terry — and dip it into hot water, lay it flat on a table and sprinkle center with flour. On the floured center, put the raisins, then the dough mixture on top of raisins. Pull towel up around all to make into a ball shape, pull tight and tie with a string. Put into a large kettle of boiling water; cover kettle. Cook for 3 hours.

Remove ball from water when ready to serve. Unwrap, place on platter and slice. Serve with a butter, raisin or cherry sauce.

Note: "We always had canned beef with this. Hope this recipe helps M.D."
— *H.K of Rock Island*

Onion, Tomato Salsa

Aug. 5, 1998

L.C. of LeClaire helps with our "salsa search."

- 2 tablespoons vegetable oil
- 1 jumbo (1¼ pounds) sweet Texas or Vidalia onion, finely chopped
- 2 cloves garlic, finely chopped
- 1 fresh jalapeno pepper, halved, seeded and finely chopped
- ¼ cup chopped fresh oregano
- 3 medium-large (1½ pounds) ripe tomatoes, peeled, halved, seeded and finely chopped
- 2 tablespoons lime juice
- ¼ teaspoon salt
- ¼ teaspoon ground black pepper
- Fresh oregano sprigs
- Tortilla chips, optional

In large skillet, heat oil over medium heat. Add onion and sauté until soft, about 10 minutes. Add garlic and jalapeno; sauté 1 minute. Stir in chopped oregano until well mixed. Remove from heat.

Stir tomatoes into onion mixture until well combined. Add lime juice, salt and black pepper. Spoon into airtight container. Refrigerate until cold.

To serve: Spoon some salsa into small serving bowl and garnish with oregano sprigs. Place bowl on platter and surround with tortilla chips, if desired. Makes about 3 cups. — *L.C. of LeClaire*

Praline Sweet Potatoes

June 12, 1996

D.S.F. shares a favorite recipe and note with Curious Cook and her readers.

"I am a male who loves to cook and garden but disabled by cancer last year. Recovery is somewhat slow but numbness from chemotherapy and radiation still lingers; even so I do as much as I can."

Actually, D.S.F. of Davenport sent Curious Cook three of his recipes. Unfortunately his two dessert recipes called for raw eggs. We food editors no longer publish nor recommend using any recipes that require raw eggs because of the risk of salmonella.

However, the gentleman from Davenport also includes the following recipe for Praline Sweet Potatoes.

- 1 can (28 ounces) sweet potatoes, medium or large, drained (See directions)
- 1 can (14 ounces) sweetened condensed milk
- 1 cup brown sugar, packed hard
- ½ cup butter or margarine "I prefer and use butter."
- ½ teaspoon maple flavor extract
- Pecan pieces

Cut large pieces of sweet potatoes in half. Sweet potatoes depend on size of your baking dish and how many you need to serve. I usually use a Corningware casserole that is approximately 8½x11x1½-inches, but a 9x13x2-inch pan would work, too.

In a heavy saucepan, mix together the sweetened condensed milk, brown sugar and butter. Cook to boiling point. When it boils, remove from heat and add maple flavor extract.

Pour mixture over potatoes. Evenly try to coat all potatoes before filling gaps with sauce. Garnish with pecan pieces.

Bake at 350 degrees for 30 to 45 minutes so all is thoroughly heated. Serve.

— *D.S.F. of Davenport*

Salsa

Aug. 5, 1998

We're still on our "salsa search" for D.L.K. of Donahue, Iowa.

As we pointed out in a recent column, there are so many individual recipes for salsa, the Spanish word for sauce.

Southwestern and Mexican cuisines, popular in recent years, have inspired the increased use of salsa as a condiment, a flavorful complement to many foods.

"Here is a recipe for the Salsa Search," writes C.W. of Davenport. "I got it from a friend while living in southern California.

"This is a mild salsa. Can be used as a dip or topping for eggs or baked potatoes."

- 1 can (8 ounces) tomato sauce
- 1 cup (8 ounces) water
- ½ cup chopped onion red, green or white or combination
- 2 medium-size tomatoes, chopped
- 3 cloves garlic, minced
- 1 can (4 ounces) diced green chilies (see note)
- ½ teaspoon ground cumin
- ½ teaspoon garlic powder
- ½ teaspoon fresh ground pepper
- Salt, to taste
- ¼ cup snipped fresh cilantro OR 1½ teaspoons of dried (see note)
- 1 tablespoon lemon juice

Combine ingredients and refrigerate for an hour. If needed, add more water.

Variations: "For a 'hotter' flavor, add 1 small can of diced jalapeno peppers or 1 fresh jalapeno, diced.

"Sliced black olives may be added for a color contrast.

"Crabmeat, either fresh, canned or imitation, about 2/3 cup, is another great addition to this salsa."

Notes: "Canned green chilies can be found in the Mexican food section." Also, "Fresh cilantro is definitely better and is what gives this salsa an authentic Mexican flavor." — *C.W. of Davenport*

Sandwich Filling

April 29, 1998

 After last week's column featuring Olive Nut Sandwich Spread, Curious Cook received this e-mail from W.L. of Moline. The olive-nut mixture brought back memories for her and she shares a favorite recipe. W.L. writes:

"Thought you might like this truly different sandwich filling. I have never had a recipe, as all you need to do is: shred three carrots, add ½ cup chopped peanuts can be salted, my preference, or dry roasted and just enough real mayonaise to blend with the carrots and peanuts. Spread on bread to make sandwiches. Makes a couple of sandwiches. Sandwiches are crunchy, tastes good and a way to get your veggies.

"Thought of these sandwiches, which I made years ago, when I read P.B.'s request for Petersen's Olive Nut Spread. I, too, remember those olive nut sandwiches." — *W.L. of Moline*

Scalloped Cabbage

March 8, 2000

After last week's request for Scalloped Cabbage, readers are sharing their favorite ways of preparing this dish. V.M. of Rock Island writes:

"Y.P. of Port Byron requested a recipe for Scalloped Cabbage and I'd like to share an excellent one that came from the mother of a friend."

1 head of cabbage	6 slices Velveeta cheese
4 tablespoons margarine	2 cups cheese croutons
4 tablespoons flour	½ stick margarine, melted
2 cups milk	

Chop cabbage into bite-size pieces. Cook in boiling water for 5 minutes; drain. Mix the 4 tablespoons margarine, melted, with flour and milk to make a cream sauce. Add cheese; stir to melt. Set aside. Combine croutons with ½ stick melted margarine.

In a buttered casserole, layer drained cabbage, half the croutons and all the sauce. Top with remaining croutons. Bake at 350 degrees for 45 minutes. — *V.M. of Rock Island*

Scalloped Cabbage

March 22, 2000

"Here is one that is a little different from the ones in Wednesday's paper," M.V.L. of Eldridge tells us about her recipe for Scalloped Cabbage.

20 soda crackers, coarsely crumbled	½ teaspoon salt
	¼ teaspoon celery seed
1 quart finely shredded cabbage	¼ teaspoon black pepper
	3 tablespoons butter
1-1/3 cups milk	1 tablespoon butter

Sprinkle half of the cracker crumbs over the bottom of a well-buttered casserole. Add cabbage and top with remaining crumbs.

Heat milk with salt, celery seed, pepper and 3 tablespoons butter.

Pour hot mixture over cabbage and bake at 350 degrees for about 50 minutes. Dot with an additional 1 tablespoon butter about 10 minutes before end of baking period. Makes 6 servings. — *M.V.L. of Eldridge*

Scalloped Corn

March 24, 1999

"Here is a recipe for Scalloped Corn as requested by E.M. of Aledo. This is a family favorite at all gatherings and is easy to prepare," promises K.M. of Geneseo.

- 2½ cups soda cracker crumbs
- 2 sticks butter
- 2 tablespoons minced onion sautéed in small amount of butter
- 4 tablespoons flour
- 2 cups milk
- 1 can (14¾ ounces) cream-style corn
- 1 can (14¾ ounces) whole-kernel corn, drained
- 1 teaspoon salt
- 2 teaspoons sugar
- 4 eggs
- 1 tablespoon chopped green pepper (optional)

Melt 2 sticks butter and combine with cracker crumbs. Press ¾ of mixture into 13x9-inch pan. Sauté onion in a small amount of butter; then add flour and milk. Cook until thick.

To the white sauce, add cream-style corn, whole-kernel corn, salt, sugar and eggs. Also, add green pepper if desired.

Pour mixture over crumb crust then sprinkle with remaining crumbs. Bake at 400 degrees for 1 hour.

Note: Bottom will burn if baked too low in oven or if pan is brown.

— *K.M. of Geneseo*

Souffle Potatoes

Feb. 15, 1995

Culinary congratulations are in order for the Junior Board of Quad City Symphony Orchestra Association and Phyllis Hallene of Moline.

Mrs. Hallene's recipe for soufflé potatoes, which she submitted for the local "Return Engagement" cookbook, was chosen to be included in "Best-Loved Community Recipes," a new Better Homes and Gardens book published by Meredith Corp., Des Moines, Iowa.

"Return Engagement" is the popular community cookbook of the Junior Symphony Board. A collection of favorite recipes of the Quad-Cities area's best cooks, "Return Engagement" was published in 1989 as a sequel to the Junior Board's equally popular "Standing Ovations." The symphony organization has been working with Better Homes and Gardens for a couple of years.

"Best-Loved Community Recipes" is a beautifully illustrated, hard-cover cookbook that features community classics from all over the United States. A full-color photograph and technique photos for the dish accompany each recipe.

About Mrs. Hallene's recipe, the cookbook editors commented:

"Phyllis Hallene tasted her sister-in-law's recipe for soufflé potatoes about 20 years ago and immediately requested the recipe. Phyllis suggests if you're a garlic lover, like she is, that you add a little extra to the dish. Although soufflé potatoes deflate slightly if not served immediately, Phyllis assures us that they'll still be absolutely delicious."

- 3 cups cooked, mashed potatoes (5 or 6 potatoes)
- 1 cup cream-style cottage cheese
- ½ cup dairy sour cream
- 3 egg yolks, well beaten
- 3 tablespoons chopped onion
- 3 tablespoons chopped pimiento, optional
- 2 tablespoons butter or margarine, melted
- 1 clove garlic, minced
- ½ teaspoon salt
- Dash pepper
- 3 egg whites, stiffly beaten
- 1 tablespoon butter or margarine

Preheat the oven to 350 degrees. Grease a 2-quart casserole; set aside.

In a large mixing bowl, stir together the mashed potatoes, cottage cheese, sour cream, egg yolks, onion, pimiento if using, the 2 tablespoons melted butter or margarine, garlic, salt and pepper.

Beat with an electric mixer on medium speed until the mixture is light and fluffy, scraping the sides of the bowl. Gently fold in the beaten egg whites. Carefully spoon the mixture into the prepared casserole. Dot with the 1 tablespoon butter or margarine.

Bake in the 350 degree oven about 1 hour or until the casserole is puffed and the top is golden. Serve immediately. Makes 8 servings.

— *Phyllis Hallene of Moline*

Southern Sweet Potato Pie

May 22, 1996

"Here is a great Sweet Potato Pie that is extra tasty. Almost like pumpkin pie," reports J.M.N.

1½ cups mashed, cooked sweet potatoes
½ cup sugar
½ teaspoon salt
½ teaspoon nutmeg
1 teaspoon cinnamon
¼ teaspoon cloves
2 eggs, well beaten
½ teaspoon vanilla
¼ cup butter
1 cup milk
1 (9-inch) unbaked pastry shell

 Combine sweet potatoes, sugar, salt, nutmeg, cinnamon, cloves, eggs and vanilla.

Melt butter in milk, gradually pour into potato mixture, stirring constantly. Beat gently with mixer until well blended and smooth. Pour into pie shell.

Bake at 450 degrees for 10 minutes; reduce heat to 350 degrees for 45 minutes or until knife comes out clean.

— *J.M.N. of Wheatland, Iowa*

Spinach Soufflé

Aug. 14, 1996

- 1 bag (10 ounces) fresh spinach
- ¼ cup butter or margarine
- ¼ cup all-purpose flour
- ¼ teaspoon pepper
- 1 cup milk
- 1 teaspoon dried minced onion
- 1 teaspoon salt
- 1/8 teaspoon ground nutmeg
- 3 eggs, separated
- ¼ teaspoon cream of tartar

Wash and trim spinach, leaving the water that clings to the leaves. Place in a large skillet and steam just until wilted, about 3 to 5 minutes. Drain and chop; set aside.

Melt butter in a small saucepan over medium heat. Blend in flour and pepper. Cook and stir until bubbly. Slowly add milk; bring to a boil, stirring constantly. Cool and stir 1 minute. Remove from the heat. Stir in onion, salt and nutmeg.

In a large mixing bowl, beat egg whites until soft peaks form. Add cream of tartar, continuing to beat until stiff peaks form. In another bowl, beat egg yolks until thick and lemon-colored; stir into white sauce. Gently fold into egg whites along with spinach.

Pour mixture into a greased 1½-quart casserole or souffle dish. Place casserole in a larger pan; fill larger pan with 1 inch of water.

Bake, uncovered, at 350 degrees for 50 to 60 minutes or until a knife inserted halfway between the center and the edge comes out clean. Serve immediately. Yield: 6 servings. — *D.L.A. of Port Byron*

Spinach Soufflé

Aug. 14, 1996

- 2 pints small-curd cottage cheese
- 6 eggs, well beaten
- ½ pound Velveeta cheese, cubed
- 1 stick butter, cut in pieces
- 2 packages (10 ounces) each frozen chopped spinach, thawed and well-drained
- 6 tablespoons flour

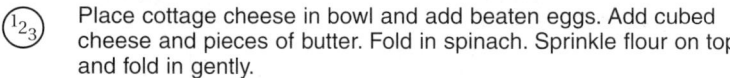

Place cottage cheese in bowl and add beaten eggs. Add cubed cheese and pieces of butter. Fold in spinach. Sprinkle flour on top and fold in gently.

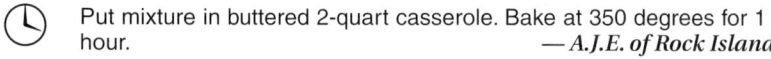

Put mixture in buttered 2-quart casserole. Bake at 350 degrees for 1 hour. *— A.J.E. of Rock Island*

Spinach Soufflé

Aug. 14, 1996

- 1 package (10 ounces) frozen chopped spinach, thawed and well-drained
- 4 large eggs
- 1 carton (16 ounces) cottage cheese
- ¼ pound butter, cut into small pieces
- 3 tablespoons flour
- 1 cup grated sharp Cheddar cheese

Heat oven to 350 degrees. Mix all ingredients together and put into greased 1½-quart souffle dish.

Bake at 350 degrees for 1 hour. Yield: 6 servings. *— R.N.L. of Silvis*

Spinach Soufflé a la Randall's

Oct. 6, 1993

From E.A. of Davenport regarding the request for a Randall's recipe:

"I saw in your column that J.C.M. of Rock Island was looking for a Spinach Souffle recipe that was in the Randall Grocery monthly recipe sheets. I had gotten my monthly sheets from Randall's in Davenport and had saved them.

"My recipe only calls for 1 package of frozen spinach, but sure hope this is the one she was looking for. Enjoy your column every week. Thank you."

- **1 package (10 ounces) frozen chopped spinach**
- **3 eggs, beaten**
- **1 cup flour**
- **1 teaspoon baking soda**
- **½ teaspoon salt**
- **Dash black pepper**
- **Dash cayenne pepper**
- **½ pound grated sharp Cheddar cheese**
- **½ pound grated Monterey Jack cheese**
- **¼ cup butter or margarine, melted**
- **Pimiento, for garnish**

Cook frozen spinach according to package directions; drain thoroughly. Beat eggs and stir in flour, baking soda, salt, black pepper and cayenne pepper. Add drained spinach and grated cheeses.

Melt butter or margarine in a 11-x-7-inch pan. Spoon in spinach mixture. Bake in preheated oven, 350 degrees, for 35 minutes. Let stand 10 minutes before serving. Garnish each portion with pimiento.

Note: "May be enjoyed piping hot or cooled to room temperature."

— *E.A. of Davenport*

Sunshiny Carrot Bake

Nov. 29, 1995

"I hope that this Sunshiny Carrot Bake may add a recipe for the reader who was fortunate enough to have a nice crop of carrots this year," writes L.M.L. of Taylor Ridge.

"Years ago my sister-in-law sent this recipe and noted that with a salad it could be a meal.

"Thanks to you and all of your readers for the help I've had from the column."

- 3 cups coarsely shredded carrots
- 2 cups cooked rice
- 2 cups (8 ounces) shredded Cheddar cheese
- 2 tablespoons chopped onion
- 1 teaspoon salt, optional
- ¼ teaspoon caraway seed
- 1/8 teaspoon white pepper
- 2 eggs, beaten
- 1½ cups milk

Preheat oven to 325 degrees. In a large bowl, place carrots, rice, 1¼ cups of the cheese, onion, salt, caraway seed and pepper. Combine eggs and milk. Mix lightly with rice mixture.

Turn mixture into a buttered square baking dish. Sprinkle remaining cheese on top. Bake at 325 degrees for 30 to 35 minutes. Test with a knife near the center. Makes 6 to 9 servings. — *L.M.L. of Taylor Ridge*

Sweet Potato Pie

Dec. 27, 1995

- 3 eggs
- 2 cups sieved cooked sweet potatoes
- 1 cup brown sugar
- 3 tablespoons molasses
- ¼ teaspoon salt
- ½ teaspoon ginger
- 1 teaspoon cinnamon
- ¼ teaspoon cloves
- 1 teaspoon nutmeg
- 1½ cups half-and-half
- 9-inch unbaked deep-dish pastry shell

Beat eggs in medium-size mixing bowl until foamy. Thoroughly beat in sweet potatoes, brown sugar, molasses, salt, spices and half-and-half. Pour into unbaked pastry shell and bake in preheated 450 degrees oven for 15 minutes. Reduce heat to 325 degrees and bake 30 minutes, or until filling appears set. — *D.C. of Bettendorf*

desserts

save the **best for last**

Dear Curious Cook

10-Minute Fruitcake Ring

June 19, 2002

"J.G. of Geneseo requested a recipe for Apricot Fruitcake," e-mails P.R. of Sherrard. "The following does not include all the ingredients she requested, but my great-aunt always requested this cake for her December birthday."

"It is very good," P.R. promises.

- **8 ounces chopped dates**
- **8 ounces maraschino cherries, well-drained and quartered**
- **1 cup chopped dried apricots**
- **1 cup walnuts (large pieces)**
- **¾ cup unsifted flour**
- **¼ cup sugar**
- **½ teaspoon baking powder**
- **¼ teaspoon salt**
- **3 eggs**
- **½ cup Grandma's Unsulphured Molasses**
- **1 teaspoon vanilla**

In large bowl, mix together dates, drained cherries, apricots and nuts.

Mix together flour, sugar, baking powder and salt. Add to fruit mixture and mix well.

Beat eggs; beat in molasses and vanilla. Add to fruit and dry ingredients. Stir until dry ingredients are completely moistened.

Spoon into very well-greased 6-cup ring mold. Bake at 300 degrees for 1 hour. Cool for 10 minutes; then turn out of pan to cool.

Note: Sliced almonds could probably be substitued for the walnuts.

— *P.R. of Sherrard*

Apricot Fruitcake

July 3, 2002

We're celebrating the Independence Day holiday this week, but D.A.R. of Silvis looks ahead to Christmas when she answers a recent request from J.C. of Moline.

J.C. is interested in a recipe for Apricot Fruitcake, and the Silvis cook has a recipe, an original one, of which she is very proud.

D.A.R. writes: "This is to answer the request for Apricot Fruitcake from J.C. of Geneseo. This is a recipe that I created myself for a friend who wanted a fruitcake without glazed fruit.

"I cannot keep up with the orders for the holidays. Perhaps J.C. would like to try this one," D.A.R. suggests.

So, dear cooks, here's the Silvis cook's original recipe. Clip and save, please. Tomorrow's the Fourth of July mid-summer holiday. The way time flies, the Christmas holidays are just around the corner!

4 tablespoons margarine, melted
2 cups sugar
5 eggs
1½ teaspoons vanilla
2 cups apricot nectar

5 cups flour
1½ teaspoons baking powder
2 pounds dates, cut in halves
1½ pounds dried apricots, cut in quarters
1½ pounds pecans, broken in half

Melt margarine. Add sugar, eggs, vanilla and apricot nectar. Beat well. Add flour and baking powder. Pour over mixed fruit and nuts and mix thoroughly. If batter is too thick, add a little more apricot nectar.

Pour batter into four greased-and-wax-paper-lined small pans.

Bake at 325 degrees for 1½ hours or until a toothpick inserted in the center comes out clean.

Note: "Put a pan of water in the oven while baking fruitcakes. They will be more moist. I also cover loosely after 45 minutes so they don't get too brown." — *D.A.R. of Silvis*

Banana Bread Pudding

Sept. 12, 2001

"I have been reading in your column about the Bread Puddings with Raisins," writes D.L.N. of Moline. "My mother always made them like that when we were children and I always loved them.

"But I found the following recipe in a magazine some time ago and have made it several times. It is very good. I think perhaps some of your readers might like to try it.

"I have gotten quite a few recipes from your column that I enjoy so much. It is the first thing I look at when I get the paper."

Curious Cook thanks D.L.N. for the following recipe and her kind words.

4 cups cubed, day-old French bread
¼ cup butter, melted
3 eggs
2 cups milk
½ cup sugar
2 teaspoons vanilla
½ teaspoon cinnamon
½ teaspoon nutmeg
½ teaspoon salt
1½ cups firm, sliced banana

Place bread cubes in a greased 2-quart casserole. Pour melted butter over cubes and toss to coat.

Lightly beat eggs; add milk, sugar, vanilla, cinnamon, nutmeg and salt. Stir in bananas and pour over bread; stir to coat.

Bake, uncovered, at 350 degrees for 40 minutes or until a knife inserted in center comes out clean. Makes 6 servings.

Note: "May serve with the following sauce, if desired. Personally I like mine with a little cream or whipped topping."

SAUCE:

3 tablespoons butter
2 tablespoons sugar
1 tablespoon cornstarch
¾ cup milk
¼ cup light corn syrup
1 teaspoon vanilla

In a small saucepan, melt the butter. Combine sugar and cornstarch and add to butter. Stir in milk and syrup.

Cook over medium heat until mixture comes to a boil; cook 1 minute. Remove from heat and add vanilla. Serve warm over warm pudding.

— *D.L.N. of Moline*

Best Ever Pineapple Cake

April 7, 1999

Pineapple Cake answers to many names. Best Ever Cake. Granny's Cake. Pineapple Sheet Cake. Pineapple Bars. Hawaiian Wedding Cake. Pineapple Walnut Squares. No Shortening Pineapple Cake.

Take your choice, dear cooks. With only a few variations, these cakes are the same. And Curious Cook thanks all who contributed recipes to answer this request.

- 1 cup chopped pecans
- 2 cups granulated sugar
- 2 eggs, slightly beaten
- 2 cups flour
- 2 teaspoons baking soda
- 1 can (20 ounces) unsweetened crushed pineapple, undrained

Put all ingredients in a bowl and stir until blended; do not beat. (At first you wonder how it will mix together, but very soon it just goes together nicely.)

Put batter in a greased 9x13-inch pan. Bake at 350 degrees for 35 to 40 minutes. Cake will be a nice golden brown on top and will be pulling away from the sides of the pan when it is done. Prepare the icing while the cake is baking.

ICING:

- 2/3 stick of margarine "which is pretty close to 1/3 cup"
- 1 package (8 ounces) cream cheese, softened
- 1-1/3 cups powdered sugar
- 1 teaspoon vanilla

Beat in mixer until smooth. Spread on hot cake. (This turns out to look kind of messy but is fine after it has been in the refrigerator.) Cool in the refrigerator several hours overnight. Keep any leftover cake in the refrigerator.

— *M.H. of Moline*

Bird's Nest Apple Pie

Sept. 27, 2000

E.H. of Davenport kindly sent a copy of her recipe file card on Bird's Nest Apple Pie. This answers a recent request of P.J.H. of Bettendorf for Crow's Nest Apple Dessert.

P.J.H.'s brother-in-law from New York state yearned to find a recipe that he called Crow's Nest Apple Dessert because he remembers his mother preparing it. Fond memories, I am sure. P.J.H. couldn't find the recipe anywhere, she wrote, but sure enough she's found it here in Curious Cook's column!

E.H.'s version of the dessert is called Bird's Nest Apple Pie and here 'tis:

- **5 medium-size apples, cored, peeled and sliced**
- **2 cups flour**
- **1 cup sugar**
- **½ teaspoon baking soda**
- **½ teaspoon cream of tartar**
- **1 cup sour milk (see note)**
- **1 egg**
- **¼ cup sugar**
- **½ teaspoon cinnamon**
- **¼ teaspoon nutmeg**

Coat two 9-inch pie plates with spray. Divide apples between the two plates.

Combine flour, 1 cup sugar, baking soda, cream of tartar, sour milk and egg; mix well. Pour batter over apples slices in pie plates.

Bake at 350 degrees for 25 to 30 minutes until lightly browned and apples are done. Invert on serving plates so apples are on top.

Combine ¼ cup sugar, cinnamon and nutmeg; sprinkle over top of pies. Yield: two 9-inch pies.

Note: For sour milk, combine 1 tablespoon white vinegar and milk to 1 cup; let stand 5 minutes.   *— E.H. of Davenport*

Black Walnut Jiffy Cake

May 2, 2001

"I have used the recipe and liked it very much," writes D.L.N about Black Walnut Jiffy Cake to answer the request of Mrs. K.R.S. of Davenport. "I cut it out of a newspaper a long time ago and the note to the recipe reads:

"This recipe came from the Black Walnut Festival in Stockton, Mo. When using large pieces of nutmeats, they are broken up while mixing the cake and the flavor is diffused throughout the cake.

"The aroma of the cake baking is only surpassed by the flavor."

- **2 cups sugar**
- **1 cup butter, softened**
- **2 cups sifted flour**
- **¼ teaspoon salt**
- **1 cup large black walnuts**
- **1 teaspoon lemon extract**
- **1 teaspoon vanilla**
- **5 large eggs**

Place ingredients into mixing bowl in order given. Beat at high speed for 5 minutes. Pour into a greased and floured 10-inch tube pan.

Bake at 350 degrees for 1 hour and 15 minutes. Cool upright before removing from pan. Serve plain or frost with whipped topping and chopped walnuts.

— *D.L.N. of Moline*

Blarney Stones Peanut Bars

Feb. 19, 1997

Curious Cook's mailbox has been packed lately with responses to various requests. We have received quite a number of variations of the Blarney Stones.

Today we'll start with N.S. of Long Grove, via e-mail:

"About 15 years ago, I requested a recipe for Blarney Stones from Pat Hundahl at the North Scott Press. The response was terrific. I am enclosing what I consider to be the best and most complete recipe," N.S. writes.

"This was a favorite dessert in Clinton County for bridal showers, wedding receptions, wedding anniversaries, and just special occasions."

4 eggs, separated
1 cup sugar
1 cup cake flour
1½ teaspoons baking powder

1 teaspoon vanilla
½ cup boiling water
1 pound ground, salted, blanched peanuts without skins

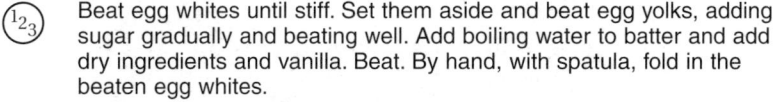

Beat egg whites until stiff. Set them aside and beat egg yolks, adding sugar gradually and beating well. Add boiling water to batter and add dry ingredients and vanilla. Beat. By hand, with spatula, fold in the beaten egg whites.

Line a 15x10½x1-inch jelly-roll pan with wax paper. Pour in the cake batter. Bake at 375 degrees for about 15 minutes. Let cool. Cut into 24-28 pieces. Remove from wax paper. Frost with thin powdered sugar frosting on all sides. Roll in ground peanuts. Can be frozen.

FROSTING:
3 cups powdered sugar
1 teaspoon vanilla

¼ cup margarine, softened
Milk or half-and-half

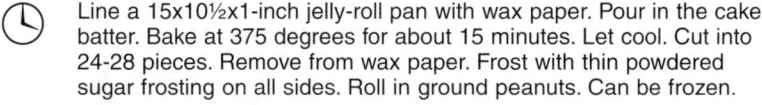

Combine powdered sugar, vanilla and margarine; mix well. Stir in milk or half-and-half until of desired consistency.

— *N.S. of Long Grove, Iowa*

Blarney Stones

Feb. 19, 1997

3 egg yolks
1½ cups sugar
1½ teaspoons lemon extract
½ cup hot water
1½ cups flour

2¼ teaspoons baking powder
¼ teaspoon salt
3 egg whites
Chopped peanuts

Beat egg yolks and add sugar, lemon extract, water, flour, baking powder and salt. Whip egg whites until stiff and fold into first mixture. Pour into greased oblong 9x12-inch cake pan and bake at 325 degrees for 45 minutes. Cool. Frost 3x1-inch oblongs of cake with white butter frosting and roll in chopped peanuts.   — *B.H. of Clinton*

Blarney Stones

March 5, 1997

"I read your request for Blarney Stones. My mother made them when I was a little girl 80 years ago. I make them especially for St. Patrick's Day — they are unusual and good.

"Her recipe was just a little list of ingredients but I use the Betty Crocker Sponge cake recipe. I think any light yellow cake mix could be used. The cake needs to be about an inch thick. I use one 9x12-inch pan and one square pan. When cool, cut in bars or squares any size you prefer.

"Then frost with a plain powdered sugar icing on the top and all four sides. Then roll in chopped peanuts and let dry. I have never known the origin, but I have not known anyone else making them either. Enjoy!"   — *C.G. of East Moline*

Blarney Stones

March 5, 1997

Blarney stones. A white or yellow sheet cake, cut in squares, frosted and rolled in ground peanuts. Webster's Dictionary says. "A stone in Blarney Castle in the county of Cork, Ireland, said to impart skill in blarney to those who kiss it."

"My way of making Blarney stones: Grease and flour cupcake pans. Prepare 1 box of cake mix and fill cupcake pans about half full. Bake about 18 minutes. Cool.

"Frost using ¾ stick of margarine, 1-pound box powdered sugar, enough milk to thin out frosting so it spreads easy. Add 1 jar dry-roasted peanuts, ground fine. Frost cupcakes and roll in peanuts. No waste or crumbs using this method." — *P.H.P of La Salle*

Sponge Cake for Blarney Stones

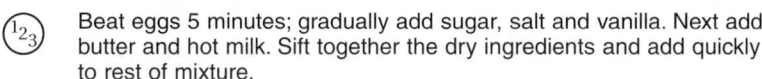

March 5, 1997

4 eggs
2 cups sugar
½ teaspoon salt
2 teaspoons vanilla
2 tablespoons butter, melted in the hot milk

1 cup boiling hot milk
2 cups sifted flour
2 teaspoons baking powder
Powdered sugar frosting
Ground peanuts

Beat eggs 5 minutes; gradually add sugar, salt and vanilla. Next add butter and hot milk. Sift together the dry ingredients and add quickly to rest of mixture.

Grease and flour 9x13-inch pan and bake at 350 degrees for 25 to 35 minutes. Frost with powdered sugar frosting and cover with ground peanuts. Can also be used unfrosted as shortcake for any fresh fruit. — *B.H. of Clinton*

Blueberry Brunch Cake

July 31, 2002

Curious Cook has received a delightful letter and several recipes from M.M. of Rock Island, a charming almost 92-year-old, who collects recipes and cooks. Curious Cook remembers well interviewing this cook for a food article quite a number of years ago.

M.M. was kind enough to send recipes from her personal collection to answer recent requests. Answering a request for Blueberry Coffee Cake, M.M. sends her Blueberry Brunch Cake recipe.

"I worked out the recipe myself," M.M. writes, "and have used it for years. It can be doubled, tripled, etc., and freezes like a charm."

2 cups buttermilk baking mix
4 tablespoons sugar
1 large egg
1/3 cup oil

1/3 cup milk
1 tablespoon lemon juice
Blueberries

Measure buttermilk baking mix in mixing bowl. Measure the oil and milk in cup but do not mix.

To baking mix, add sugar, egg and liquids. Beat until smooth. Pour into a 9-inch-square baking pan greased with cooking spray. Sprinkle blueberries over batter and press in lightly. Sprinkle with streusel-mix topping.

STREUSEL MIX

1/3 cup flour
1/3 cup brown sugar
1 teaspoon cinnamon

2 tablespoons firm butter or margarine
1/3 cup chopped nuts, optional

Mix flour, sugar, cinnamon and butter with pastry blender until mixed. Add nuts if desired.

Bake at 350 degrees until done, about 35 minutes, or until tester inserted in center comes out clean. Remove from oven and cool a few minutes. Then drizzle with confectioners' sugar frosting: 1 cup confectioners' sugar and 1 or 2 tablespoons water or milk.

Note: "This recipe can be doubled for 9x13-inch pan and one 8-inch pan. Freezes well." — *M.M. of Rock Island*

Blueberry Strata

July 15, 1998

Several weeks ago, B.B. of Davenport e-mailed a plea for help with a Blueberry Strata recipe which he apparently had misplaced. But then he found the recipe and is kind enough to share with fellow cooks.

"I completely enjoy making and eating this strata!" B.B. writes. "It is so good! I hope your readers will enjoy it, too!"

STRATA:
- 9 slices of thick Texas toast bread with crust removed
- ¾ of an 8-ounce package of cream cheese light or regular
- 8 large eggs
- 1-1/3 cups of 2 percent milk
- ¼ cup maple syrup
- ½ cup fresh or frozen blueberries

SAUCE:
- 2 tablespoons butter
- ½ to ¾ cup brown sugar
- 1 cup fresh or frozen blueberries
- 1 tablespoon cornstarch mixed in ¾ cup of water
- 1 dash black ground pepper
- 1 ounce Grand Marnier may be added for special occasions

Lightly coat a 7½x12x2-inch glass baking dish with butter. Cut all slices of bread into ¾-inch squares. Using half of the squares, line the base of the dish. Cut the cream cheese into ¾-inch cubes and spread evenly among the bread base.

Sprinkle the blueberries evenly over the bread and cream cheese and then cover with the remaining squares of bread.

Mix the eggs, milk and maple syrup together and pour evenly over the dish and slightly firm the mixture with a fork. Cover with aluminum foil and refrigerate overnight.

Pre-heat the oven to 350 degrees and bake casserole for 30 minutes. Remove foil and bake for another 30 minutes or until nicely browned.

Meanwhile, to prepare the sauce, combine all ingredients, except Grand Mariner, and cook in a saucepan over medium heat until a smooth consistency has been achieved. You may add a little water if sauce becomes too thick. Stir in Grand Mariner, if desired.

Remove strata from the oven and let stand for 5 to 10 minutes before cutting into servings. Pour the sauce over the baked strata and serve.

Note: If fresh blueberries are available reserve a ¼ cup to be added to sauce just before serving.

— B.B. of Davenport

Bread Pudding

Aug. 29, 2001

"This recipe is a custard bread pudding," explains R.C. of Geneseo.

"Started by my grandmother, who owned an English tea house on the east side in New York."

12-inch loaf of French bread, or heavy bread like Pepperidge Farm, cut up
1 cup raisins
½ cup pecans or walnuts
3 eggs, beaten
1 teaspoon vanilla
1 quart milk scalded with ¾ cup sugar
¼ pound butter, melted

Combine all ingredients in a 3-quart baking bowl. Place in water bath and bake at 350 degrees for 50 minutes.

Can serve warm or cold. Serve with heavy cream. — *R.C. of Geneseo*

Burnt Sugar Cake

June 9, 1999

N.P.S. of Davenport has responded to A.G's request for Burnt Sugar Cake. N.P.S. writes: "I had made one many years ago. My mother used to make them often, as it was one of her favorite cakes. She used a heavy black iron skillet to make the syrup."

1¾ cups sugar, divided	3 cups sifted cake flour
¾ cup boiling water	3 teaspoons baking powder
¾ cup butter or margarine, softened	½ teaspoon salt
	¾ cup milk
1 teaspoon vanilla	Burnt sugar frosting
2 eggs, separated	Pecan halves

In a small heavy skillet or saucepan, heat ¾ cup sugar, stirring until a brown syrup forms and mixture begins to smoke. VERY GRADUALLY stir in boiling water and remove from heat. Cool thoroughly.

Cream butter and 1 cup sugar until light. Gradually beat in ½ cup burnt sugar syrup. (Reserve remainder for frosting.) Add vanilla and then egg yolks, one at a time, beating well after each addition.

Add sifted flour, baking powder and salt alternately with milk, beating until smooth. Fold in stiffly beaten egg whites.

Pour batter into two greased 8-inch layer pans lined on the bottom with wax paper. Bake in moderate oven, 375 degrees for about 25 minutes. Cool and frost. Top with nut halves.

Burnt Sugar Frosting

1/3 cup butter or margarine	1 teaspoon vanilla
1 box (1 pound) confectioners' sugar	Burnt sugar syrup
	About 2 tablespoons cream or evaporated milk
½ teaspoon salt	

Cream the butter or margarine; beat in confectioners' sugar, salt, vanilla and remaining burnt sugar syrup and enough cream or evaporated milk to make a spreading consistency. — *N.P.S. of Davenport*

Butterscotch Pie from Scratch

Nov. 21, 2001

The late Wilma Linney of Moline was known in her circle of family and friends for her delicious Butterscotch Pie. Her recipe was published years ago in one of the early Holiday Food Guides. So to answer P.B.'s request on behalf of her mother-in-law, here's that recipe:

¼ cup butter	3 egg yolks
1¼ cups brown sugar	½ teaspoon vanilla
1/8 teaspoon salt	1 tablespoon firm butter
1/3 cup flour	3 egg whites
1 teaspoon cornstarch	6 tablespoons sugar
2 cups plus 2 tablespoons milk	9-inch baked pie shell

 Melt ¼ cup butter in heavy 2-quart saucepan and stir in half of the sugar. Heat until smooth, thick liquid forms; then boil 1 minute. Remove from heat.

 Blend remaining sugar with salt, flour and cornstarch and stir into hot mixture. Slowly stir in half the milk so as to keep mixture smooth. Then stir in rest of milk. Place over medium heat and cook and stir until thickened, 5 to 6 minutes. Remove from heat.

Beat egg yolks well; quickly add a little of hot mixture to egg yolks, return to saucepan and cook 2 minutes longer. Remove from heat and stir in vanilla and the tablespoon of firm butter. Pour into pie shell.

Beat egg whites until stiff, gradually adding the 6 tablespoons sugar a tablespoon at a time. Spread meringue on hot filling and bake at 350 degrees until meringue is lightly browned. — *Wilma Linney of Moline, originally published in an early Holiday Food Guide*

Caramel Crunch Apple Pie

Dec. 2, 1998

From A.L.M. of Alexis: "I see by the paper someone is looking for a Caramel Apple Pie. I have a very good recipe called Caramel Crunch Apple Pie.

"I have baked this pie several times and everyone thinks it is very good," reports A.L.M. of Alexis.

Our friend, S.E. of Davenport, sent in the same recipe. S.E. writes: "I have an extra copy of the Caramel Apple Pie and you're welcome to it per request in a most recent column." Here's the recipe:

Pastry for 1-crust 9-inch pie   1/3 cup sugar
24 caramels   **½ teaspoon ground cinnamon**
2 tablespoons water   **1/3 cup margarine**
4 cups sliced, peeled apples   **½ cup chopped walnuts**
¾ cup flour

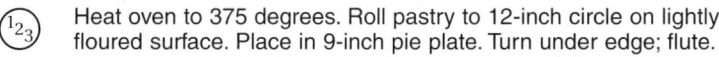
Heat oven to 375 degrees. Roll pastry to 12-inch circle on lightly floured surface. Place in 9-inch pie plate. Turn under edge; flute.

Melt caramels with water in heavy saucepan over low heat, stirring frequently until smooth. Spoon apples into crust; top with caramel sauce.

Mix flour, sugar and cinnamon; cut in margarine until mixture resembles coarse crumbs. Stir in walnuts. Sprinkle over apples.

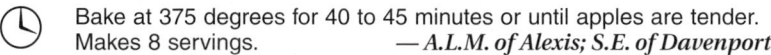
Bake at 375 degrees for 40 to 45 minutes or until apples are tender. Makes 8 servings.   — *A.L.M. of Alexis; S.E. of Davenport*

Cherry Crisp

Dec. 24, 2003

L.P. is craving a Cherry Crisp that was served at her Geneseo school a number of years ago. She recently described the cherry dessert as having a white cake layer.

So K.B.S. of Moline sent us her recipe for Cherry Crisp from the late '50s or early '60s, she says. She recalls using this recipe "a very long time ago."

Here are the directions:

Pour cherry pie filling (1 can, 21 ounces) into an 8-inch pie or cake pan. Sprinkle with 1 cup white or yellow cake mix. Pour ½ stick melted butter or margarine over all.

Bake at 400 degrees for 30 minutes. Serve hot or cold. "Serving hot with a scoop of vanilla ice cream is best!

"Also very good, 1 can (20 ounces) crushed pineapple with juice mixed into the pie filling. In this ingredients' mix, use twice the amount of cake mix and butter or margarine. For this version, use a 9x13-inch pan.

"Nuts on top of all is another choice."

— *K.B.S. of Moline*

Cherry Pudding

Nov. 13, 1996

From J.M. of Moline: "Enclosed is a recipe for Cherry Pudding. It is very good and so simple to make. The cherries will sink to the bottom.

"You may top with ice cream or whipped cream. I make this often and everyone loves it."

½ **cup sugar**	**1 teaspoon baking powder**
¼ **cup shortening**	¼ **teaspoon salt**
½ **cup milk**	**2 cups drained cherries, save juice, (20-ounce can)**
¼ **teaspoon vanilla**	
1 cup flour	**Water and juice to make 1 cup**
	½ **cup sugar**

Cream together ½ cup sugar and shortening. Add milk and vanilla; mix well. Sift together flour, baking powder and salt. Add to creamed mixture and mix well.

Pour batter into greased 6x10-inch pan. Pour 2 cups drained cherries over batter. To reserved juice, add enough water to make 1 cup. Heat until hot. Sprinkle ½ cup sugar over cherries. Add juice. Bake at 375 degrees for 40 minutes.

— *J.M. of Moline*

Chocolate Chip Cake

Sept. 11, 2002

With a recipe for Chocolate Chip Cake, C.J.S. of Walcott answers the recent request of a Prophetstown reader for a "moist cake with dates and nuts in it, with no frosting," circa 1963. C.J.S. writes:

"I'm sending you a recipe given to me in 1961 that is a moist cake with dates and nuts and has no frosting.

"It is a delicious cake and one would never know it contained chopped dates. It is a family favorite."

1 cup chopped dates	1¾ cups white flour
1 cup boiling water	1 teaspoon baking soda
1 cup margarine or shortening	1 teaspoon vanilla
1 cup white sugar	1½ cups chocolate chips
2 eggs	½ cup chopped nuts ("I use walnuts.")
1 tablespoon cocoa	

Combine dates and boiling water and let cool.

Cream margarine and sugar; add eggs and mix well.

Sift together flour, cocoa and baking soda; add alternately the dry ingredients with the dates/water; add vanilla and mix well.

Stir in 1 cup of the chocolate chips. Spread batter into a greased 9x13-inch pan. Sprinkle with remaining chocolate chips and the chopped nuts.

Bake in a preheated 350-degree oven for 35 to 40 minutes or until tests done. Cake requires no frosting.   — *C.J.S. of Walcott*

recipes to remember forever

Concord Grape Pie

Sept. 22, 1993

Here's a note from B.J.B. of Geneseo, a newcomer in our community. Welcome , B.L.B. and thank you for contributing a recipe!

"Just read in The Dispatch in The Curious Cook section about someone wanting a Grape Pie recipe. Here's mine.

"I made it the other day with fresh Concord grapes from our back yard. I shared it with our daughter and family and our new neighbor. We just moved here from Mendota, Ill., 3½ months ago.

"I acquired the recipe from a friend there a long time ago. Enjoy."

4 cups Concord grapes
1 cup sugar
1/3 cup flour
¼ teaspoon salt

1 tablespoon lemon juice
2 tablespoons margarine, melted
1 9-inch unbaked pie shell

Slip skins from 4 cups of Concord grapes. Set skins aside. Bring pulp to a boil. Reduce heat and simmer 5 minutes. Sieve to remove seeds. Add skins to pulp.

Mix sugar, flour and salt; add grape mixture. Stir in lemon juice and margarine. Mix well. Pour into 9-inch unbaked pie shell.

Bake at 400 degrees for 25 minutes. Sprinkle topping (see below) over pie; return to oven and bake 15 minutes longer.

TOPPING:
½ cup sugar
½ cup flour
¼ cup margarine

Mix well and sprinkle on top of pie.

— B.J.B. of Geneseo

Feb. 21, 1996

Cranberry Dessert with Hot Butter Sauce

"I hope this recipe is what M.L. from Davenport is looking for," writes M.B. of Erie. "I've had it for many years. A lady from Wisconsin gave it to me while we were all on vacation at a lake in that state."

1 cup sugar	2 cups flour
2 tablespoons butter	½ teaspoon salt
1 egg, beaten	2 teaspoons baking powder
1 cup milk	2 cups whole, washed cranberries

Cream together sugar and butter; add beaten egg, milk, flour, salt and baking powder. Mix well. Lastly add cranberries. Then pour into a greased 9x13-inch pan. Bake at 350 degrees for about 35 minutes.

SAUCE:

1 cup powdered sugar	½ cup butter
½ cup cream	1 teaspoon vanilla

Combine powdered sugar, cream and butter in a saucepan. Heat to boiling but do not boil. Remove from stove and add vanilla. Stir well and pour over cake in dessert dishes.

Note: "I usually have to make 1½ recipes of the sauce." — *M.B. of Erie*

Cranberry Mousse

April 30, 1997

From C.H. of Rock Island: "Requested by B.C. of Hampton. I enjoy your column and often clip recipes from it. My problem is finding the recipe again when I want to use it. I have many filed neatly in boxes but also have an overflow."

And A.R.S. of LeClaire sent the same recipe with this note: "Everyone who eats this enjoys it very much."

- 1 large package (6 ounces) sugar-free strawberry-flavored gelatin
- 1 cup boiling water
- 1 can (20 ounces) crushed pineapple in juice, no sugar
- 1 can (16 ounces) whole-berry cranberry sauce
- 3 tablespoons lemon juice
- 1 teaspoon grated lemon peel
- ½ teaspoon ground nutmeg
- 2 cups (16 ounces) light sour cream
- ½ cup chopped pecans

In a large bowl, dissolve gelatin in boiling water. Drain pineapple, setting the pineapple aside and adding juice to the gelatin. Stir in cranberry sauce, lemon juice, peel and nutmeg. Chill until mixture thickens. Fold in sour cream, pineapple and pecans.

Pour into a glass serving bowl or an oiled 9-cup mold. Chill until set, at least 2 hours. Yields 16-20 servings.

Note: The recipe from A.R.S. calls for regular strawberry-flavored gelatin and sour cream. — *C.H. of Rock Island, A.R.S. of LeClaire*

Cranberry Salad or Dessert

Nov. 19, 1997

If you want to prepare a cranberry salad for your Thanksgiving Day dinner, Curious Cook's readers have provided choices galore.

"In regard to C.P. of Davenport request for a Cranberry salad/dessert type recipe this is a very good one," reports B.L.P. of Keithsburg.

"I use Equal in place of sugar," she adds.

- 2 cups ground cranberries
- ½ cup sugar or 14 packets Equal
- 1 can (11 ounces) mandarin oranges, drain and save juice
- 1 can (20 ounces) crushed pineapple, drain and save juice
- 1 cup coconut
- 1 large banana, mashed
- 2 envelopes plain gelatin
- 1 cup lite sour cream
- 1 cup frozen whipped topping, thawed

Mix ground cranberries and sugar or Equal. Let stand until sugar dissolves, 15 minutes.

Drain oranges and pineapple. Save ¾ cup of juices. Mix oranges and pineapple into cranberries, then stir in coconut.

In saucepan, sprinkle plain gelatin over juice. Heat until gelatin is dissolved. Add to cranberries mixture. Stir in sour cream and whipped topping. Mix in banana. Mix thoroughly.

Pour into 9x9-inch pan. Refrigerate overnight. — *B.L.P. of Keithsburg*

Cream Puffs

March 19, 2003

"For S.W.G. of Rock Island from L.L. of Port Byron:

"I love making this puff pastry for special parties. I split them, put a ball of ice cream in the middle and drizzle with homemade hot fudge sauce and top with whipped cream.

"It's a good thing."

½ **cup butter or margarine**	¼ **teaspoon salt, optional**
1 cup boiling water	**4 eggs**
1 cup sifted all-purpose flour	

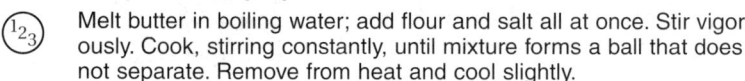

Melt butter in boiling water; add flour and salt all at once. Stir vigorously. Cook, stirring constantly, until mixture forms a ball that does not separate. Remove from heat and cool slightly.

Add eggs, one at a time, beating vigorously after each addition until smooth. Drop by heaping tablespoonsful 3 inches apart on greased cookie sheet.

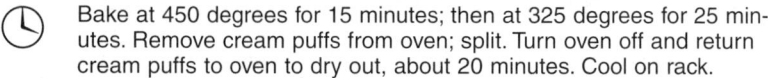

Bake at 450 degrees for 15 minutes; then at 325 degrees for 25 minutes. Remove cream puffs from oven; split. Turn oven off and return cream puffs to oven to dry out, about 20 minutes. Cool on rack.

Fill with ice cream or pudding. Drizzle with chocolate sauce and sprinkle with nuts. Yield: 10 servings. — *L.L. of Port Byron*

Creamy Pumpkin Pie

Nov. 28, 2001

M.H. of Moline sends a recipe to answer the request of S.N. of Moline and tells us its interesting history as well:.

"I've enclosed a recipe for No-Bake Pumpkin Pie made with ice cream.

"I've had this recipe since the mid-'60s. One of the men I worked with brought the pie in for our annual Christmas party. It was an instant hit with the office staff.

"Since that time, my family only wants me to make this pumpkin pie. No more baked pumpkin pie for them.

"I hope this is the pie S.N. of Moline is looking for. If not, she might want to try it anyway. I think she will be pleased with the results.

2 eggs
1 cup pumpkin
½ cup firmly packed brown sugar
1 teaspoon cinnamon
½ teaspoon salt
¼ teaspoon ginger

¼ teaspoon nutmeg
1/8 teaspoon ground cloves
1 envelope (1 tablespoon) unflavored gelatin
¼ cup cold water
1 pint vanilla ice cream
One 9-inch pie shell, baked and cooled

Beat eggs in saucepan until foamy. Add pumpkin, brown sugar, salt and spices. Stir until smooth.

Soften gelatin in cold water; add to pumpkin mixture. Cook over medium heat until mixture boils and is thickened. Remove from heat.

Beat with rotary beater until smooth and creamy. Cut ice cream into pieces. Add to pumpkin mixture and stir until melted.

Pour into baked pie shell. Chill until set, 2 hours.   — *M.H. of Moline*

Crème de Menthe Pie

April 26, 1995

- 1 pint vanilla ice cream, softened
- 2 tablespoons lemon juice
- 2 tablespoons green crème de menthe
- 2 tablespoons white crème de cacao
- 3 cups frozen whipped topping, thawed
- 1 or 2 drops green food coloring
- 1 commercial chocolate pie shell
- Additional frozen whipped topping, thawed

Mix together the ice cream, lemon juice, green creme de menthe, creme de cacao, whipped topping and green food coloring. Pour into chocolate pie shell. Chill. Serve with whipped topping.

Note: "Be very careful using the green food coloring so you don't use too much and be sure to use rubber gloves or you will have green fingers for a few days! Filling may be a little much for crust."

— *M.O. of East Moline*

Custard-like Bread Pudding

Aug. 29, 2001

"This is easy to make," writes S.F. of Moline. "The sauce is great over it."

"A soft, custard-like bread pudding," she says.

- 2 eggs
- 2 cups milk
- 1 cup sugar
- 1 tablespoon butter or margarine, melted
- 1 teaspoon ground cinnamon
- 10 slices day-old bread, crusts removed, cut into ½-inch cubes
- 1 cup raisins

SAUCE:
- 2/3 cup sugar
- 2 tablespoons all-purpose flour
- 1 cup water
- 2 tablespoons butter or margarine
- 1 teaspoon vanilla

For pudding: In a large bowl, combine eggs, milk, sugar, butter and cinnamon. Add the bread cubes and raisins; mix well. Pour into a greased 11x7x2-inch baking dish.

Bake at 350 degrees for 50 to 60 minutes or until knife inserted near center comes out clean.

For sauce: In a saucepan, combine sugar, flour and water until smooth. Add butter. Bring to a boil over medium heat; cook and stir for 2 minutes. Remove from the heat; stir in vanilla.

Serve sauce warm or cold over pudding. Yield: 8 servings.

— *S.F. of Moline*

Delicious No-Sugar Apple Pie

Oct. 22, 1997

D.R. of Bettendorf likes this recipe. She says that finding the 6-ounce can of frozen apple juice may be difficult, so she buys the 12-ounce size and uses half of it for this pie.

1 can (6 ounces) frozen apple juice concentrate
1 tablespoon margarine
2 tablespoons cornstarch
1 teaspoon cinnamon
¼ teaspoon nutmeg
6 cups peeled sliced delicious apples
Pastry for 2-crust pie

Place apple juice concentrate in saucepan; bring to a boil.

Combine margarine, cornstarch and spices in small bowl. Add a small amount of apple juice; stir until well blended. Stir cornstarch mixture into apple juice. Pour over apples; stir carefully to cover all slices.

Pour mixture into unbaked pie crust; place top crust over apples. Cut slits in top crust.

Bake at 425 degrees for about 30 minutes. Reduce temperature to 375 degrees; bake for 30 minutes longer. — *D.R. of Bettendorf*

Diplomatic Cake

Dec. 17, 2003

"This is in response to C.D. of Andalusia, who was looking for a recipe for the Most Wonderful Chocolate Cake she had in Texas," e-mails L.W. of Coal Valley.

The Andalusia cook described the cake as "a dense, very moist chocolate cake topped with custard flan, drizzled with caramel and toasted pecans." C.D. wrote that she ate this cake when she was in South Texas, but she was unsure of its name.

Here's the way L.W. responded:

"I just so happened also to recently taste a cake that sounds just like that one."

"A Hispanic co-worker had made a treat for us and I think this is what C.D. is looking for," L.W. adds.

Here's that recipe:

- 1 large jar of Smucker's Caramel Ice Cream Topping (see note)
- 1 can (14 ounces) sweetened condensed milk
- 1 can (12 ounces) evaporated milk
- 3 eggs
- 1 tablespoon vanilla
- 1 box chocolate cake mix (any brand)

Coat bottom of 9x13-inch cake pan with no-stick cooking spray. Spread caramel over the bottom.

In a blender, combine the milks, eggs and vanilla and pour over the caramel.

Mix the cake as directed and pour over the milk layer, being careful not to mix it too much.

Set this pan inside another cake pan with some water (similar to double boiler) and bake at 350 degrees for 45 minutes to 1 hour. Test with toothpick after 45 minutes.

Cool slightly and turn over onto a platter to serve. You also may sprinkle with nuts after turning onto platter. "Moist and delicious."

Note: "Caramel topping is not available in the large size in many stores so it would probably be best to use two of the 12-ounce size."

— *L.W. of Coal Valley*

D.J.'s Bread Pudding

March 11, 1998

Curious Cook still has family-favorite bread pudding recipes to share with readers. This one is from D.J.N. of Davenport.

"I'm writing about the bread pudding request. This is mine. We all like it, and I have no bad press about it so far.

"Here's a new thing I've done for quite awhile: Don't limit it to raisins. My daughter doesn't like raisins, so I use chocolate chips in her half of the pudding.

"How about chopped pears tossed with a teaspoon of cinnamon? Or fresh apples sauteed with apple pie spice? Then there are peaches, large can, tossed with three tablespoons flour.

"So, see we can go on and on. Like the man says, 'It's yours; do whatever you yourself like and you will get that, 'Ooh, it's so good!' '

"P.S. When I use pears or peaches from the can, I reduce the milk to 2½ cups."

¾ cup raisins, softened in boiling water and drained

6 slices bread, toasted, buttered and cubed to equal 6 ounces

3 eggs

3 cups milk, scalded

1/3 cup sugar

1 teaspoon vanilla

1 teaspoon butter flavoring liquid

2 tablespoons cinnamon sugar

2 tablespoons margarine

Prepare raisins and set aside. Prepare bread cubes.

Place cubes in 2-quart casserole sprayed with no-stick cooking spray. Or cubes may be placed in a 2-quart baking dish — 8x8x2½.

Whisk eggs. Add sugar, vanilla, and butter flavoring. Whisk. Then add scalded milk and whisk. Set aside.

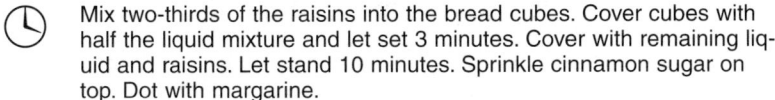

Mix two-thirds of the raisins into the bread cubes. Cover cubes with half the liquid mixture and let set 3 minutes. Cover with remaining liquid and raisins. Let stand 10 minutes. Sprinkle cinnamon sugar on top. Dot with margarine.

Bake at 350 degrees for 40 minutes or until done knife inserted in center comes out clean. — *D.J.N. of Davenport*

Real Easy Bread Pudding

Aug. 29, 2001

Today we'll continue our "discussion" of bread puddings because Curious Cook has received additional contributions from bread pudding devotees.

It's interesting to learn how bread pudding recipes vary from cook to cook, family to family.

To answer the request of E.M.K. of East Moline, readers write about their favorite — and delicious — puddings.

"Here's a real easy Bread Pudding recipe with raisin bread," writes C.A. of Milan to answer the recent request of E.M.K. of East Moline.

"I make it with sugar-free pudding and it is still sweet enough," she advises.

1 loaf cinnamon raisin bread, cubed or torn   **2 cups milk**

 Place bread in a buttered 9x13-inch pan. Pour 2 cups milk over bread and set aside.

4 cups milk   **1 teaspoon vanilla**
2 small packages cook-and-serve vanilla pudding   **Ground cinnamon, if desired**

 Prepare pudding according to package directions, using the 4 cups of milk. Stir in vanilla.

Pour the pudding mixture over the bread mixture; sprinkle on more cinnamon if deserved.

 Bake at 375 degrees for 45 minutes or until pudding sets up and knife or toothpick comes out clean. Very good and easy.

Note: Can use sugar-free pudding   — *C.A. of Milan*

Dried Apricot Pie

Aug. 13, 1997

We have so many Dried Apricot Pie recipes for J.S. of DeWitt that she will have to prepare a different one every week for weeks on end.

Curious Cook is delighted at the response to the DeWitt cook's request. For a recipe that seemingly was difficult to locate, we received many interesting contributions.

"Here's a recipe for a Dried Apricot Pie my Mom makes. She won a pie contest with it but didn't want me to tell you that," writes S.T. of Moline.

- 2 cups uncooked dried apricots, cut into 2 to 3 pieces each
- 1½ cups water used to soak fruit and cook in later
- 1 tablespoon lemon juice
- 4 tablespoons flour
- 1 cup sugar
- ½ teaspoon salt
- 1 tablespoon butter or margarine
- 1 double pie crust recipe

Preheat oven to 350 degrees. Cover cut-up apricots with the 1½ cups water and soak overnight.

In the morning, add the lemon juice and simmer apricots, water and lemon juice about 10 minutes. Mix flour, sugar and salt and add to entire apricot mixture. Continue simmering another 8 to 10 minutes until desired thickness.

Pour mixture into an unbaked pie shell, dot with butter and cover with top crust. Seal crust and cut slits in top crust.

Bake at 350 degrees for approximately 30 minutes or until golden brown and bubbly. Cool and ENJOY! — *S.T. of Moline*

Easy Cake

Sept. 7, 1994

The easy cake recipe that M.C. of Lynn Center recently requested apparently has a number of titles! That won't surprise recipe collectors at all.

We have heard from several readers who give the cake rave reviews. But they each give the recipe a different name! Cake bakers will enjoy comparing the similarities and differences in these treasured recipes.

We'll start with C.D. of Moline, whose recipe doesn't even have a title but it matches the description provided by the Lynn Center cook! C.D. writes:

"This may be similar to the lost cake recipe M.C. of Lynn Center was looking for."

CAKE	FROSTING
2 eggs	5 tablespoons brown sugar
1 cup sugar	3 tablespoons cream
1 teaspoon vanilla	Coconut
1 cup sifted cake flour	
1 teaspoon baking powder	
½ cup milk	
1 tablespoon butter	

For cake: Beat the eggs; add sugar, vanilla, sifted cake flour and baking powder. Boil milk with butter. Add hot milk mixture to first mixture.

Bake in ungreased 8x8-inch pan at 375 degrees for 30 minutes.

For frosting: Combine brown sugar and cream; heat together and boil for 3 minutes. Spread frosting on cake when taken out of oven. Sprinkle generously with coconut and brown under broiler. — *C.D. of Moline*

Easy Oil Pie Crust

March 30, 1994

1½ cups flour
1 teaspoon salt
1½ tablespoons sugar

½ cup cooking oil
2 tablespoons milk

In a pie plate, combine flour, salt and sugar. Add oil and milk. Stir to combine all. Then press into the bottom and sides of the pie plate.

"I usually end by putting wax paper over the crust and pressing another pie plate on top of it to flatten it more evenly. Flute around the edge."

For a single-crust pie to be filled with a cream filling, bake at 375 degrees for 15 to 20 minutes or until golden. — *M.S. of Rock Island*

Eggnog Cake

Jan. 25, 1995

1 package yellow cake mix without pudding
1 package instant vanilla pudding mix

4 eggs
1 cup eggnog
¼ cup oil
1 cup chopped pecans

Blend all ingredients except pecans. Beat at medium speed for 5 minutes.

Grease a 10-inch tube pan. Sprinkle chopped nuts on bottom. Pour in batter.

Bake at 350 degrees for 50 to 60 minutes. Cool 10 minutes in pan. When cool, dust cake with powdered sugar or drizzle with thin icing.

Note: "Be sure to grease pan real well." — *J.L. of Bettendorf*

Fresh Peach Pie

June 17, 1998

"I am hoping one of your readers can help me find a recipe I thought I would never lose," writes J.P. of East Moline.

"It is a Fresh Peach Pie. It took three or four peaches. The crust, I believe, had oil and sugar in, and you pressed it in a pie pan and baked it. When it was cool, you cooked, I believe, white syrup, sugar and when you took it off the stove you added 3 tablespoons peach gelatin.

"I poured the sliced peaches in this mixture, when it cooled some, then poured it in the shell. Then you refrigerate this.

"I think I have forgotten some of the other ingredients; this is what I remember. Thank you very much."

Curious Cook has had this recipe for Fruit Pie in her recipe files for many years, since it was published a long time ago on Dispatch food pages. Surely it is the recipe requested by J.P. Indeed, it is an excellent pie.

The No-Roll Pastry recipe came from my cousin, the late Sister Frances Clare McCarthy, O.S.F., who was at Immaculate Conception Convent in Peoria. She had marked her hand-written recipe "Suellen's No-Roll Pastry."

I have no idea who Suellen is, but her pastry crust is easy and excellent!

1 quart fresh fruit (6 peaches; or raspberries or strawberries), sliced
1 cup granulated sugar
3 tablespoons cornstarch
¼ teaspoon salt

1 cup water
2 tablespoons light corn syrup
½ package of gelatin (use peach, raspberry or strawberry, depending on which fruit is used)

Wash, peel and slice peaches; set aside. Blend sugar and cornstarch. Add salt, water and corn syrup to sugar mixture, blending well. Bring to a boil and boil a minute or two or until clear.

Remove from heat and stir in dry gelatin. Cool slightly and gently blend with prepared fruit.

Pour mixture into baked no-roll pastry crust and refrigerate.

NO-ROLL PASTRY CRUST
1½ cups all-purpose flour
1 teaspoon salt

1 tablespoon sugar
½ cup vegetable oil
2 tablespoons milk

Mix together the flour, salt and sugar. Mix ½ cup oil and 2 tablespoons milk; pour over flour mixture and mix with fork. Press with fingers to line bottom and sides of pie pan. Flute around edge with fingers and thumb.

For pie shell: Bake at 425 degrees for 10 to 12 minutes. Be sure crust has been pricked many times with fork before baking. Makes one 9-inch crust. "A good crust for open-face pies." — *from Curious Cook's files*

Fresh Pear Crumble Pie

Dec. 8, 1999

- 5 cups peeled, sliced fresh pears (about 2½ pounds)
- 3 tablespoons lemon juice
- ½ cup sugar
- 2 tablespoons all-purpose flour
- 1 teaspoon finely shredded lemon peel
- ½ cup all-purpose flour
- ½ cup sugar
- ½ teaspoon ground ginger
- ½ teaspoon ground cinnamon
- 1/8 teaspoon ground mace
- ¼ cup butter or margarine
- 3 slices American or Cheddar cheese, cut into triangles, optional
- Pastry for single crust 9-inch pie

In a bowl, sprinkle pears with lemon juice. In a large mixing bowl, combine ½ cup sugar, the 2 tablespoons of flour and lemon peel; stir in sliced pears. Spoon pear-sugar mixture into a 9-inch pastry-lined plate.

In another mixing bowl, combine the ½ cup flour, ½ cup sugar, ginger, cinnamon and mace. Cut in butter or margarine until mixture resembles coarse crumbs. Sprinkle crumb mixture over pear filling.

To prevent overbrowning, cover edge of pie with foil. Bake at 375 degrees for 25 minutes. Remove foil; bake for 25 to 30 minutes more, or until pie is bubbly and crust is golden. Cool on rack before serving.

Garnish with cheese triangles, if desired.   *— G.H. of Davenport*

Nov. 28, 2001

Frozen Pumpkin Pie

"I have used this recipe for many years, J.J. of Moline tells us in her e-mail, answering the Pumpkin Ice Cream Pie request. "It came from my mother. It is very good and easy."

1 cup canned pumpkin
½ cup granulated sugar
½ teaspoon salt
½ teaspoon nutmeg
½ teaspoon ginger
1 quart vanilla ice cream
One 9-inch baked pie shell
12 walnut or pecan halves

Mix pumpkin, sugar, salt, nutmeg and ginger. Then stir ice cream to soften and then fold in the pumpkin mixture.

Put mixture into the pie shell, decorate with nut halves, and freeze for 6 hours or more.

Note: "If you wish, you may use the already spiced pumpkin. You also can use a graham cracker crust or the oatmeal one below that I usually use." — *J.J. of Moline*

Oatmeal Pie Crust

1 cup oats
2/3 cup butter, melted
3 tablespoons brown sugar
2/3 cup finely chopped nuts

Mix together and pat into pie plate. Bake at 350 degrees for 10 minutes or until done. — *J.J. of Moline*

Gooseberry Pie with Meringue

June 6, 2001

Fresh gooseberry pie is a popular dessert. D.B. of New Windsor should be delighted with the response to her request for information/recipes regarding fresh gooseberries.

We're continuing our gooseberry discussion this week with a letter from L.H. of Rock Island, who also identifies herself as "a faithful reader."

L.H. writes: "I've used this gooseberry pie recipe for years but, of course, I couldn't find it now." This often happens to cooks! It's the culinary gremlins!

But L.H. persevered: "I called my sister out-of-town and she sent me a copy," she continues. "I did get all of my recipes sorted and organized better, though, while looking for it," she admits!

"I had added the 'green' since D.B. of New Windsor didn't know if she was to use them when green or red.

"Even my grandchildren like this pie. Hope she does."

Then L.H. added this tip: "Raw gooseberries freeze well. Stem and wash them. I usually spread them out on a towel and blot excess water. Freeze 2 cups in each freezer bag and they are ready for another pie."

1 pre-baked pie shell
2 cups green gooseberries
½ cup water
1 cup sugar
½ teaspoon salt
¼ cup flour

Cook gooseberries in water until tender. Mix dry ingredients and add to the gooseberry mixture. Cook until thick. Cool.

Pour gooseberry mixture into the pre-baked crust and cover with meringue. Bake at 350 degrees for 15 to 20 minutes, until brown.

MERINGUE:

2 egg whites   **4 tablespoons sugar**

Beat egg whites until frothy, gradually adding sugar a little at a time until sugar is dissolved and meringue forms peaks.   — *L.H. of Rock Island*

Curious Cook's note: L.H.'s recipe doesn't call for cream of tartar in the meringue, but to improve stability and volume, ¼ teaspoon may be beaten in with the egg whites until frothy.

recipes to remember forever

Grandma Bingman's Butter Pie

Feb. 2, 2000

A recipe for Butter Pie, along with a delightful note from an 81-year-old widower will warm your hearts, dear readers, just as it did Curious Cook's. J.A.A. of Davenport answered the recent request for Butter Pie with the following:

"Here is my grandmother's recipe for Butter Pie. My mother made it often, and so do I. The ingredients are always on hand and the pie is DELICIOUS.

"My grandmother was born in 1875, died in 1964, so this recipe is about 100 years old.

"I always make it as my contribution to my grandchildren's Christmas dinner. I am an 81-year-old widower. I hope L.W. of Annawan enjoys this pie."

¾ **cup sugar**	**1 cup milk or more**
2 eggs	**Vanilla or lemon flavoring**
2 tablespoons flour	**Nutmeg**
1 teaspoon butter	**Pastry for single crust pie**

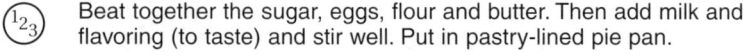

Beat together the sugar, eggs, flour and butter. Then add milk and flavoring (to taste) and stir well. Put in pastry-lined pie pan.

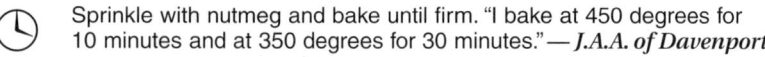

Sprinkle with nutmeg and bake until firm. "I bake at 450 degrees for 10 minutes and at 350 degrees for 30 minutes." — *J.A.A. of Davenport*

Granny's Cake

April 7, 1999

"This is delicious and everyone requests the recipe," writes E.L.K. of Coal Valley. Her recipe calls for both baking soda and baking powder.

- 1½ cups white sugar
- 2 eggs
- 1 can (20 ounces) crushed pineapple, undrained
- 2 cups all-purpose flour
- 1 teaspoon baking soda
- 1 teaspoon baking powder
- ½ teaspoon salt
- ½ cup brown sugar
- ½ chopped nuts

Beat eggs slightly and add crushed pineapple.

Sift together white sugar, flour, baking soda, baking powder and salt. Add to egg and pineapple mixture. Blend well. Do not beat hard. Do not use mixer.

Pour batter into greased 9x12-inch pan. Sprinkle with ½ cup brown sugar and ½ cup chopped nuts on top of cake.

Bake at 350 degrees for 30 to 35 minutes or until toothpick comes out clean. While cake bakes, make glaze.

GLAZE:
- ¾ cup evaporated milk
- ¾ cup butter or margarine
- ½ cup white sugar
- 1 teaspoon vanilla, add after boiling

Put milk, butter and sugar in heavy pan; mix and boil gently until thick, which will take about 20 minutes. Stir often, burns easy.

Pour over warm cake.

— *E.L.K. of Coal Valley*

Grasshopper Pie

Dec. 21, 2001

- 24 Oreo sandwich cookies, finely crushed
- ¼ cup margarine, melted

Combine cookie crumbs and margarine and press into pie pan, reserving ½ cup cookie crumbs for topping. Chill crust.

- ¼ cup milk
- 24 large marshmallows
- 2 cups whipping cream, whipped
- ¼ cup green creme de menthe
- 2 tablespoons creme de cacao, optional
- Few drops of green food coloring

Heat milk to boiling; add marshmallows, mixing until well blended. Fold in whipped cream, creme de menthe and creme de cacao. May add few drops of green food coloring.

Pour into crust; sprinkle with reserved ½ cup crushed cookies. Freeze. Yield: 8 to 10 servings.

— *M.P. of Moline*

Hummingbird Cake

Sept. 10, 1997

"Could you help me please?" asks A.M. of East Moline of Curious Cook. "Lost my recipe for a cake that was in The Dispatch in 1995. It was called the Hummingbird Cake.

"Some of the ingredients were bananas, crushed pineapple and pecans. The frosting had cream cheese in it.

"It was a very moist cake and very good. Hope you can help me," she adds.

Curious Cook's note: We searched the files and came up with the following recipe (on facing page), which was published Oct. 4, 1995, in Curious Cook's column.

At that time, M.S. of East Moline, who sent in the cake recipe, wrote:

"My husband was once affiliated with a real estate company named Hummingbird and we served this cake at one of our promotional affairs. It's delicious — and even better the third and fourth day — if it lasts that long!"

- **3 cups all-purpose flour**
- **2 cups sugar**
- **1 teaspoon soda**
- **1 teaspoon salt**
- **1 teaspoon cinnamon**
- **3 eggs, beaten**
- **1 cup vegetable oil**
- **1½ teaspoons vanilla extract**
- **1 teaspoon butter-flavor extract**
- **1 can (8 ounces) crushed pineapple, undrained**
- **1 cup chopped pecans**
- **2 cups chopped bananas**
- **Cream cheese frosting (see recipe below)**
- **½ cup chopped pecans**

Combine flour, sugar, soda, salt and cinnamon in large mixing bowl. Add eggs and oil, stirring until dry ingredients are moistened. Do not beat.

Stir in vanilla extract, butter-flavor extract, pineapple, pecans and bananas.

Spoon batter into three 9-inch, round, greased and floured cake pans. Bake at 350 degrees for 25 to 30 minutes or until a wooden toothpick inserted in center comes out clean. Cool in pans for 10 minutes; remove from pans and cool completely.

Spread frosting between layers and on top and sides of cake; then sprinkle the half-cup of chopped pecans on top. Refrigerate. Flavors blend and intensify upon standing for 24 hours after baking. Makes one 3-layer cake.

Curious Cook's note: In the Hummingbird Cake recipe shared by several area cooks in the Curious Cook's column of Wednesday, June 8, 1994, these baking directions were given: Pour batter into greased 9x13-inch pan. Bake at 350 degrees 40 to 45 minutes, until cake tests done. A cup of chopped nuts may be sprinkled on top of the icing. Also, one contributor bakes her cake in a greased 11x18-inch pan at 350 degrees for 30 to 40 minutes.

CREAM CHEESE FROSTING:

1 package (8 ounces) cream cheese, softened

½ cup butter or margarine, softened

1 package (16 ounces) powdered sugar, sifted

1 teaspoon vanilla-nut extract

Combine cream cheese and butter, beating until smooth. Add powdered sugar and vanilla-nut extract; beat until light and fluffy. Makes enough frosting for one three-layer cake.   — *M.S. of East Moline*

Lamb Cake

Sept. 11, 1996

Lamb cakes are far more popular than any of us thought. Responses to a request for directions for using a lamb mold to bake a novelty cake have been beyond our expectations.

Read through them this week and next; the details and advice are very interesting.

We'll start with a Lamb Cake recipe from our friend B.K. of Rock Island.

1½ cups sugar
½ cup shortening
2 eggs
1 cup sour milk
1 teaspoon cinnamon
1 teaspoon cloves
1 teaspoon nutmeg

1 cup raisins optional
1 teaspoon baking powder
1 teaspoon baking soda
1 teaspoon salt
2½ cups flour
1 cup nuts

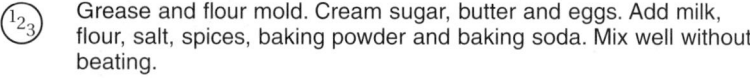

Grease and flour mold. Cream sugar, butter and eggs. Add milk, flour, salt, spices, baking powder and baking soda. Mix well without beating.

Fill face and ears of mold with plain batter, no nuts or raisins. Add nuts and raisins to remaining batter. Fill pan level. Place toothpick in each ear and neck.

Fit upper pan on and bake at 350 degrees for 1 hour or until upper pan comes off easily. Let cool in lower pan. Frost with favorite white icing.
— *B.K. of Rock Island*

Lamb Mold ($3.95)

Sept. 11, 1996

"I have a cast-aluminum lamb mold but it is quite heavy," B.H. of Atkinson tells us in her letter.

"I purchased it in Chicago about 1945. The ad enclosed gives the price $3.95. It also states tested Lady Baltimore recipe in exact proportions included. The size is 8x13 inches. Following is the enclosed recipe."

2 cups sifted flour	**½ cup shortening**
2½ teaspoons Calumet baking powder	**¾ cup milk**
	1 teaspoon vanilla
¾ teaspoon salt	**3 egg whites, beaten**
1 cup sugar	

Sift all dry ingredients together. Stir shortening in mixing bowl to soften. Mix in sifted dry ingredients. Add milk and vanilla and beat with electric mixer for 2 minutes. Fold in beaten egg whites and beat for 1 minute.

Grease lamb mold very well; flour and fill the half containing the lamb's face. Insert a toothpick in the nose for reinforcement and cover with the other half of mold, being sure the edges "lock" together.

Bake cake at 370 degrees for 50 to 60 minutes and let cool slightly before removing from mold. Frost with white icing, sprinkle with coconut and decorate with cherry for nose, raisins for eyes and a ribbon or flowers around neck.

Note: "A good way to ensure against leaking is to bake with nose down for 25 minutes, then turned to the back to finish the baking time.

"I have never used this mold but my mother did. I remember she said she also had to use toothpicks to reinforce the ears. She also colored coconut with green food coloring to place the lamb cake on. It looked as if it were in the grass. I hope this helps. Have fun!"

— *B.H. of Atkinson*

Lamb Cake

Sept. 18, 1996

This recipe from D.M. of Davenport is similar to the one submitted by M.E. of Davenport and published in last week's column. D.M. adds some bits of advice based on her own experience baking Lamb Cakes.

D.M. tells us, "This is in answer to L.M. of Davenport who requested the recipe for the two-piece, cast-iron lamb mold. I have the mold and have the original recipe that came with it some 40 or 50 years ago. The recipe, in my opinion, is not as important as the instructions which came with the mold on how to use and care for it. The following is almost verbatim.

"To prepare mold for use: Wash mold, scour inside and outside, rinse, wipe and dry on hot stove. Apply good coating of fresh fat. I use Crisco to both inside and outside of molds. Keep molds well warmed thru for half an hour or more. Wipe grease out clean and mold is ready for use."

D.M. points out: "The above is for first-time use and your reader's mother probably has already done this."

Here's the recipe for the cake. However, be sure to read D.M.'s note:

½ cup shortening	2½ cups flour
1½ cups sugar	4 teaspoons baking powder
3 eggs, separated	½ teaspoon salt
1 cup milk	1 teaspoon vanilla

Cream shortening; add sugar gradually. Cream well. Add well-beaten yolks and cream again. Alternately add dry ingredients, which have been sifted together, and then milk to which flavoring has been added. Lastly, carefully fold in beaten egg whites.

To bake cake: Grease molds with butter or any preferred fat, sift small film of flour over interior of molds. "My mold is well-seasoned from many, many years of use and I now use Baker's Joy, which both greases and flours the molds."

Fill bottom mold about level full. Placing a meat skewer or popsicle stick through the body — to help support the neck, and a toothpick in each ear will support these parts of cake. Put empty top mold in place.

Bake in pre-heated moderate oven, 350 degrees, about 45 minutes on grate in middle of oven. Set bottom mold, face down, on cookie sheet or any flat surface so mold rests level on oven grate.

Bake with mold face-down for 25 minutes, then turn entire mold over and bake with mold back-down for 20 minutes. Can test with toothpick through top vent holes if in doubt that cake is finished. Remove from oven and cool in bottom mold, carefully removing top mold after letting entire mold set for about 10 minutes. Cool and frost with decorator's frosting or frosting of choice.

Note: "This recipe produces a rather heavy cake. I use the purchased cake mix-with-pudding-in-it and it works just as well and is a better tasting cake in my opinion. Have fun." — *D.M. of Davenport*

Lemon-Glazed Nectar Cake

July 7, 1999

"This is a quick, easy and refreshing cake with a nice tang," A.W. promises.

1 package lemon cake mix
½ cup sugar
4 eggs
½ cup oil

1 cup apricot nectar
¼ cup lemon juice
1¾ cups powdered sugar, sifted

Preheat oven to 350 degrees.

Mix cake mix and sugar. Blend in eggs, oil and nectar; beat 6 minutes. Pour into greased and floured 10-inch tube pan.

Bake at 350 degrees for 50 minutes or until toothpick comes out clean. Cool on cake rack for 10 minutes. Remove from pan onto cake rack; place rack on wax paper.

Mix lemon juice and powdered sugar; beat until smooth. Pour glaze over, allowing it to drizzle down sides. Servings: 10.   — *A.W. of Erie*

Lemon Poppyseed Pound Cake

April 19, 1995

Dear cooks, you will be amazed at the variations of the Poppy Seed Cake recipe received by Curious Cook.

Let's start with L.L. of Rock Island: "To S.T. of East Moline, Poppy Seed Cake is one of my favorites, too. I acquired this wonderful recipe from my mother-in-law in Colorado Springs."

1¾ cups sugar
1 cup Wesson oil
1 tablespoon grated lemon rind
4 eggs
2½ cups all-purpose flour
2 teaspoons baking powder
½ teaspoon nutmeg
½ teaspoon salt
2/3 cup milk
1/3 cup lemon juice
1½ tablespoons poppy seeds

FOR GLAZE:
1 cup powdered sugar
2½ tablespoons lemon juice
1 teaspoon grated lemon rind
½ teaspoon poppy seeds

For cake: In a large bowl, mix sugar, oil and rind until well blended. Add eggs and beat until mixture is thick and pale.

In medium bowl, combine flour, baking powder, nutmeg and salt. In small bowl, combine milk and lemon juice. Heat oven to 350 degrees.

Mix flour and milk mixtures alternately into oil mixture, beginning and ending with flour mixture. Beat until smooth, about 2 minutes. Stir in poppy seeds.

Spoon batter into a 12-cup oiled and floured Bundt pan. Bake at 350 degrees for 1 hour or until cake tests done. Invert on rack; cool in pan for 10 minutes. Remove and cool completely.

In a small bowl, whisk together glaze ingredients until smooth. Smooth glaze over cake. Enjoy! — *L.L. of Rock Island*

Mandarin Orange Cake

Aug. 21, 1996

Mary Lambert of Moline sent this recipe to Curious Cook. "I do not have the date on this recipe, but a note that I got it from The Dispatch. It is a favorite at our house," she reports. Note: There's no shortening in this cake batter.

- 1 cup granulated sugar
- 1 cup all-purpose flour
- 1 egg
- 1 teaspoon baking soda
- 1 teaspoon salt
- 1 teaspoon vanilla
- 1 can (11 ounces) mandarin oranges, well drained
- ½ cup brown sugar
- 2 tablespoons margarine
- 2 tablespoons milk

Combine granulated sugar, flour, egg, baking soda, salt, vanilla and oranges in a mixing bowl and beat 3 minutes. Pour into a lightly greased 8x8-inch pan. Bake at 350 degrees for 25 minutes.

In a saucepan, bring to a boil the brown sugar, margarine and milk. Remove cake from oven 5 minutes before done. Prick cake and pour topping over it. Bake 5 minutes more. — *M.L. of Moline*

Feb. 21, 1996

Michigan Cranberry Cake with Vanilla Sauce

Curious Cook has interesting Cranberry Cake recipes for you today to answer a recent request. Hope you have cranberries in your freezer so you can try these dishes. Our readers rave about them. This recipe is from E.B. of Geneseo.

- 1 cup sugar
- ½ cup butter, at room temperature
- 2 eggs
- 1 cup milk
- 2 cups flour
- 2½ teaspoons baking powder
- ½ teaspoon salt
- 1 teaspoon vanilla
- 2 cups fresh or frozen whole cranberries
- ¼ cup chopped pecans, optional

Preheat oven at 350 degrees. Cream sugar and butter. Add eggs. Mix in milk, flour, baking powder and salt. Add vanilla. Fold in cranberries and nuts. Bake in greased 9x12-inch cake pan or two 9-inch pie pans at 350 degrees for 25 minutes. Test for doneness with toothpick.

VANILLA SAUCE

- 1 cup hot water
- 1 cup sugar
- ½ cup butter
- 1 or 2 tablespoons flour
- 2 teaspoons vanilla

Mix first four ingredients in saucepan and cook over medium heat, stirring constantly until thickened. Remove from heat; add vanilla. Serve hot sauce over warm cake. Serves 12. Delicious! — *E.B. of Geneseo*

Miss American Pie

May 1, 2002

L.C. of Bettendorf answers a recent request from East Moliner R.P,. who wanted a recipe for Triple Layer Cheesecake Dessert. L.C.Y. writes:

"I don't know if this is what R.P. of East Moline is looking for, but here is a red, white and blue recipe I have called Miss American Pie."

One 10-inch pie pastry, baked	1 cup powdered sugar, sifted
1 can (21 ounces) blueberry pie filling	1 carton (12 ounces) frozen non-dairy whipped topping, thawed
1 package (8 ounces) cream cheese, softened	1 can (21 ounces) cherry pie filling

 Bake the 10-inch pie pastry. Cool. Pour blueberry pie filling in bottom of crust. Chill 30 minutes.

Beat softened cream cheese, adding powdered sugar until smooth. Fold in whipped topping.

 Spread cheese mixture on top of blueberry pie filling. Chill 30 minutes.

 Gently spread cherry pie filling on top. Chill at least 4 hours.

— *L.C.Y. of Bettendorf*

Mock Apple Pie

Sept. 1, 1999

J.H. of Bettendorf has a slightly different version of the Mock Apple Pie. Here 'tis:

4 cups zucchini, peeled and sliced like apples	1 teaspoon nutmeg
Boiling water	¼ teaspoon salt
¾ cup white sugar	4 tablespoons flour
½ cup brown sugar	3 tablespoons lemon juice
2 teaspoons cinnamon	1 teaspoon water
	Double pie pastry

 Cover zucchini with boiling water and cook for a few minutes. Drain well. Combine zucchini, white sugar, brown sugar, cinnamon, nutmeg, salt, flour, lemon juice and water; mix well. Fill a 9-inch pie shell.

 Cover with top crust; cut slits in top. May dust the top of crust of pie shell with sugar. Bake at 425 degrees for 15 minutes and reduce heat to 350 degrees and bake for 1 hour. — *J.H. of Bettendorf*

Mock Apple Pie

Oct. 6, 1993

"Reading your column is a weekly must!" writes L.G. of Davenport in answering a recent request.

"I'm writing to share a favorite mock apple pie from our church cookbook that I have successfully used and fooled my kids!"

She adds, "Hope your readers will enjoy this recipe."

1 large zucchini, peeled, quartered, and seeds removed
Salted water
Pie dough for a 2-crust pie (see note)
1 scant cup sugar
¼ teaspoon nutmeg
1 teaspoon cinnamon
1½ teaspoons cream of tartar
3 tablespoons cornstarch or 6 tablespoons flour
1 tablespoon margarine
1 tablespoon lemon juice

Slice zucchini, cover with salted water and boil for 2 minutes; drain and rinse. Prepare pie crust for a 2-crust pie. Or see directions below for streusel topping.

Combine sugar, spices, cream of tartar and cornstarch or flour. Layer zucchini and sugar mixture in the crust, ending with the dry mixture. Dot with margarine and lemon juice. Cover with top crust and bake at 400 degrees for 50 minutes.

Note: "This pie looks and tastes just like an apple pie. Sometimes I omit the top pie crust and add a streusel topping of:

½ cup flour
1/3 cup sugar
½ to 1 teaspoon cinnamon
¼ cup margarine

Combine flour with cinnamon and sugar. Cut in margarine until crumbly. — *L.G. of Davenport*

Mystery Apple Pie

Feb. 26, 1997

From R.K. of Durant: "Someone asked for the Mystery Apple Pie with soda crackers. I'm sending the one I have. I made them a lot when my family was all home. I took one to work and they didn't believe it wasn't apple."

1½ cups water	Cinnamon
1½ cups sugar	2 tablespoons butter
2 teaspoons butter	Sugar
1 teaspoon cream of tartar	Pie pastry for double-crust pie
16 soda crackers, broken in quarters	

Combine water, 1½ cups sugar, 2 teaspoons butter and cream of tartar; boil for 2 minutes and pour over broken soda crackers in unbaked pie shell.

Sprinkle with cinnamon and dot with 2 tablespoons butter. Put top crust on and cut 2 strips in crust to vent. Sprinkle with sugar. Bake at 425 degrees for 30 to 35 minutes. — *R.K. of Durant*

Mom's Date Cake

Aug. 21, 1996

Mary Lambert of Moline treasures her unfrosted cake recipes, which came from the collection of her 87-year-old mother, Mabel Mosinski of East Moline. "This is another of my mother's recipes I've used all my married life," Mrs. Lambert says.

1 cup dates, chopped	1½ cups sifted all-purpose flour
1 cup boiling water	½ teaspoon salt
½ cup shortening (Crisco)	1 teaspoon soda
1 cup sugar	1 teaspoon baking powder
1 egg	½ cup chopped nuts optional
1 teaspoon vanilla	

Chop 1 cup dates and cover with 1 cup boiling water. Set aside to cool. In mixing bowl, cream together shortening, sugar and egg. Add dates with water and vanilla. Sift together the flour, salt, soda and baking powder; add to date mixture. Put in greased 9x13-inch pan. Bake at 350 degrees for 35 to 40 minutes. — *M.L. of Moline*

Mom's Gingerbread

Aug. 21, 1996

"This recipe for gingerbread is from my mother's collection and a favorite of my family," Mary Lambert wrote in answer to a request in Curious Cook's column for unfrosted cakes.

½ cup shortening (Crisco)
½ cup granulated sugar
1 egg
1 cup molasses
2½ cups sifted flour
1½ teaspoons soda
1 teaspoon ginger
1 teaspoon cinnamon
1 teaspoon nutmeg
1 teaspoon cloves
1 cup boiling water

Cream together the shortening, sugar and egg. Add molasses. Sift together the flour, soda, ginger, cinnamon, nutmeg and cloves. Add last the 1 cup boiling water and mix gently. Pour into a greased 9x13-inch pan.

Bake at 350 degrees for 35 to 40 minutes. Test for doneness with a toothpick.

Note: If gingerbread is served as a dessert, cut in squares and top with lemon sauce.

LEMON SAUCE

2 tablespoons cornstarch
½ cup granulated sugar
1 cup boiling water
2 tablespoons butter or margarine
1 tablespoon grated fresh lemon rind OR 1 teaspoon dried lemon rind
3 tablespoons fresh lemon juice

Mix cornstarch and sugar; add boiling water and mix well. Cook, stirring, until clear.

Remove from heat and add butter or margarine, grated rind and lemon juice. Mix well.

Serve hot or cold on cakes, puddings or gingerbread. Yield: 1½ cups.

— *M.L. of Moline*

Perfect Chocolate Cake

Dec. 26, 2001

"If I remember right, someone recently requested a recipe for Perfect Chocolate Cake," writes D.T. of Moline.

"I have made this cake many times, baking it in a 9x13-inch pan and frosting it with a white, buttercream icing. Would also work well in a large sheet-cake pan.

"I don't recall where this recipe came from, perhaps my mother's recipe file," D.T. adds. "It is a favorite of mine and my family."

- 1 cup unsifted, unsweetened cocoa
- 2 cups boiling water
- 2¾ cups sifted all-purpose flour
- 2 teaspoons baking soda
- ½ teaspoon salt
- ½ teaspoon baking powder
- 1 cup butter or regular margarine, softened
- 2½ cups sugar
- 4 eggs
- 1½ teaspoons vanilla

Grease well and lightly flour three 9x1½-inch layer pans.

Combine cocoa and water in a bowl and mix with wire whisk until smooth. Cool completely.

Sift together all-purpose flour, baking soda, salt and baking powder.

In large bowl of electric mixer, beat together the butter, sugar, eggs and vanilla, scraping bowl occasionally until mixture is light and fluffy, about 5 minutes.

On low speed, beat in flour mixture, ¼ at a time, alternately with cocoa mixture, in thirds, beginning and ending with flour mixture. DO NOT OVERBEAT.

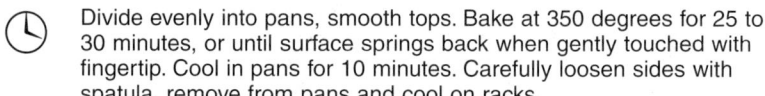

Divide evenly into pans, smooth tops. Bake at 350 degrees for 25 to 30 minutes, or until surface springs back when gently touched with fingertip. Cool in pans for 10 minutes. Carefully loosen sides with spatula, remove from pans and cool on racks.

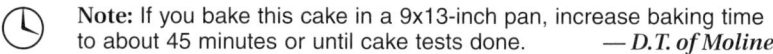

Note: If you bake this cake in a 9x13-inch pan, increase baking time to about 45 minutes or until cake tests done.   — *D.T. of Moline*

Perfect Chocolate Cake Frosting and Filling

1 package (6 ounces) semi-sweet chocolate chips
½ cup light cream

1 cup butter or regular margarine
2½ cups powdered sugar

 Stir chocolate chips, cream and butter in saucepan over medium heat until smooth.

Remove from heat and with wire whisk, blend in 2½ cups powdered sugar. In bowl, set over ice, beat well until mixture holds shape.

FILLING:

1 cup heavy cream, chilled

¼ cup unsifted powdered sugar
1 teaspoon vanilla

Whip cream with the powdered sugar and vanilla. Refrigerate

— *D.T. of Moline*

Old Time Lemon Pie

Feb. 24, 1999

1 baked 9-inch pie shell
1-1/3 cups sugar
1¾ cups water
2 tablespoons butter
1/3 cup cornstarch
½ cup cold water
4 egg yolks
3 tablespoons milk
½ cup fresh lemon juice
1½ teaspoon grated rind fresh

MERINGUE:
4 egg whites
1/2 cup sugar
1 teaspoon fresh lemon juice

Combine sugar, 1¾ cups water and butter and heat until sugar dissolves. Blend cornstarch and ½ cup cold water and add to hot mixture; cook slowly until clear.

Beat together egg yolks and milk. Slowly stir into other mixture. Cook 2 minutes. Remove from heat and add lemon juice and grated rind.

For meringue, beat whites slowly adding sugar until stiff. Add juice.

Pour lemon mixture into baked shell and top with meringue. Brown at 350 degrees. — *B.R. of Moline*

Peanut Butter Cake

Dec. 16, 1998

"I've always enjoyed your column; as I was reading it, I came across a lady from Davenport searching for a Peanut Butter Cake," writes J.P. of East Moline.

"Well, you're in luck, I just happen to have one. My mother made it for me when I was a child, so I hope J.R. of Davenport enjoys it also!! Here it is. It's really good."

½ cup peanut butter
½ cup shortening
1 cup white sugar
½ cup brown sugar
1 egg

1½ cups flour
¼ teaspoon salt
1 teaspoon baking powder
½ teaspoon vanilla

Cream together peanut butter, shortening, sugars and egg. Add rest of ingredients. Mix well. Bake in greased 9x13-inch pan at 375 degrees for about 25 minutes or until done. — *J.P. of East Moline*

Peanut Butter Streusel Pie

May 7, 1997

We've always known that Quad-Cities area cooks are generous with their recipes and eager to help others. Curious Cook's mail is proof enough!

Quite of number of you promptly answered the urgent plea of B.J. of Davenport for a recipe for Baked Peanut Butter Pie. B.J.'s husband, who is seriously ill, is hungry for the pie.

J.L. of East Moline sent in this first recipe. "I only hope this helps her, she writes.

1/3 cup peanut butter	3 egg yolks, slightly beaten
¾ cup confectioners' sugar	2 tablespoons butter or margarine
1 pastry shell (9-inch), baked	½ teaspoon vanilla flavoring
1/3 cup flour	3 egg whites
1 cup granulated sugar, divided	¼ teaspoon cream of tartar
1/8 teaspoon salt	1 teaspoon cornstarch
2 cups milk, scalded	

Blend peanut butter and confectioners' sugar to mealy consistency. Sprinkle two-thirds of mixture in pie shell.

Combine flour, ½ cup granulated sugar and salt in top of double boiler; stir in milk. Cook over boiling water, stirring constantly, until thickened. Stir a small amount of cooked custard into egg yolks. Combine egg mixture with remaining custard; cook several minutes longer. Remove from heat. Add butter and vanilla. Pour into pie shell.

Beat egg whites until stiff, adding cream of tartar. Gradually add remaining sugar blended with cornstarch. Continue beating until meringue is stiff and shiny. Spread on top of custard-filled shell. Sprinkle with remaining crumbs.

Bake at 350 degrees for 15 to 20 minutes. Chill before serving.

— *J.L. of East Moline*

Pear and Apple Pie

Dec. 8, 1999

Curious Cook has received quite a number of recipes for the requested Pear Pie.

We thank all who contributed recipes. We'll start with J.H. of Bettendorf. She writes:

"D.F. of Milan wanted a pear pie recipe. I make this pie with pears from my dad's pear tree.

"Make sure the pears are ripe or the pie will be crunchy!"

- 3 cups thinly sliced peeled pears
- 3 cups thinly sliced peeled apples
- ¾ cup sugar
- 3 tablespoons flour
- ¼ teaspoon salt
- ½ teaspoon cinnamon
- 1 (9-inch) unbaked pie shell

Combine pears, apples, sugar, flour, salt and cinnamon; place mixture in pie shell.

TOPPING:
- ½ cup brown sugar
- ¼ cup flour
- ½ cup finely chopped pecans
- ¼ cup butter or margarine, melted

Combine brown sugar, flour, pecans and butter; sprinkle over top of pie. Fold foil loosely over top and around sides of pie.

Bake at 400 degrees for 40 minutes. Remove foil and bake another 20 minutes.

— *J.H. of Bettendorf*

Pecan Fruitcake

Nov. 29, 2000

"I saw the request by A.E.L. of Davenport for a German Fruitcake," writes M.W. of East Moline. "Mine isn't called that, but it's different.

"I got the recipe from a friend at work over 40 years ago. She came from a small town in Iowa. I've made it lots of times and love it.

"She told me to sprinkle it with the cherry juice several times to keep it moist and wrap in wax paper before the foil. Hope A.E.L. enjoys this cake.

"I photocopied the recipe because I wanted you to see how it was written. My copy is yellow with age."

- ¾ **cup sifted flour**
- ¾ **cup sugar**
- ½ **teaspoon salt**
- ½ **teaspoon baking powder**
- **3 cups pecan halves**
- **2 packages of pitted dates (about 1 pound)**
- **1 cup well-drained maraschino cherries**
- **3 eggs**
- **1 teaspoon vanilla**

Start heating oven — 300 degrees. Grease and line with wax paper a 9x5x3-inch loaf pan. In sifter, place first four ingredients.

In large bowl or pan, place nuts, dates and cherries. Sift flour mixture over these. Mix with hands until well coated. Beat eggs until foamy. Add the teaspoon of vanilla and add to nut mixture. Stir until nut mixture is well mixed. Spread evenly in pan.

Bake at 300 degrees for 1 hour and 45 minutes or until done. Cool on wire rack in pan for 15 minutes. Then remove from pan. Tear off paper and finish cooling. Then wrap in aluminum foil. Store in refrigerator. "This recipe makes one big loaf."

Note: "Will keep five weeks or more if you don't nibble too much."

— *M.W. of East Moline*

Perfect Pie Crust

March 30, 1994

"In response to J.G. of Moline, I have a recipe for a pie crust using egg and vinegar, and it turns out perfectly — even when handled excessively," advises D.C. of Bettendorf.

"However, my recipe states specifically not to use lard, but solid shortening," she adds.

- 4 cups flour, lightly spooned into cup
- 1 tablespoon sugar
- 2 teaspoons salt
- 1¾ cups solid shortening — not lard or oil
- ½ cup water
- 1 tablespoon white or cider vinegar
- 1 large egg

Put first three ingredients in large bowl and mix well with fork. Add shortening and mix with fork until ingredients are crumbly.

In small bowl, beat together, with fork, ½ cup water, the vinegar and egg. Combine the two mixtures, stirring with fork until ingredients are moistened.

Divide dough into 5 portions and, with hands, shape each portion into a flat round patty ready for rolling. Wrap each in plastic or wax paper and chill at least ½ hour. Each patty will make a 9-inch crust.

The dough may be kept in the refrigerator up to 3 days or frozen until ready to use. Roll out and use dough as you would any other pie crust.
— *D.C. of Bettendorf*

Prune Cake

Sept. 19, 2001

From E.B. of Davenport:

"Inside the notepaper is my mom's Prune Cake recipe. It's very good and a favorite of mine."

½ **pound prunes**	**1 teaspoon cinnamon**
2 cups flour	**1 teaspoon nutmeg**
1½ cups sugar	**¼ teaspoon cloves**
1¼ teaspoons baking soda	**½ cup salad oil**
1 teaspoon salt	**3 eggs**

Cook prunes. Save 2/3 cup of liquid. Pit and chop prunes; set aside.

Sift dry ingredients. Add prune liquid and salad oil. Mix to blend. Beat vigorously for 2 minutes.

Add eggs; beat 1 minute more. Stir in prunes.

Pour batter into greased and floured 13x9-inch pan. Sprinkle with crumb topping. Bake at 350 degrees for 50 minutes.

CRUMB TOPPING:

½ cup sugar	**2 tablespoons butter**
2 tablespoons flour	**½ cup nuts**

Combine ingredients for crumb topping; mix well. — *E.B. of Davenport*

Prune Cake

Sept. 12, 2001

From E.C.G. of Davenport: "Answering your request for Prune Cake recipe. This recipe was handed down from my mother and I am a senior citizen.

"Have always thought it was a delicious cake!"

½ cup (1 stick) butter or margarine
1½ cups firmly packed brown sugar
2 eggs
½ cup cooked, pitted prunes, chopped
1½ cups flour

1 teaspoon baking soda
¼ teaspoon salt
½ teaspoon cinnamon
½ teaspoon nutmeg
½ teaspoon allspice
¼ teaspoon cloves
2/3 cup buttermilk
½ cup chopped walnuts

Cream together butter and sugar until light and fluffy. Add eggs one at a time, beating well after each addition. Stir in prunes.

Combine flour, baking soda, salt and spices and add alternately with buttermilk to creamed mixture. Stir in walnuts.

Pour into greased and floured 9-inch square pan. Bake at 350 degrees for 40 to 45 minutes.
— *E.C.G. of Davenport*

Val's Prune Cake

Sept. 26, 2001

"I'm responding to the request for a Prune Cake recipe," writes C.P. of Davenport.

"The recipe was my Mom's and during the Depression Days, neighbors would donate whatever they could of the ingredients so Mom could bake the Prune Cake and they'd gather on a Saturday night to play cards, have some little trinkets for prizes and then finish the evening with some cold meat sandwiches, coffee and prune cake."

½ cup shortening
1 cup sugar
1 egg
1 cup unsweetened prune juice
1 cup chopped, cooked prunes
2 cups sifted flour

1 teaspoon baking powder
1 teaspoon baking soda
½ teaspoon salt
1½ teaspoons cinnamon
½ teaspoon allspice
¼ teaspoon cloves
Chopped nuts, optional

Cream shortening and sugar. Add egg and beat until fluffy. Add prune juice and all dry ingredients. Beat 2 minutes if by hand. Then stir in chopped prunes. Chopped nuts also may be added.

Bake in a 9x12-inch greased pan at 350 degrees for 35 to 40 minutes.

ICING:
2 cups confectioners' sugar
Pinch of salt

3 drops maple flavoring
1 tablespoon butter
Enough hot prune juice to mix

Combine all ingredients. Stir to mix well and frost Prune Cake.

— *C.P. of Davenport*

Pumpkin Chiffon Pie

Jan. 15, 2003

Although pumpkin pies are especially popular during the Thanksgiving/Christmas season, there's no reason not to enjoy a piece of Pumpkin Chiffon Pie in January. The pie might very well chase away the winter blues.

E.M. of Moline shares a long-time favorite recipe to answer the request of F.L. of East Moline. E.M. writes:

"I have had this recipe for many years," she explains. "It's always a hit with my family. It's light and perfect after a meal, especially during the holidays.

"Look forward to your column each week. Thank you."

- **1 envelope unflavored gelatin**
- **½ cup granulated sugar**
- **½ teaspoon salt**
- **½ teaspoon nutmeg**
- **½ teaspoon ginger**
- **1 teaspoon cinnamon**
- **¼ teaspoon ground cloves**
- **2/3 cup evaporated milk**
- **3 egg yolks**
- **1¼ cups canned pumpkin**
- **3 egg whites**
- **¼ cup granulated sugar**
- **1 (9-inch) baked pastry pie shell**
- **Whipped cream or frozen whipping topping, thawed, for topping**

In saucepan, combine gelatin, ½ cup granulated sugar, salt and spices. Stir in evaporated milk and egg yolks and blend well.

Cook slowly, stirring constantly, until gelatin dissolves and mixture thickens slightly. Remove from heat and stir in pumpkin. Chill in refrigerator, stirring occasionally until mixture starts to set.

Beat egg whites until stiff but not dry and gradually add ¼ cup sugar. Beat until very stiff. Fold into pumpkin mixture; turn mixture into pie shell. Chill until firm.

Top with whipped cream or whipping topping. Yield: 6 to 8 servings.

— *E.M. of Moline*

Pumpkin Custard Pie

Dec. 26, 2001

A.D. of Rock Island answers the request of M.K. of Moline for a Pumpkin Custard Pie with this recipe.

"This is excellent"

- ¾ cup dark brown sugar
- 1 teaspoon salt
- 1 teaspoon cinnamon
- ½ teaspoon ginger
- ¼ teaspoon cloves
- ¼ teaspoon nutmeg
- 3 eggs, slightly beaten
- 1¾ cups pumpkin
- 1½ cups milk
- 9-inch, deep-dish, pie shell, unbaked

Combine sugar, salt, spices. Add eggs and mix well. Stir in pumpkin, then milk. Stir until smooth.

Pour into 9-inch deep-dish pie shell. Bake in hot oven, 425 degrees, on shelf just below center of oven for 45 minutes or until tester comes out clean. Protect edge of pie crust. — *A.D. of Rock Island*

Pumpkin Spice Angel Food Cake

Feb. 24, 1999

"I enjoy all the 'oldies' that reappear in your column," writes M.B.H. of Davenport.

"During the Christmas season, in a local paper, I saw a recipe for Pumpkin Angel Food Cake. The first ingredient was a package of Betty Crocker One-Step Angel Food Cake mix. There also were pumpkin and spices.

"I didn't cut it out immediately, so it is gone. If any of your readers has it, I would really appreciate getting it. …

"As you can see I'm a year-round pumpkin lover. Thanks."
— *M.B.H. of Davenport*

Curious Cook found the following cake recipe in our files. It matches the description given by M.B.H.

The recipe was published Dec. 2, 1998, along with other extra dessert recipes submitted for the 1998 Holiday Cookbook.

- 1 box Betty Crocker 1-step angel food cake mix
- 1¼ cups water
- ½ cup canned pumpkin
- ¼ teaspoon cinnamon
- ¼ teaspoon ginger
- ½ teaspoon nutmeg
- Orange sherbet, for topping

Preheat oven to 350 degrees. Using electric mixer, beat cake mix, water, pumpkin and spices. Pour batter into ungreased tube pan and bake at 350 degrees for 35 to 40 minutes. Cool cake completely before removing from pan. Serve with orange sherbet as a topping.
— *1998 Holiday Cookbook*

recipes to remember forever

Raw Apple Cake

April 11, 2001

"Does anyone have a recipe for Apple Cake using cold coffee?" asks B.K. of Davenport. "Would appreciate it very much. Thank you." — *B.K. of Davenport*

We found this recipe for Raw Apple Cake in our files:

1 cup shortening	2 teaspoons cinnamon
2 cups granulated sugar	1 cup cold coffee
2 eggs	4 cups chopped apples
3 cups flour	½ cup brown sugar
2 teaspoons baking soda	1 cup chopped nuts

Cream together the shortening and granulated sugar; add eggs and beat well. Sift together the flour and soda; add cinnamon. Add flour mixture to creamed mixture alternately with the cold coffee. Stir in chopped apples.

Pour batter into buttered 13x9-inch pan. Sprinkle brown sugar and nuts on top. Bake at 350 degrees for approximately 1 hour, until cake tests done. — *from Curious Cook's files*

Rice Pudding

Dec. 6, 2000

Well, dear cooks, we have received quite a wonderful response to the request of S.W. of Rock Island for directions for baking Rice Pudding with custard on top!

Many of you shared treasured family recipes and lovely sentiments about this traditional Swedish dish.

And although the recipes are similar, each has its own characteristics and history.

We'll start with E.P. of Andover:

"A reader requested Rice Pudding with a custard on top. Here is my mother's J.A.P. recipe."

2/3 cup regular rice	½ teaspoon salt
2 cups water	½ cup sugar
1 quart milk (whole or fat-free)	½ teaspoon vanilla
4 large eggs	Nutmeg

Cook rice in the 2 cups of water for 20 minutes or until water is absorbed. Scald milk. Beat eggs slightly in a 2-quart casserole. Add salt, sugar and vanilla. Then add scalded milk and cooked rice; stir. Sprinkle with nutmeg.

Set casserole in a pan of water and bake at 350 degrees for 1¼ to 1½ hours. To test if it is done, insert a silver knife in the middle and see if it comes out clean. — *E.P. of Andover*

Swedish Rice Pudding

Dec. 6, 2000

D.B.E. of Moline has fond memories of her mom's Rice Pudding: "I remember my mom gently stirring the pudding half way through the baking to help mix the rice with the custard.

"Growing up in the '50s and '60s, Swedish Rice Pudding was the staple of every church picnic, family gathering, holiday and bereavement dinner I attended," she recalls.

"My own family is now multi-ethnic and requests different foods, so I have learned to adapt with the times.

"I only hope that there will be one recipe that I leave for my family that provides the bittersweet memories as my mom's Rice Pudding does for me."

1 cup rice, uncooked
3 eggs
4 cups whole milk
½ teaspoon vanilla
½ cup sugar
Butter
Nutmeg

Cook rice until done. Rinse with water to remove the starch.

In a bowl, beat eggs; add milk, vanilla and sugar and stir until well blended. Stir in cooked rice. Pour into a buttered 1½- to 2-quart glass casserole dish.

Bake at 325 degrees for 1 hour or until inserted knife comes out clean. Half way through the baking, gently stir, dot with butter and sprinkle with nutmeg. — *D.B.E. of Moline*

Sauerkraut Cake

Oct. 2, 1996

4 eggs
1 cup sugar
½ cup packed brown sugar
1 can (14 ounces) sauerkraut, rinsed and drained
1 large tart apple
1 cup vegetable cooking oil

1 cup chopped walnuts
2 cups all-purpose flour
2 teaspoons baking powder
2 teaspoons cinnamon
1 teaspoon baking soda
1 teaspoon salt
½ teaspoon ground nutmeg

In a large bowl, beat eggs and sugars; set aside. Squeeze sauerkraut until dry; finely chop and add to egg mixture. Peel and finely grate apple; squeeze dry. Stir into egg mixture. Add oil and walnuts.

Combine dry ingredients and stir into egg mixture. Line the bottom of two 8-inch greased and floured pans with wax paper. Make sure to grease and flour the sides. Pour batter into pans.

Bake at 350 degrees for 35 to 40 minutes. Cool slightly in pans before removing. Frost with cream cheese frosting. Makes 10 to 12 servings.

FROSTING:

1 package (8 ounces) cream cheese, softened
2 to 3 tablespoons whipping cream, divided
4½ cups confectioners' sugar

1 tablespoon grated orange peel
½ teaspoon ground cinnamon
1 teaspoon vanilla
Chopped nuts, optional

Beat cream cheese and 2 tablespoons cream in a small bowl. Add sugar, beating until fluffy. Add orange peel, cinnamon and vanilla. Mix well. Add remaining cream, if necessary.

Spread frosting between layers and over entire cake. Garnish with chopped nuts. Store in refrigerator. — *J.E. of Utica*

Strawberry Cake

June 12, 2002

1 box white or yellow cake mix (2-layer size)
4 eggs
2/3 cup oil
1/3 cup water
1 box (4-serving size) strawberry gelatin
1 package (10 ounces) frozen strawberries, thawed (see note)
Small carton frozen whipped topping, thawed

Mix first five ingredients and beat 4 minutes. Add some of the strawberries, saving rest to put in whipped topping.

Bake in a greased 9x13-inch pan at 350 degrees for 40 minutes.

When cooled, put whipped topping with added strawberries on top of cake. Refridgerate.

Note: "Very good. I have to make it for my kids' birthdays. I use my frozen strawberries and use more than 10 ounces." — *D.L.L. of Geneseo*

Swedish Apple Pie

Sept. 6, 2000

B.S. of Moline asked Curious Cook for help because she lost a Swedish Apple Pie recipe, which she clipped several years ago from one of the "Quad-Cities Holiday Cookbooks."

"We just love it," she told us of the pie and promised never to lose the recipe again if Curious Cook could find it for her.

We have good news for B.S. A little research led us to the 1993 edition of the "Holiday Cookbook" and the following recipe for Swedish Apple Pie.

7 medium-size apples, cored, peeled and sliced
1 tablespoon sugar
2 teaspoons cinnamon
¾ cup margarine, melted
1 cup sugar
1 cup flour
1 egg, beaten
1 cup chopped nuts
¼ teaspoon salt

Fill a 9-inch pie pan full of sliced apples; sprinkle with 1 tablespoon sugar and 2 teaspoons cinnamon.

In medium-size bowl, combine melted margarine, 1 cup sugar, flour, beaten egg, chopped nuts and salt. Mix well. Spread over apples in the pie pan to cover. Bake at 350 degrees for 45 minutes. — *1993 Quad-Cities Holiday Cookbook*

Sweet Potato Pie

June 10, 1998

"I have made this Sweet Potato Pie and love it," writes O.M. of Andalusia. "So hope D.W. of Davenport will like this one.

"I also read the recipes, and find them most enjoyable. I also make a lot of the food, too. No mistake. I'm a bake-a-holic."

2 eggs	TOPPING:
1 can (12 ounces) evaporated milk	1/3 cup butter
1 teaspoon vanilla	1/3 cup all-purpose flour
1¼ cups sugar	½ cup packed brown sugar
½ teaspoon cinnamon	½ cup shredded coconut
½ teaspoon nutmeg	½ cup chopped pecans
1½ cups mashed, cooked sweet potatoes	
1 unbaked pie crust (9 inches)	

 In a mixing bowl, beat eggs; add milk and vanilla. Combine sugar, cinnamon, and nutmeg, add to the egg mixture. Stir in potatoes; beat until smooth. Pour into pie shell.

 Bake at 425 degrees for 15 minutes. Reduce heat to 350 degrees and bake for 30 minutes longer.

 Combine topping ingredients; sprinkle over pie. Return to the oven for 10 to 15 minutes or until topping is golden brown. Cool on wire rack. Store in refrigerator.

Serve with whipped topping or ice cream. Yield 6 to 8 servings.

— *O.M. of Andalusia*

Dec. 20, 1995

Sweet Potato Pie

"Saw the request for sweet potato pie, and since my recipe was still out decided to send it. We all enjoy this through the holidays. Someone even said, 'If we have to eat sweet potatoes, this is the way to have them.'

"The recipe came from Mississippi when our oldest daughter lived there many years ago. Enjoy your column and have tried many of the ideas sent in. Thank you."

- 3 cups cooked, peeled and mashed sweet potatoes
- 1 cup raisins
- 3 eggs
- 1 teaspoon vanilla
- ¼ cup margarine
- 1 teaspoon pumpkin pie spice
- ¼ cup margarine
- ¼ cup flour
- 1 cup chopped pecans
- 1 cup brown sugar

Mix mashed sweet potatoes, raisins, eggs, vanilla, ¼ cup margarine and pumpkin pie spice; put mixture into a greased 9x13-inch pan. Combine ¼ cup margarine, flour, chopped pecans and brown sugar. Sprinkle over potatoes. Bake at 325 degrees for 25 to 30 minutes, until brown and crusty.

— *S.S. of Colona*

Dec. 20, 1995

Sweet Potato Custard Pie

From A.L. of Rock Island "I thought I read in your article about a week ago that someone was looking for a Sweet Potato Pie recipe. I have found the one I used while I lived out in North Carolina. It's very good."

- 1 cup cooked, mashed sweet potatoes
- 1/3 cup sugar
- ½ teaspoon salt
- ½ cup milk
- 1 egg, beaten slightly
- ½ teaspoon cinnamon
- ½ teaspoon nutmeg
- ¼ teaspoon ground cloves
- 1 tablespoon butter or margarine, melted
- 8- to 9-inch unbaked pastry shell

Mix sweet potatoes, sugar, salt, milk, egg, cinnamon, nutmeg, cloves and melted butter in order listed. Pour into unbaked pie shell. Bake at 400 degrees for about 40 minutes or until custard is set. Take out of oven and let cool.

— *A.L. of Rock Island*

Texas Sheet Cake

June 8, 2005

D.C. of Bettendorf sent a Texas Sheet Cake recipe with an interesting variation for the frosting. D.C. writes:

"The brownie recipe B.B. of Davenport is seeking, I think, is what I've always called Texas Sheet Cake. My mother-in-law also called it Brownies. Whatever a person chooses to call it, it's delicious — especially with the chocolate/peanut butter frosting."

1 cup (2 sticks) margarine	½ cup buttermilk
1 cup water	1 teaspoon baking soda
4 tablespoons cocoa	2 eggs
2 cups flour	1 teaspoon vanilla
2 cups sugar	½ teaspoon cinnamon

Bring margarine and water to a boil in a medium saucepan. Blend flour, sugar and cocoa in a large mixing bowl. Pour on boiled mixture and beat thoroughly. Mix in buttermilk, soda, eggs, vanilla and cinnamon. Pour batter into greased jelly-roll pan (10x16x1-inch, or 11x16x1-inch). Bake in a preheated 350-degree oven for 25 to 30 minutes.

FOR FROSTING:

½ cup (1 stick) margarine	4 tablespoons cocoa
6 tablespoons milk	1 pound powdered sugar
1 teaspoon vanilla	½ cup coarsely chopped walnuts (optional)

Boil margarine, milk and vanilla in a small saucepan. Blend powdered sugar and cocoa in large mixing bowl. Pour on boiled mixture and beat until smooth. Stir in walnuts. Spread over cake as soon as it comes out of the oven.

Note: "I like to add 2 tablespoons peanut butter and ½ cup chopped peanuts to this frosting, because if chocolate is good, chocolate and peanut butter are even better." — *D.C. of Bettendorf*

Texas Sheet Cake

June 14, 2000

C.P. of East Moline has requested the recipe for Texas Sheet Cake, a very good cake indeed.

The Texas Sheet Cake has become a classic. It's always welcome, always delicious. Because results are best if the cake is mixed by hand, this cake is quick and easy to prepare.

If you don't want to buy a quart of buttermilk in order to have ½ cup for the cake, powdered buttermilk is an excellent investment. The powder works well and may be kept on hand because it stores in the refrigerator. Just follow directions on the can.

- 2 cups sugar
- 2 cups flour
- 2 sticks margarine
- 4 tablespoons cocoa
- 1 cup water
- ½ cup buttermilk
- 1 teaspoon baking soda
- 2 eggs
- 1 teaspoon vanilla

Mix sugar and flour in a large bowl.

Melt margarine, cocoa and water in saucepan. Bring just to a boil and add to mixture in bowl. Mix baking soda into buttermilk. Add to flour mixture with remaining ingredients and blend.

Pour batter into lightly greased 15½x10½x1-inch jelly-roll pan and bake at 400 degrees for 20 minutes.

While cake is baking, prepare the frosting, which is a major part of the presentation.

FROSTING:
- 1 stick margarine
- 6 tablespoons milk
- 4 tablespoons cocoa
- 1 box (1 pound) confectioners' sugar
- 1 teaspoon vanilla
- 1 cup chopped nuts, optional

Melt margarine, milk and cocoa in saucepan. Remove from heat and blend in sugar and vanilla. Mix in nuts and spread on cake while cake and frosting are still warm. Cool; cut into squares.

Yield: About 15 squares 3x3½-inches.

— *Curious Cook's files*

Tres Leche Cake (Three Milk Cake)

Oct. 29, 2003

CAKE:
- 6 eggs, separated
- 2 cups sugar
- 2 cups flour
- 3 teaspoons baking powder
- ½ cup milk
- 2 teaspoons vanilla

SAUCE:
- 1 can (12 ounces) evaporated milk
- 1 can (14 ounces) sweetened condensed milk
- ½ pint whipping cream

FROSTING:
- 2 egg whites
- 2 tablespoons white corn syrup
- 1½ cups sugar
- 2 teaspoons vanilla
- Dash of salt
- 1/3 cup water

For cake: Beat egg whites until peaks form. Add sugar gradually. Add yolks; beat 3 minutes.

Combine flour and baking powder; add to egg mixture alternately with milk. Add vanilla.

Pour into well-greased 9x13-inch pan. Bake at 350 degrees for 30 to 40 minutes.

For sauce: Pour sauce ingredients into blender and blend until smooth. With toothpick, punch holes in warm cake just out of oven, then pour sauce over cake. Allow cake to cool in refrigerator before frosting.

For frosting: Mix all ingredients in top of double boiler. Cook for 7 to 10 minutes while beating constantly with electric mixer. Frost cake. Keep refrigerated.   — *C.M. of Galesburg*

Three Milk Cake

K.B. of East Moline offers an easier version of the Three Milk Cake. She writes:

"A friend gave me her recipe for Three Milk Cake. It's not detailed but is very good. This is what she gave me."

- 1 package (2-layer size) Betty Crocker French vanilla cake mix
- ½ cup half-and-half
- ½ cup evaporated milk
- ½ cup sweetened condensed milk
- Rum or other flavoring, as desired
- Whipped cream for topping

Prepare cake mix following package directions for 13x9-inch pan.

Bake cake as directed. While cake is cooling, mix and then boil together half-and-half, evaporated milk and condensed milk. Remove from heat and add rum or whatever flavoring you want to milks (no certain measurement).

Poke holes in cake and pour milk mixture over cake. Whip up some real whipping cream for top after cake is completely cooled. Keep cake refrigerated. — *K.B. of East Moline*

Three Milk Cake / Tres Leches Cake

Nov. 12, 2003

L.M. of Bettendorf was so fascinated by the recipe for Three Milk Cake recently featured in this column that she wanted to experiment a bit with one of the three milks. She explains:

"When I was visiting my daughter in Garland, Texas, my son-in-law brought home a cake from a Hispanic deli called Tres Leches Cake, which means Three Milk Cake in Spanish. It was delicious!

"We were trying to figure out the three milks and were sure that one of the ingredients was coconut milk. Not so. Like the lady who requested the recipe said, it contained evaporated milk, sweetened condensed milk and heavy cream.

"Now being not satisfied, I have purchased a can of light coconut milk available in the oriental section at your supermarket and will try to see how it works as one of the milks. I'm enclosing the recipe."

Well, dear cooks, true to her word, L.M. baked the Three Milk Cake, substituting light coconut milk for the heavy cream. Here's her report/opinion on that experimentation:

"I made the Three Milk Cake," she writes. "I used the light coconut milk instead of the 1 cup heavy cream. It was delicious!

"Now, the sweetened condensed milk does overpower the coconut taste. So for those who want coconut, some don't, I'd also use 1 teaspoon coconut flavoring instead of the almond flavor."

Here's the recipe submitted by L.M.:

1½ cups all-purpose flour
2 teaspoons baking powder
½ teaspoon salt
6 large eggs, separated
½ teaspoon cream of tartar
1½ cups granulated sugar
1/3 cup cold water
1 teaspoon vanilla extract
1 teaspoon almond extract
1 cup (8 ounces) heavy cream
1 can (14 ounces) sweetened condensed milk
1 small can (5 ounces) evaporated milk
2 teaspoons vanilla extract
Whipped cream, for frosting
Fresh fruits, for garnish

In a medium-sized bowl, whisk flour, baking powder and salt. Separate eggs. In a separate bowl, beat egg whites and cream of tartar until stiff. In another bowl, beat egg yolks until they are pale yellow and fluffy. Add sugar gradually and continue beating until mixture is very thick and falls from beaters in ribbons. Add the 1/3 cup cold water, 1 teaspoon vanilla extract and 1 teaspoon almond extract to the egg-yolk mixture. Then stir in dry ingredients. Gently whisk in beaten egg whites. Spoon batter in greased and floured 9x13-inch baking pan. Bake cake at 350 degrees for about 30 minutes or until toothpick inserted in the center comes out clean. Let cool in pan for 15 minutes. Using fork, poke holes all over top of cake. Mix the heavy cream, sweetened condensed milk and evaporated milk and 2 teaspoons vanilla. Pour slowly over top of cake, allowing milks to sink in. Refrigerate several hours before frosting with whipped cream. Decorate with fresh fruit on top of whipped cream.   *— L.M. of Bettendorf*

Very Berry Cheesecake Trifle

June 12, 2002

R.P. of East Moline reports that a friend was "kind enough to give me the recipe" for the red, white and blue dessert which R.P. recently requested in Curious Cook's column!

So R.P shares with other cooks, too.

"It's called Very Berry Cheesecake Trifle," R.P. adds. "And the recipe follows."

- 2 packages (8 ounces each) cream cheese, softened
- ¾ cup powdered sugar
- 1 teaspoon almond extract
- 1 container (8 ounces) frozen whipped topping, thawed
- 1 angel food cake (10½ ounces), cut in bite-size pieces
- 1 can (21 ounces) strawberry pie filling
- 1 can (21 ounces) blueberry pie filling

Beat together the cream cheese, powdered sugar and almond extract for at least 2 minutes. Add thawed whipped topping. Fold in angel food cake pieces.

Using a large glass bowl, spread strawberry pie filling on the bottom. Next put in the cream cheese mixture and top with blueberry pie filling. Chill. Serves about 20.

— *R.P. of East Moline*

Vinegar Pie

Aug. 7, 1996

- ¼ cup butter, softened
- 2 cups sugar
- ½ teaspoon cinnamon
- ½ teaspoon allspice
- ¼ teaspoon cloves
- 4 eggs, separated
- 3 tablespoons cider vinegar
- 1 cup seedless raisins
- Dash of salt
- Pastry for 9-inch single crust pie

Heat oven to 425 degrees. Cream butter and sugar; add spices and blend well. Beat in egg yolks until smooth and creamy. Add vinegar and beat again. Stir in raisins with wooden spoon.

Beat egg whites with dash of salt until stiff; then fold into vinegar mixture. Turn into pastry-lined pan.

Bake at 425 degrees for 15 minutes; then reduce heat to 300 degrees and bake 20 minutes longer or until top is nicely browned and center of filling is jelly-like. Cool on wire rack for 2 to 3 hours before cutting.

— *A.J.E. of Rock Island*

Feb. 16, 2000

White Chocolate Cake

Good news! Curious Cook has had the recipe for the White Chocolate Cake for years. This recipe was published in The Dispatch in 1969! Needless to say, it's a super-delicious cake, a dessert classic that's still welcome after 30 years!

¼ pound white chocolate
½ cup boiling water
1 cup butter or margarine
2 cups sugar
4 eggs, separated
1 teaspoon vanilla
2½ cups cake flour
1 teaspoon baking soda
1 cup buttermilk
1 cup chopped pecans or almonds
1 cup flaked coconut

Melt white chocolate in boiling water; cool. Cream together butter and sugar until fluffy. Mix in 4 egg yolks, one at a time, beating well after each addition. Add melted white chocolate and vanilla.

Sift together the cake flour and baking soda. Add to white chocolate mixture alternately with 1 cup buttermilk. DO NOT OVERMIX.

Beat 4 egg whites, but not too stiff, and fold into batter. Gently stir in chopped pecans or almonds and flaked coconut. Pour batter into three 9-inch cake pans which have been well greased and floured. Bake at 350 degrees for approximately 30 minutes until cake layers test done. Cool and frost.

White Chocolate Cake Frosting

1 cup evaporated milk
1 cup sugar
¼ cup butter or margarine
3 egg yolks, slightly beaten
1 teaspoon vanilla
1 can (1-1/3 cups) flaked coconut
1 to 1½ cups chopped pecans

Mix together the evaporated milk, sugar and butter; bring to a boil, stirring constantly. Remove from heat. Have ready the 3 slightly beaten egg yolks; blend (carefully) into cooked mixture in usual manner. Add vanilla. Return to heat. Cook, stirring, over low heat until thick, about 15 minutes. Remove from heat and add flaked coconut and chopped pecans. Beat frosting until fluffy and of spreading consistency.

Note: White Chocolate Cake may be completely frosted. Or spread the frosting between the layers, like a filling, and swirl it across the top to give the cake a torte-like appearance. — *The Dispatch, 1969*

White Texas Sheet Cake

March 8, 1995

Curious Cook received another version of the white cake from N.F.D. of Geneseo. She calls it "a delightful cake."

Here the White Texas Sheet Cake recipe:

- 1 cup butter or margarine
- 1 cup water
- 2 cups all-purpose flour
- 2 cups sugar
- 2 eggs, beaten
- ½ cup sour cream
- 1 teaspoon almond extract
- 1 teaspoon salt
- 1 teaspoon baking soda

FROSTING:
- ½ cup butter or margarine
- ¼ cup milk
- 4½ cups confectioners' sugar
- ½ teaspoon almond extract
- 1 cup chopped walnuts

For cake: Melt margarine in water. Bring to boil; remove from heat. Stir dry ingredients together. Add to water. Add sour cream and almond extract. Beat eggs and add to cake mix.

Pour batter into greased 15x10-inch jelly-roll pan. Bake at 375 degrees for about 20 minutes or until tests done. Ice cake while warm.

For frosting: Bring margarine and milk to a boil. Remove from heat and add sugar and extract. Mix well. Fold in walnuts and frost cake while warm.

— *N.F.D. of Geneseo*

Zucchini Chocolate Cake

Oct. 2, 1996

J.E. of Utica submitted this Zucchini Chocolate Cake recipe to answer the request of B.A.S. of Davenport:

½ cup butter
½ cup cooking oil
1¾ cups sugar
2 eggs
2 teaspoons vanilla
½ cup sour milk
2½ cups unsifted flour
4 tablespoons cocoa

½ teaspoon baking powder
2 teaspoons baking soda
½ teaspoon ground cinnamon
¼ teaspoon ground cloves
½ teaspoon salt
2 cups grated zucchini
¼ cup chocolate chips

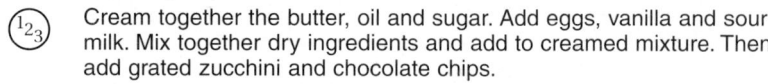

Cream together the butter, oil and sugar. Add eggs, vanilla and sour milk. Mix together dry ingredients and add to creamed mixture. Then add grated zucchini and chocolate chips.

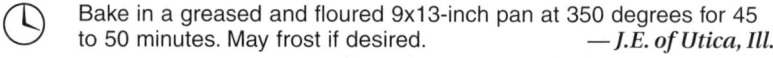

Bake in a greased and floured 9x13-inch pan at 350 degrees for 45 to 50 minutes. May frost if desired. — *J.E. of Utica, Ill.*

cookies & candies

sweet tasty morsels

Dear Curious Cook

'1932' Candy Apples

Dec. 18, 1996

"Recipe from 1932," reports Mrs. F.F.F. of Rock Island of her candied apples.

- 8 medium-size red apples
- 8 flat wooden skewers or spoons
- 2 cups granulated sugar
- 1 cup white corn syrup
- ½ cup water
- ¼ cup red cinnamon candies
- 10 drops red food coloring

Wash and dry apples; remove stems and insert skewers into stem ends.

Combine sugar, syrup and water in heavy 2-quart saucepan. Stirring constantly, cook over medium heat until mixture boils and sugar is dissolved. Then cook without stirring until temperature reaches 250 degrees or until small amount of syrup dropped into very cold water forms a ball which is hard enough to hold its shape yet plastic.

Add cinnamon candies and continue cooking to 285 degrees or until small amount of syrup dropped into very cold water separates into threads which are hard but not brittle. Remove from heat. Stir in red food coloring.

Hold each apple by skewer and quickly twirl in syrup, tilting pan to cover apple with syrup. Allow excess to drop off; then twirl to spread syrup smoothly over apple.

Place on a lightly buttered cookie sheet to cool. Store in a cool place. Serves 8.

— *Mrs. F.F.F. of Rock Island*

Alma's Old-Fashioned Sugar Cookies

June 2, 1999

B.M. of Geneseo shares her grandmother's cookie recipe with us. She writes:

"I enjoy your cooking columns in The Dispatch. A recent request from M.L. of Moline was for sugar cookies with the shortening cut in, like pie crust. Here's my grandmother's recipe, shared by my mother.

"They are not hard to assemble, and do not need to be refrigerated before rolling out. They are so good, I 'invent' occasions to make them for!"

4 cups flour
1½ cups sugar
1 cup butter or margarine
1 teaspoon baking soda

1 teaspoon hot water
2 eggs, beaten
4 tablespoons cream (or milk)

Sift together into a large bowl: 4 cups flour, 1½ cups sugar. Add 1 cup butter or margarine and blend like pastry.

Dissolve 1 teaspoon baking soda in 1 teaspoon hot water and stir into 2 beaten eggs. Stir in 4 tablespoons cream (or milk). Add to flour and butter mixture. Use your hands to knead the dough until well blended.

Dough does not need to be refrigerated. Roll out and cut into cookie shapes. (Use ½ flour and ½ sugar to "flour" the rolling pin and cutting board.) Bake on lightly greased cookie sheet at 375 degrees for 5 to 8 minutes. Makes 6 to 8 dozen.

Sugar the cookie tops before baking. Or, after cookies have cooled, frost with favorite frosting. — *B.M. of Geneseo*

Baked Caramel Corn

March 21, 2001

6 quarts popped popcorn
1 cup butter
2 cups firmly packed brown sugar

¼ cup corn syrup
1 teaspoon salt
½ teaspoon baking soda
1 teaspoon vanilla

Cook butter, brown sugar, corn syrup and salt; bring to boil, stirring constantly. Boil without stirring for 5 minutes. Remove from heat; stir in baking soda and vanilla.

Gradually pour mixture over popped popcorn; mix well. Turn into a roaster pan. Bake at 250 degrees for 1 hour, stirring every 15 minutes.

Remove from oven and cool completely. Break apart and store in tightly covered container. "Enjoy." — *M.I.L. of Orion*

Belgian Lukken

Jan. 14, 1998

"I've answered your readers' requests over the years. Now I need help," writes M.M.S. of Orion.

"I would like a cookie called Belgian Lukken made in a mold on top of stove. Part of ingredients: butter, flour, sugar white and brown, jigger of whiskey. Thank you very much." — *M.M.S. of Orion*

Curious Cook's Note: My treasured copy of the "Belgian Cook Book," published by the Center For Belgian Culture of Western Illinois, contains two recipes for Belgian Lukken. There could be no better source than this cookbook. The recipes, which were collected from area cooks, preserve Belgian food history in general and from our community in particular.

My copy of the "Belgian Cook Book" is dated 1976, but the book has been reprinted and still is available at the Center for Belgian Culture of Western Illinois, 712 18th Ave., Moline.

If you're interested, lukken irons also are available at the Belgian Culture Center.

Here is the Lukken recipe:

1 pound butter	2 teaspoons vanilla
1 cup brown sugar	2 ounces whiskey
1-1/3 cups white sugar	5 cups flour
2 eggs	

Stir butter until creamy. Add eggs, mix. Add brown and white sugar and mix well. Add vanilla and whiskey; mix well.

Add flour very gradually and keep mixing with wooden spoon.

Place in refrigerator for several hours or overnight for easier handling. You can, however, use mixture immediately.

Form dough into little balls, or if you use mixture immediately, spoon out, and place one at a time on a lukken iron. Brown each side for 5 to 10 seconds, turning iron and counting to yourself.

Place each baked lukken on wax paper on a flat surface until it is cool. Do not place on top of each other. The wafers are very fragile.

Can be kept several months in freezer.
   — *Contributed to the "Belgian Cook Book" by Mrs. Gentiel Sercu*

Black Walnut Cookies

Aug. 28, 1996

"These are very good cookies," writes L.V. of Atkinson, who is answering the recent request for black walnut cookies. "Hope this recipe is what your reader is looking for."

6 cups sifted, all-purpose flour
1 teaspoon salt
½ teaspoon baking soda
1 teaspoon cream of tartar
1¾ cups butter
2¼ cups firmly packed brown sugar
½ cup granulated sugar
2 eggs, lightly beaten
2 teaspoons vanilla
1½ cups black walnut meats
1½ cups shredded coconut, optional

Sift flour, measure, sift again with salt, baking soda and cream of tartar. Cream butter, adding sugars gradually. Beat until fluffy. Add eggs and vanilla.

Grind nuts and coconut together in blender; add to creamed mixture. Add sifted flour mixture; blend well. Chill dough slightly and then shape into four rolls about 2 inches in diameter. Wrap in wax paper. Chill.

Cut rolls into 1/8-inch thick slices and place on ungreased cookie sheet. Bake at 350 degrees for 10 to 12 minutes. Makes 8 to 9 dozen cookies.

— *L.V. of Atkinson*

Busy Day Drop Cookies

Dec. 11, 2002

R.H. of Davenport recently requested a recipe for Busy Day Drop Cookies but she was concerned the long-ago recipe might not be found. Not to worry!

The following note/recipe from C.S.H. of Bettendorf is the second response we've had to R.H.'s request for the recipe for cookies her mother baked years ago.

"I saw R.H.'s request for Busy Day Drop Cookies in The Leader," writes C.S.H. "I received this recipe from my mother-in-law in the early '70s when I was a newlywed, and thought it might be the one R.H. is looking for.

"Hope this is a help.:

½ cup shortening
1 cup brown sugar
1¾ cups flour
½ teaspoon baking powder
½ teaspoon baking soda

½ teaspoon salt
¼ cup buttermilk
1 egg
¾ cup chopped nuts
1 teaspoon vanilla

Thoroughly cream shortening and brown sugar.

Sift flour, baking powder, baking soda and salt together. Blend the buttermilk and egg and add alternately with the flour to the creamed shortening and sugar mixture. Stir in the vanilla and nuts.

Drop dough 3 inches apart on greased baking sheet. Bake at 350 degrees for 12 to 15 minutes. Makes about 3½ dozen cookies.

— *C.S.H. of Bettendorf*

Butterscotch Ground Raisin Cookies

Jan. 8, 1997

Cookie-baking surely isn't restricted to the holiday season. Home-baked cookies are all-year favorites. Today, in answer to a recent request, we have raisin cookie recipes for our readers. We'll start with K.M.H. of Geneseo:

"Saw in The Dispatch you wanted a recipe for Butterscotch Ground Raisin Cookies. Got this recipe from a friend who has passed on and these cookies are very good."

2/3 cup brown sugar
1 stick margarine or butter
1 egg, beaten
1 teaspoon vanilla
1-1/3 cups flour (see note)

1 teaspoon baking soda
½ teaspoon cream of tartar
½ cup nutmeats
½ cup ground raisins

Cream together the brown sugar and margarine; add beaten egg and vanilla and mix well. Mix flour, soda and cream of tartar together. Then add nutmeats and add to creamed mixture. Add ground raisins last. Mix well.

Shape dough into 1½-inch diameter, long rolls. Wrap in wax paper. Put in refrigerator overnight. Cut in thin slices and place on lightly greased cookie sheet.

Bake at 350 degrees for 8 to 10 minutes or until done. Cookies should be brown on edges.

Note: "If dough is too thin, add a little more flour. Some different brands make a difference." — *K.M.H. of Geneseo*

Aug. 16, 2000

California White Fudge

M.J.M. of Rock Island recently asked for a White Fudge recipe. Curious Cook searched the electronic library and found this one in the 1997 Quad-Cities Holiday Cookbook, which was published in November of that year by The Dispatch, The Rock Island Argus and The Leader.

- 2 cups sugar
- ¾ cup sour cream
- ½ cup margarine
- 1 package (12 ounces) white bark, chopped
- 1 jar (7 ounces) marshmallow cream
- ¾ cup chopped walnuts
- ¾ cup chopped dried apricots

In a heavy saucepan, combine sugar, sour cream and margarine. Bring to a full boil, stirring constantly. Continue boiling for 7 minutes over medium heat or to 234 degrees on candy thermometer, stirring constantly.

Remove from heat. Stir in white chocolate until melted. Add the apricots, nuts and marshmallow cream. Beat until well blended.

Pour mixture into a greased 9x13-inch pan. Cool at room temperature. Cut into squares.

— *From "Holiday Cookbook" 1997*

Feb. 6, 2002

Can't Fail Five-Minute Fudge

"I have written 'revised' on this recipe so I don't remember what I changed from the original recipe," admits E.S. of Moline. "Anyway, this fudge recipe works for me!"

- 2/3 cup (small can) undiluted evaporated milk
- 1¼ cups sugar
- ½ teaspoon salt
- 2 cups small marshmallows
- 1 cup chocolate chips
- 1 teaspoon vanilla
- 1/3 cup chopped nuts

Mix undiluted evaporated milk, sugar and salt in saucepan over low heat. Heat to boiling. Cook 5 minutes, stirring constantly. Remove from heat.

Add small marshmallows, chocolate chips, vanilla and chopped nuts. Stir 1 to 2 minutes or until marshmallows melt.

Pour into buttered 9-inch square pan. Cool; cut in squares.

— *E.S. of Moline*

Grandma's Fudge

Sept. 28, 1994

We'll start out on a sweet note today with a treasured fudge recipe from C.D. of Andalusia:

"I saw your request for fudge recipes. I am very sure you will be deluged with many recipes but I just had to send my grandma's recipe. The entire family looks forward to Christmas just for her fudge."

2/3 cup cocoa	1½ cups milk (whole milk)
3 cups sugar	¼ cup real butter
1/8 teaspoon salt	1 teaspoon vanilla

Thoroughly combine dry ingredients in heavy 4-quart saucepan. Stir in milk and bring to bubbly boil over medium heat. Boil WITHOUT STIRRING to 234 degrees soft-ball stage.

Remove from heat and add butter and vanilla. Cool to room temperature about 110 degress. Beat until fudge loses its gloss. Quickly spread in lightly buttered 8x8-inch pan. Cool thoroughly before cutting.
— *C.D. of Andalusia*

Non-Chocolate Fudge

April 7, 1999

M.L.H. of Moline sent this non-chocolate fudge recipe of her sister, B.W. of Rock Island, because "my sister can't have chocolate."

2 cups sugar	Dash of salt
¼ cup butter	1 teaspoon vanilla
½ cup milk	¼ cup peanut butter
¼ cup white corn syrup	

In a 1½-quart saucepan, combine sugar, butter, milk, corn syrup and salt; boil. Cook at a rolling boil for exactly 7 minutes. Remove from heat. Add vanilla and peanut butter. Beat until mixture loses its gloss. Pour into buttered 9-inch pan.
— *B.W. of Rock Island*

Old-Fashioned Fudge

Oct. 18, 2000

"In response to J.S. from DeWitt, asking for a good fudge recipe, I am submitting one that we've used in my family just about forever," writes A.J.E. of Rock Island. "In fact, it's the only one we've ever used.

"My mother, who lived until 95, and I, who am 71, have probably made it hundreds of times and its name tells the story — Old-Fashioned Fudge.

"The one important thing to remember is to always use 'pure cane sugar.' Some sugars are made from beets and using this just does not result in a good product.

"I hope this will help her. It results in a very creamy and delicious candy."

2 cups pure cane sugar
2/3 cup milk
¼ cup cocoa powder
1 tablespoon white corn syrup
1 tablespoon butter or margarine
1 teaspoon vanilla

Place first four ingredients — sugar, milk, cocoa and white corn syrup — in a heavy, 2-quart saucepan.

Cook over medium heat until a few drops placed in a small dish of cool water forms a soft ball which can be picked up with the fingers; or cook to soft-ball stage, 240 degrees on a candy thermometer.

Remove from heat and place pan in cold water in sink to cool. While pan is cooling, add vanilla and butter.

When bottom of pan feels cool to the touch, beat the fudge with a spoon until it loses its gloss or begins to feel it is getting thicker.

Pour into an 8-inch greased pan or glass dish. Cool (see note) and cut in squares. Nuts of your choice may be added before beating.

Note: When fudge is placed in dish to cool, it doesn't mean refrigerate. Just let set on kitchen counter until it is set.   — *A.J.E. of Rock Island*

Old-Fashioned Fudge

Nov. 1, 2000

V.N. of Davenport shares this fudge recipe and advice to answer the recent request from J.S. of DeWitt:

"I cut this out of the Moline paper years ago and it's very good. You just have to be sure you mix it very thoroughly before you cook it."

2 cups sugar	1 tablespoon butter
2 tablespoons cocoa	1 teaspoon vanilla
1 tablespoon white Karo syrup	Dash of salt
¾ cup milk	Nuts, if desired

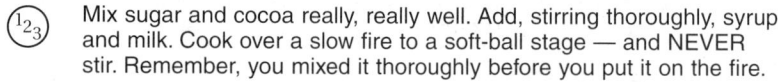
Mix sugar and cocoa really, really well. Add, stirring thoroughly, syrup and milk. Cook over a slow fire to a soft-ball stage — and NEVER stir. Remember, you mixed it thoroughly before you put it on the fire.

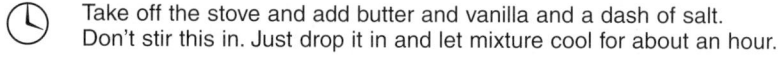
Take off the stove and add butter and vanilla and a dash of salt. Don't stir this in. Just drop it in and let mixture cool for about an hour.

Then beat by hand until the fudge loses its shine and keeps its shape when dropped by teaspoon on wax paper. Or pour into an 8-inch buttered pan. If you desire nuts, add just before you drop or pour it.
— *V.N. of Davenport*

Peanut Butter Fudge

Dec. 22, 1993

"Here is my mother's recipe for peanut butter fudge cooked on top of the stove," writes L.J.H. of Rock Island. "I hope it is what S.J.H. wants."

1 cup brown sugar	1 cup miniature marshmallows
1 cup white sugar	"plus a couple handfuls"
2/3 cup milk	1 cup crunchy peanut butter

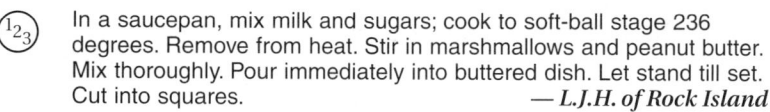
In a saucepan, mix milk and sugars; cook to soft-ball stage 236 degrees. Remove from heat. Stir in marshmallows and peanut butter. Mix thoroughly. Pour immediately into buttered dish. Let stand till set. Cut into squares.
— *L.J.H. of Rock Island*

Pumpkin Fudge

Jan. 25, 1995

1 cup sugar
¼ cup canned pumpkin
½ teaspoon pumpkin pie spice
½ teaspoon cornstarch

½ stick butter
1 small can (5-1/3 ounces) evaporated milk
1 teaspoon vanilla
1 cup chopped pecans

In a heavy saucepan, combine all ingredients except vanilla and pecans. Cook, stirring constantly, until mixture forms a soft ball when a small amount is dropped into cold water. Remove from heat; add vanilla and pecans.

Beat until thickened and pour into a buttered 8x8-inch pan. Cool and cut into squares.

Note: Do not overcook. If overcooked, add a few drops of milk and heat; then pour into pan. — *J.E. of Utica, Ill.*

Pumpkin Fudge

Jan. 25, 1995

3 cups sugar
¾ cup butter or margarine
1 can (5.33 ounces) or 2/3 cup evaporated milk
½ cup solid pack pumpkin
1 teaspoon pumpkin pie spice
1 package (12 ounces) butterscotch flavored morsels

1 jar (7 ounces) marshmallow creme
1 cup chopped almonds, toasted
1 teaspoon vanilla extract

In a heavy saucepan, combine sugar, butter, milk, pumpkin and spice. Bring to a boil, stirring constantly until mixture reaches 234 degrees on candy thermometer, about 10 minutes.

Remove from heat; stir in morsels. Add marshmallow creme, nuts and vanilla, mixing until well blended. Quickly pour into greased 13x9-inch baking pan, spreading just until even.

Cool at room temperature. Cut into squares. Store tightly wrapped in refrigerator. Yields 3 pounds candy. — *J.E. of Utica, Ill.*

recipes to remember forever

Ruth Lucas' Fudge

Date Unknown

A very, very special candy recipe has arrived on The Curious Cook's desk just in time for the holiday season when candy-making's so much a part of our cooking tradition.

A few weeks ago, N. K. of Moline wrote to The Curious Cook, pleading for the recipe for the "marvelous fudge" that was sold at Hafner's in Moline a number of years ago.

Every person in town seemed to remember that popular fudge, and gave Marti Lucas Jesuit of East Moline full credit.

Indeed, Marti Jesuit is the fudge-maker par excellence, following in the footsteps of her mother, the late Mrs. Clarence L. Lucas of Moline. Ruth Lucas was recognized throughout the area as the best candy-maker ever. Gift boxes of her special, homemade candies were coveted by her legions of friends.

After N. K.'s request for the recipe, Marti Jesuit said she had to practice making the fudge again. She sent a note along with the requested recipe:

"I'd love to share my mother's fudge recipe with you. But I had to practice a couple of times to make sure I hadn't forgotten.

"Tell your readers it's a kind of 'practice makes perfect fudge.' The secret is in the cooking to a soft-ball stage, as well as in the beating. The first few times I made it, I ended up with chocolate sauce!"

So, dear cooks, for your recipe collections, and for your candy trays during the holidays, here's Ruth Lucas' best fudge recipe, courtesy of her daughter, Marti Jesuit.

2 cups sugar   **2 heaping cook spoons cocoa**

Mix together. Then add:

1 tablespoon light corn syrup   **¾ cup milk**

Mix thoroughly. Cook slowly over low flame (never stir) to soft-ball stage.

Take off stove. Drop 1 teaspoon vanilla into pan along with 1 tablespoon butter. Don't stir. Let cool 1 to 2 hours.

Beat by hand after cooled until fudge loses its shine and will hold its shape when dropped by teaspoon into individual pieces onto wax paper.

Note: Marti Lucas Jesuit shares her mother's original recipe, which calls for "two heaping cook spoons of cocoa." Mrs. Jesuit says that should be equal to 4 heaping measuring tablespoons of cocoa.

— *Ruth Lucas of Moline*

Cherry Cookies

Oct. 17, 2001

From D.A.R. of Silvis: "I'm not sure that this Cherry Cookie recipe is the one D.A.H. of Moline wants, but I have had it for years. It is a soft drop cookie, nice and moist.

"For the holidays, I double the recipe and add chopped dates and candied pineapple. It makes a pretty cookie for cookie trays."

½ cup shortening
1 cup brown sugar
1 egg
¼ cup sour cream
1¾ cups flour

½ teaspoon salt
½ teaspoon soda
1 cup pecans (see note)
1 cup green and red candied cherries (see note)

Cream shortening and sugar. Add egg and beat well. Stir in sour cream.

Mix dry ingredients and add to first mixture. Fold in pecans and cherries.

Drop from a spoon onto ungreased cookie sheet and bake at 350 degrees F. for about 10 to 15 minutes, until light, golden brown. Check the timing carefully because ovens vary.

Note: D.R. says she cuts the cherries in halves or quarters and breaks the pecans in pieces.   — *D.R. of Silvis*

Chocolate Kisses

April 26, 1995

"I believe I have the recipe C.C. is looking for Chocolate Kisses," writes J.L.M. of Durant.

"Arlene Hering's grandmother, Mrs. Schult from Germany, made these and they looked like policemen's hats. The egg white is the leavening agent. C.C. had all the ingredients."

J.L.M. told Curious Cook that these Chocolate Kisses puff up and look a lot like chefs' hats as well as policemen's hats.

2 tablespoons cocoa   **2 egg whites, unbeaten**
3 cups powdered sugar, plus

Mix well cocoa and powdered sugar. Beat in egg whites, beating until mixture is very stiff. Add enough powdered sugar so dough can be handled.

Place powdered sugar on surface and pat or roll dough, which still will be a little sticky. Cut into small, 1½-inch rounds with a glass. With spatula, place on greased cookie sheet which has been lined with greased wax paper.

Bake at 325 degrees for 20 minutes. Then leave in oven another 10 minutes with heat turned off. Half a batch makes about 12 cut with 2-inch glass.   — *J.L.M. of Durant*

Chocolate-Oatmeal Cookies

Oct. 4, 1995

From M.W. of Bettendorf: "T.B. of Davenport wrote looking for a No-Cook Cookie Recipe. The following is cooked in a saucepan first, but might be what you're looking for.

"My kids always wanted to help in the cookie making process and this was one recipe they could handle beautifully. No hot cookie pans in and out of the oven."

2 cups sugar   **½ cup peanut butter (crunch**
4 tablespoons (¼ cup) cocoa   **style)**
½ cup milk   **3 cups quick-cooking oats**
1 stick (¼ pound) butter or   **1 teaspoon vanilla**
  margarine   **½ cup coconut, nuts or raisins**

In a heavy saucepan, combine sugar, cocoa, milk and butter; place on medium heat. Stir until sugar is dissolved and butter melted. Bring to a boil. Boil 1 minute; remove from heat. Quickly add peanut butter, oats, vanilla and coconut, nuts and/or raisins. Mix well and drop by teaspoonsful on wax paper. Cookie will become firm immediately.   — *M.W. of Bettendorf*

Chocolate Pinwheel Cookies

Sept. 23, 1998

E.S. of Davenport sent this recipe to answer a recent request of B.W. of Viola who wanted some old-fashioned cookie recipes which had been published in the newspaper many years ago.

1 square unsweetened chocolate, melted	½ cup butter or margarine, softened
1¼ cups flour	¾ cup sugar
¼ teaspoon baking powder	1 teaspoon vanilla
¼ teaspoon salt	1 egg

Melt chocolate over hot water and let cool. Mix flour, salt and baking powder; set aside.

Put sugar, butter, egg and vanilla in bowl and beat until light and fluffy. Add flour mixture and stir until blended.

Divide dough in half and add chocolate to one half. Wrap each half in plastic and chill several hours or until firm enough to roll.

Roll plain dough on lightly floured plastic wrap to form 16x6-inch rectangle. Repeat with chocolate dough. Invert chocolate dough on plain dough and peel off wrap. Press gently with rolling pin to seal together. Roll up like jelly-roll. Roll to make center the same diameter as ends, about 1½ inches. Wrap in plastic and chill overnight.

Slice dough 1/8-inch thick, put slices on a lightly greased cookie sheet. Bake at 350 degrees for 10 to 12 minutes until lightly brown. Remove at once to wire racks. Store airtight. Freezes well. Makes 7 to 8 dozen. — *E.S. of Davenport*

Chocolate Turtle Cookies

Sept. 3, 1997

"This is a recipe I've had for years," writes B.K.S. of Davenport.

2 eggs, beaten	1½ teaspoons vanilla
¾ cup sugar	½ teaspoon salt
5 tablespoons cocoa	1 cup flour
½ cup margarine	

Mix ingredients in order given. Drop by tablespoonsful onto greased waffle iron set at medium. Bake 1½ minutes. Remove with fork and frost.

FROSTING:

1 cup sugar	¼ cup milk
¼ cup margarine or shortening	½ cup semisweet chocolate chips

Boil sugar, shortening and milk until sugar dissolves completely. Remove from heat and beat in chocolate chips. Will thicken as it cools. — *B.K.S. of Davenport*

Mildred Poppy's Turtle Cookies

Aug. 20, 1997

As usual, our Quad-Cities area cooks have responded enthusiastically to the request for Waffle Cookies. Again, the variations are interesting.

"Several years ago, the mother of a good friend of mine won a prize for the best molded cookie catagory at the Henry County Homemakers Extension with her Turtle Cookies made on a waffle iron," D.F.G. of Cambridge writes in her note to Curious Cook.

"The lady's name was Mildred Poppy of Cambridge and I have in my scrap-cookbook a newspaper clipping picture of her with her prize and a plate of her cookies. She died a few years ago," D.F.G. adds.

¾ cup sugar
2 eggs
½ cup butter
1 cup flour

6 tablespoons cocoa
¼ teaspoon salt
1 teaspoon vanilla

Beat sugar and eggs. Melt butter and add to sugar mixture. Add remaining ingredients.

Set waffle iron on medium heat. Drop dough by teaspoon 2 inches apart on the waffle iron. Close lid and bake 30 to 45 seconds. Frost.

FROSTING:
6 tablespoons butter
6 tablespoons cream

1½ cups sugar
½ cup chocolate chips

Boil all together 30 seconds. Frost cookies when cool.

— *D.F.G. of Cambridge*

Turtle Cookies

Sept. 3, 1997

As we conclude our discussion of the waffle, or turtle cookies, this note came to Curious Cook from C.M. in Darien, Ill.:

"My mother in Geneseo frequently saves the Curious Cook section of The Dispatch for me. I recently saw J.H.'s request for Chocolate Waffle Cookies. I believe these are what she is looking for but are called Turtle Cookies.

"I found the recipe in the 1976 Andover Lutheran Church cookbook and have been making them for several years.

"The kids love them, and they can be frosted. I have written down a doubled recipe from what the original was."

1½ cups sugar
4 eggs
1 cup margarine
2 cups flour
½ cup cocoa
¼ teaspoon salt
1½ teaspoons vanilla

Beat sugar and eggs. Melt margarine and add to sugar mixture. Add rest of ingredients.

Drop by teaspoon on waffle iron on medium setting for about 45 seconds.

"I spray waffle iron once with a small amount of no-stick cooking spray. They are easy to remove using a fork." — *C.M. of Darien, Ill.*

Turtle or Waffle Cookies

April 19, 2000

"In August of 1997, in The Rock Island Argus, were a few recipes for the Turtle or Waffle Cookies," reports B.M.S. of Rock Island.

"The following recipe I used is very good. Made them for Christmas and church cookie sale."

Curious Cook checked the 1997 library files. Sure enough, the following recipe was there with attribution to the late Mildred Poppy who had won a prize for the best molded cookie category at Henry County Homemakers Extension with her Turtle Cookies made on a waffle iron.

And B.M.S. also tells us: "I was a teenage girl living in rural Cambridge. I knew this lady, Mildred Poppy, from Cambridge."

¾ cup sugar
3 eggs
½ cup butter
1 cup flour

6 tablespoons cocoa
¼ teaspoon salt
1 teaspoon vanilla

Beat sugar and eggs. Melt butter and add to sugar/egg mixture. Add remaining ingredients.

Set waffle iron on medium heat. Drop dough by teaspoons 2 inches apart on waffle iron. Close lid. Bake 30 to 45 seconds. Watch that iron isn't too hot.

FROSTING:

6 tablespoons butter
6 tablespoons cream

1½ cups sugar
½ cup chocolate chips

Combine ingredients in saucepan and boil 30 seconds. Frost cookies when cool.

Curious Cook's note: The 1997 recipe calls for 2 eggs while B.M.S. lists 3 eggs.
— *B.M.S. of Rock Island*

Club Cracker Cookies

Oct. 22, 1997

From B.L.P. of Keithsburg: "In the Oct. 1, 1997, paper M.K. of Moline was looking for a soda cracker cookie recipe. This one is Club Cracker Cookies a friend gave me years ago. It is very good."

- Whole club crackers
- 1 cup crushed graham crackers
- ½ cup white sugar
- ¾ cup brown sugar
- ½ cup margarine
- 1/3 cup milk
- 1 cup semi-sweet chocolate chips
- 2/3 cup peanut butter

Grease 9x13-inch pan with margarine. Line the bottom with whole crackers.

Put graham crackers, white sugar, brown sugar, ½ cup margarine and milk in cooking pan. Cook until mixture starts to boil. Watch carefully, cooking for 4 minutes, stirring all the time.

Spread mixture over club crackers. Add another layer of crackers. Melt chocolate chips and peanut butter in double boiler. Pour over crackers. Spread with knife. Refrigerate until cold. Cut into squares. Keep in refrigerator. — *B.L.P. of Keithsburg*

No-Bake Club Cracker Cookies

Oct. 22, 1997

"I hope this is the cracker recipe the ladies are looking for," writes W.B. of Davenport.

- Club crackers
- ¾ cup brown sugar
- ½ cup sugar
- 1/3 cup milk
- ½ cup margarine
- 1 cup crushed graham crackers
- ½ cup chocolate chips
- ½ cup butterscotch chips
- 2/3 cup peanut butter

Line a jelly-roll pan with whole crackers.

Combine sugars, milk, margarine and graham crackers; boil 5 minutes. Pour over crackers. Put another layer of crackers on top.

Combine chocolate and butterscotch chips and peanut butter and melt together. Spread mixture on top of crackers. — *W.B. of Davenport*

Soda Cracker Cookies

Oct. 22, 1997

"I don't know if these cookies are what M.K. of Moline is looking for, but these are delicious," promises S.I. of Rock Island.

"When I first saw this recipe I thought, 'How could a soda cracker make a good cookie?' I was wrong because these are easy to make and everyone loved them."

Put 24 soda crackers on a cookie sheet. Put in 400-degree oven for 1 minute. Mix 2 cups sugar and 1 cup margarine in a pan and boil 3 minutes. Put this mixture over the crackers and bake 5 minutes. Remove from oven and sprinkle with chocolate chips and nuts. Delicious.
— *S.I. of Rock Island*

Soda Cracker Cookies

Oct. 22, 1997

2 sticks butter **Club crackers**
1 cup sugar **Pecans or almonds**

Melt butter and sugar in saucepan until boiling. Lay club crackers in 13x18-inch glass, greased pan and pour sugar and butter mixture over crackers. Sprinkle with pecans or almonds.

Bake at 350 degrees about 12 minutes. Remove from pan while still warm.
— *C.P. of Moline*

Country Life Cookies

Oct. 4, 1995

From D.V.W. of Moline: "In your Sept. 6 column, T.B. of Davenport asks for a No Cook Chocolate Oatmeal Cookie. The recipe I have is 'No Bake,' but does require stove-top cooking.

"It's an older recipe — probably 35 to 40 years old. I loved it as a kid, but as an adult, it's a great summer time treat — easy to make, a no-oven-baking to heat up the kitchen. They're very tasty, too."

2 cups sugar
½ cup butter or margarine
½ cup milk
3 cups quick-cooking oatsl

6 tablespoons cocoa
1 cup coconut
1/8 teaspoon salt
1 teaspoon vanilla

In a medium saucepan, combine sugar, butter and milk. Bring to a boil over medium flame. Boil for 3 minutes. Remove from heat and add remaining ingredients. Mix well. Drop by teaspoons onto wax paper. Let cool. Make 4 dozen.

Note: For vanilla cookies, omit cocoa and substitute 1 cup of brown sugar for 1 cup of regular sugar. — *D.V.W. of Moline*

No Bake Cookies

Oct. 4, 1995

2 cups sugar
½ cup milk
¼ cup margarine
¼ cup peanut butter

¼ cup cocoa
3½ cups oats
¼ teaspoon salt
1 teaspoon vanilla

Combine and bring to a boil for 1 minute: sugar, milk, margarine, peanut butter and cocoa. Add oats, salt and vanilla; mix well. Drop by tablespoons onto wax paper. — *L.I.W. of Port Byron*

No Bake Cookies

Oct. 4, 1995

2 cups sugar
½ cup butter
½ cup milk
3 cups oats

1 cup coconut
6 teaspoons cocoa
1 teaspoon vanilla

Boil sugar, butter, and milk for 1 minute, hard-rolling boil. Remove from heat and add dry ingredients and vanilla. Stir until stiff enough to drop onto wax paper. — *B.C. of Hampton*

No Bake Fudge Cookies

Oct. 4, 1995

2 cups sugar
2 cups brown sugar
1 cup butter
1 cup milk
2 cups chocolate chips
4 cups quick-cooking oats
1 cups nuts
1 cup coconut

Bring sugars, butter and milk to a boil, boiling 2 minutes. Place remaining ingredients in a large bowl. Pour hot mixture over oat mixture. Mix well. Drop from a teaspoon onto wax paper. Makes 8 dozen.
— *B.C. of Hampton*

No-Bake Chocolate Oatmeal Cookies

Oct. 4, 1995

From B.K. of East Moline: "Enclosed is the No-Bake Oatmeal Cookie. I got the recipe about 30 years ago from a girlfriend.

"They are good to mail to service people as they do not crumble easily and do not need refrigeration."

2 cups sugar
½ cup milk
1 stick margarine
2 tablespoons cocoa
3 cups quick-cooking oats
1 teaspoon vanilla
¾ cup nuts, optional

Combine sugar, milk, margarine and cocoa; boil 1 minute. Add quick-cooking oats, vanilla and nuts. Stir well. Drop by teaspoon onto wax paper or foil.
— *B.K. of East Moline*

Sept. 27, 1995

Unbaked Chocolate Oatmeal Cookies

Quad-Cities area cooks always are so generous. Curious Cook has received many recipes for the unbaked chocolate cookies. And we'll be sharing endless variations with our readers. Cooks will be amazed at all the different versions. Here's a start.

From P.M.L. of Rock Island: "I saw that someone was asking for the recipe for Unbaked Chocolate Oatmeal Cookies. I have the original recipe that came out in 1943:

"You may be interested in the origins of this recipe. It was formulated by the British Ministry of Food during World War II. We did not have a cookie ration because there were no cookies to ration!! And we had very little to make them with ourselves.

"We had only 4 ounces of sugar and 4 ounces of butter for each person per week and so usually only people with large families could spare any for baking cookies.

"This recipe was a godsend because not only were we able to make a few cookies, but they tasted like the chocolate we couldn't get either. That is why the quantity is so small.

"I gave the recipe out to dozens of people when I came to this country and my children used to like to make them when they were quite small to take to school for treats.

"Nowadays most people also add nuts. Also, 1-ounce square of chocolate can be used for cocoa."

½ stick margarine
½ cup sugar
2 tablespoons milk
2 tablespoons cocoa
½ teaspoon vanilla
1 cup regular oats

Slowly melt the margarine, sugar and milk. Remove from heat. Stir in cocoa, vanilla and oats. Mix thoroughly. Drop in rough heaps on wax paper. Allow to set overnight. Makes about 25 or so.

— *P.M.L. of Rock Island*

recipes to remember forever

Crunchy Chocolate Chip Cookies

April 27, 1994

Curious Cook's readers are fantastic! D.C. of Mineral quickly came forward with the recipe for the Crunchy Chocolate Chip Cookies for D.H. of Bennett, Iowa.

D.H. had written to Curious Cook, lamenting, "I was going to bake the Crunchy Chocolate Chip Cookies that D.D. of Moline had sent in and found I had only the first eight ingredients. I had pasted the recipe in my scrapbook and the rest of the ingredients were on the other side."

Within a few days of publication of the plea from D.H. in the column, Curious Cook received this note and recipe from the Mineral cookie-baker. D.C. writes:

"Enclosed is the recipe for Crunchy Chocolate Chip Cookies I think D.H. is searching for. It is a favorite of mine! My college daughter bakes a batch for her roommates whenever she comes home. They love them.

"I have made cookie recipe copies from the original, so sent it to you."

Indeed, the recipe did come from Curious Cook's column but unfortunately there's no date on the clipping. However, there's a notation that these cookies are delicious but "really tender, really fragile."

The recipe, which the sender said she had used for years, was submitted in answer to a request for a crisp chocolate chip cookie. Here goes:

3½ cups sifted all-purpose flour
3 teaspoons baking soda
1 teaspoon salt
½ cup butter
½ cup margarine
1 cup packed brown sugar
1 cup granulated sugar
1 egg
1 tablespoon milk
2 teaspoons vanilla
1 cup vegetable oil
1 cup cornflakes
1 cup quick-cooking oats
1 package (12 ounces) chocolate chips
½ cup chopped pecans, optional

Sift flour, soda and salt onto wax paper. Preheat oven to 350 degrees.

Beat butter and margarine and brown and granulated sugars, egg, milk and vanilla in a bowl until well blended.

Stir in flour mixture, alternating with oil until mixture is thoroughly mixed. Stir in cornflakes, oats, chocolate chips and pecans if desired.

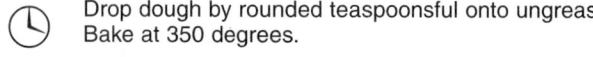

Drop dough by rounded teaspoonsful onto ungreased cookie sheet. Bake at 350 degrees.

D.D. (the original contributor of the recipe) says she doesn't time the cookies, just bakes them until they are "golden brown."

— *D.C. of Mineral, Ill.*

Double Chocolate and Pearl Cookies

Nov. 22, 2000

D.C. of Bettendorf answers another cookie request, this one from Mrs. G.A. of Moline.

In her request, Mrs. G.A. described the requested cookies as "chocolate cookies with chunks of white chocolate and nuts in them."

D.C. explains: "Though my title is not Chewy Chocolate Supreme Cookies, they are delicious and fit the criteria Mrs. G.A. of Moline outlined."

1 cup (2 sticks) margarine	1 teaspoon baking soda
¾ cup sugar	2/3 cup cocoa
½ cup firmly packed brown sugar	6 ounces semi-sweet chocolate chips
1 teaspoon vanilla	6 ounces premiere white chocolate, coarsely chopped
2 eggs	
2¼ cups flour	½ cup coarsely chopped walnuts optional

In large mixing bowl, beat margarine, sugars and vanilla until creamy. Add eggs, one at a time, beating well after each.

Mix flour, baking soda and cocoa in small bowl. Then gradually mix into previous mixture. Stir in chocolates and nuts.

Drop by rounded measuring tablespoons on ungreased cookie sheet and bake in preheated oven, 350 degrees for 12 minutes.

Remove from oven and allow to stand on baking sheet for 2 to 3 minutes. Remove to paper towels to cool thoroughly. — *D.C. of Bettendorf*

Easter Egg Nests

April 3, 1996

6 ounces white almond bark	Green food coloring
1-1/3 cups flaked coconut	1 bag tiny jelly beans
½ teaspoon milk	

In a small mixing bowl, stir together a few drops of food coloring and the milk. Add coconut and stir until it is evenly tinted; set aside.

Place almond bark in a 4-cup measure. Microwave until almond bark is melted, stirring often. Mix the tinted coconut with melted almond bark.

Place a spoonful of the mixture on wax paper, shaping into little nests. After they have cooled, place a few jelly beans in the center of each nest. Makes about 12 nests. — *E.M. of Moline*

Easter Egg Nests

April 3, 1996

From D.S. of East Moline: "In response to a request for Easter Egg Nests, I have enclosed a recipe I clipped from The Dispatch March 28, 1979, for Easter Egg Nests.

"There were a lot of Easter treats in that article. I have used some of them every year since."

5½ cups (14-ounce bag) flaked coconut

1 can (14 ounces) sweetened condensed milk

2 teaspoons vanilla

8 to 10 drops food coloring

Small jelly beans

Combine coconut, sweetened condensed milk, vanilla and food coloring, mixing well. Drop from teaspoon one-inch apart on well-greased baking sheets.

Bake at 350 degrees for 10 to 12 minutes. Remove at once from baking sheets, using moistened spatula. Place small jelly beans on cookies while still warm. Makes 5 dozen. — *D.S. of East Moline*

Nests

April 3, 1996

1 jar (7 ounces) marshmallow creme (2 cups)

¼ cup creamy peanut butter

2 tablespoons margarine or butter, melted

1 can (5 ounces) chow mein noodles (3 cups)

1 cup chopped M&M candies

Powdered sugar

Combine marshmallow creme, peanut butter and melted margarine; mix well. Add noodles and M&M candies. Drop on greased cookie sheet and form into nests. Put candies in nests for Easter.

Note: Sprinkle bottom inside of nests with powdered sugar, if desired. — *D.L. of Geneseo*

Egg White Cookies

Dec. 9, 1998

"I have, in past, baked and sold them," S.A.W. of Aledo tells us of her Egg White Cookies. "They are delicious.

"This came from The Rock Island Argus a number of years ago." She is answering a recent request of P.S. of Cambridge.

2 egg whites

1/8 teaspoon cream of tartar

¾ cup white sugar

1 teaspoon clear vanilla

1 bag (12 ounces) chocolate chips

Beat together egg whites and cream of tartar, gradually adding the sugar. Add vanilla. Beat until stiff. Fold in chocolate chips. Drop by teaspoonsful onto baking paper on cookie sheet. Bake at 300 degrees for 20 minutes. Makes 3½ dozen cookies. — *S.A.W. of Aledo*

Oct. 21, 1998
Heidi's Port Byron Chocolate Chip Cookies

H.H. of Port Byron responded quickly to the request for the recipe used for the chocolate chip cookies that were sold recently at a craft show in Port Byron. She writes:

"In regards to the request from the Dispatch on Sept. 30, 1998, from the Curious Cook section: These cookies were sold at the Port Byron Craft Show on Sept. 19."

They're now called Heidi's Port Byron Chocolate Chip Cookies and here's the recipe:

- 1 cup margarine
- 1 cup granulated sugar
- ¾ cup brown sugar
- 1½ teaspoons vanilla
- 2 medium-size eggs
- 3 cups flour
- 1½ teaspoons baking soda
- 1 teaspoon salt
- 1 cup chocolate chips

Cream margarine and gradually add sugars. Cream until light and fluffy.

Add eggs and vanilla gradually. Cream until light and fluffy.

Stir together flour, baking soda and salt. Add gradually to creamed mixture, blending after each addition. Stir in chocolate chips.

Drop on ungreased baking sheet with a No. 20 dipper. The dipper is an ice cream scooper. Press cookies slightly down.

Bake in a preheated oven, 375 degrees, for approximately 8 to 10 minutes. Let cookies set on cookie sheet a minute or so after removing from oven. "Eat and enjoy!" — *H.H. of Port Byron*

Holiday Fruit Drops

Oct. 17, 2001

From M.M.K. of Geneseo: "I think I can help D.A.H. of Moline with the soft drop cookie with maraschino cherries and nuts.

"The flavor of these cookies is wonderful and they are so pretty on a tray of assorted cookies for the holidays.

"I got the recipe from my husband's aunt in NW Iowa, 28 years ago."

- **1 cup shortening**
- **2 cups brown sugar**
- **2 eggs**
- **½ cup buttermilk or soured milk**
- **3½ cups flour**
- **1 teaspoon baking soda**
- **1 teaspoon salt**
- **1½ cups broken pecans**
- **2 cups candied cherries, halved**
- **2 cups cut-up dates**
- **Pecan halves**

Cream shortening, sugar and eggs. Stir in buttermilk. Blend dry ingredients; then stir into creamed mixture. Add broken pecans, cherries and dates. Chill 1 hour.

Drop rounded teaspoon of dough 2 inches apart on lightly greased baking sheet. Place pecan half on each cookie.

Bake at 400 degrees for 8 to 10 minutes, until almost no imprint remains when touched lightly.

Makes 8 dozen cookies. Store in tight container. — *M.M.K. of Geneseo*

Huxley Kringla

Sept. 4, 1996

A recent request from a reader for "Wonderful Unknowns" certainly stirred "wonderful" memories for other readers.

Curious Cook will share those memories, and recipes, with you today. The "Wonderful Unknowns" have been identified as Kringla, a Norwegian cookie!

M.M.H. of Geneseo sent Curious Cook a postcard to tell us that the "Wonderful Unknowns" are Norwegian cookies. "We lived in Huxley, Iowa, where our dear Norwegian babysitter brought Kringla to our children. Thanks for the memories!"

Curious Cook then called the Geneseo cook to ask for that recipe. M.M.H. responded with two recipes. (See one recipe below.) And not only that! "I wanted to make both recipes before I mailed them to you," she wrote. "It brought back many good memories."

Curious Cook thinks our area cooks are the greatest and M.M.H. is a perfect example of how generous they are in sharing recipes and advice.

"Both these recipes from my Huxley, Iowa, friends are great," M.M.H. adds. "It is a soft cookie and delicious. Some people put butter on them before they eat them. We like them just the way they are from the oven.

"Thanks for the nudge to make Kringla again," she adds. And Curious Cook thanks M.M.H. for the extra effort!

1 cup sugar	**3 cups flour**
½ cup margarine	**Dash of salt**
1 egg	**2½ teaspoons baking powder**
1 cup buttermilk	**1 teaspoon vanilla**
1 teaspoon soda	

Cream sugar, margarine and egg. Add buttermilk and soda; mix. Add the dry ingredients: flour, salt and baking powder. Continue mixing. Add vanilla and mix. Refrigerate overnight in covered bowl.

To shape, use a floured pastry cloth. "I use a cookie scoop to get a more uniform amount of dough. The Norwegian grandma would say 'about the size of a walnut.' "

Roll into rods about ½-inch thick and 8 to 10-inches long. Place each in the shape of a figure 8 on an ungreased baking sheet. Bake at 400 degrees for 8 to 10 minutes, only until lightly browned.

Note: M.M.H. says, "In my oven, I found 375 degrees for 8 minutes worked best for both recipes." — *M.M.H. of Geneseo*

Kringla

Sept. 4, 1996

B.W. of Rock Island very kindly sent a note to Curious Cook telling her that the "Wonderful Unknowns" surely must be Kringla, "a Norwegian treat served with coffee."

B.W. tipped us off that Jean Carlson of Rock Island "serves these at our church quite often."

So we quickly contacted Mrs. Carlson, who kindly shares her recipe, which she says came from her mother. And yes, she does bake Kringla to serve at First Lutheran Church in Rock Island.

Mrs. Carlson notes that homebakers will need to experiment a bit when making these cookies, also sometimes called rolls. "They are good with coffee," she says. Here's her recipe:

2 cups sugar	4 or 5 cups flour
1 large tablespoon margarine	1 rounded teaspoon baking powder
2 eggs	
1 cup commercial sour cream	1 teaspoon nutmeg
1 teaspoon baking soda	¼ teaspoon salt
	2 cups milk

Cream together the sugar and margarine; add the eggs and beat well. Mix baking soda into sour cream and add to creamed mixture.

Combine flour, baking powder, nutmeg and salt; mix well. Alternately add flour mixture and milk to creamed mixture. Chill in refrigerator. Can be stored overnight. Dough will be soft.

On a floured surface, take pieces of dough, roll out until about the size of your ring finger. Bring two ends together; twist together to form into a figure 8. You can make Kringla any size you wish, Mrs. Carlson points out.

Bake on ungreased cookie sheet for about 10 minutes at 400 degrees. Will still be light on top, but bottom should be brownish not dark brown. Check on the bottom. You want them to be light in color on top.
— *Jean Carlson of Rock Island*

Junior High Snicker Doodles

Nov. 8, 1995

Area cooks have been most generous in sharing their recipes for the popular Snickerdoodle cookies.

Most of the recipes are identical, or at least similar, so we'll bring you a sampling from the mail bag. Curious Cook thanks all who responded to those requests. It's a joy to open the mail.

The following note and recipe — one of the first we received — came from a junior high school student. It will brighten your day, dear cooks, just as it did mine. It's from J.B.F. of Rock Island:

"I am a seventh-grade student at Washington Junior High School in Rock Island. I just completed Mrs. Lundholm's Home Economics class.

"In class, we baked the attached recipe for Snicker Doodles — as requested by S.C. of Bettendorf. They were great! My mom loves your column!"

Cream the following ingredients together in a large mixing bowl using portable electric mixer:

½ **cup shortening**   1 **egg**
¾ **cup sugar**

Sift and stir in the following ingredients:

1¼ **cups plus 2 tablespoons flour**   ¼ **teaspoon salt**
1 **teaspoon cream of tartar**   ½ **teaspoon baking soda**

Blend well. Roll into balls the size of walnuts. You should have between 2 dozen and 30 balls. Preheat oven to 375 degrees. Mix together:

1 **tablespoon sugar**   1 **teaspoon cinnamon**

Roll balls in cinnamon-sugar mixture. Place about 2 inches apart on ungreased cookie sheet. Bake at 375 degrees for 8 to 10 minutes until lightly browned but still soft.   — *J.B.F. of Rock Island*

recipes to remember forever

Lemon Whippersnappers

Nov. 20, 2002

"Here's an easy cookie recipe using cake mix," e-mails M.T. of Cambridge to answer a request. "It's quick, easy and can be varied depending on what flavor of cake mix one wants to use.

"I've used chocolate, strawberry and gingerbread mixes and all are good."

1 package lemon cake mix, or other flavor

2 cups frozen whipped topping, thawed

1 egg

Powdered sugar

Mix cake mix (dry), topping and egg. Drop by teaspoon into powdered sugar. Coat and place 1½ inches apart on greased cookie sheet.

Bake at 350 degrees for 12 to 15 minutes, until firm.

— *M.T. of Cambridge*

Macadamia Cookies

Nov. 26, 1997

From N.D. of Rock Island: "This is for F.L. of East Moline who is looking for cookie recipes using macadamia nuts." N.D. says this recipe is her own adaptation of another cookie recipe. "Hope they work for her! My kids and husband love them."

- 1 cup shortening
- 2 cups sugar
- 3 eggs
- ½ teaspoon vanilla
- 3 cups flour
- 1 tablespoon baking powder
- ¾ teaspoon salt
- 6 tablespoons milk
- 1 cup chopped macadamia nuts
- 1 package (12 ounces) white chocolate chips

Cream shortening and sugar together. Add eggs and vanilla and beat well.

Mix together dry ingredients and add to creamed mixture. Add milk. Stir in nuts and white chocolate chips. Chill for 1 to 2 hours. Shape into 1¼ inch balls. Place 2½ inches apart on lightly greased baking sheet.

Bake at 375 degrees for 11 to 13 minutes or until lightly browned, do not overbake. "I bake them for 12 minutes on my Air-Bake sheets." Cool 1 minute on pan before removing to a wire rack. Makes 5½ dozen cookies.
— *N.D. of Rock Island*

Mashed Potato Candy Basic Recipe

Dec. 27, 1995

"This recipe was given to me by a co-worker at a nursing home," M.E.R. of Andover tells us.

- ¾ cup cold mashed potatoes
- 4 cups confectioners' sugar
- 4 cups shredded coconut
- 1½ teaspoons vanilla
- ½ teaspoon salt
- 8 squares baking chocolate

Mix potatoes and confectioners' sugar. Stir in coconut, vanilla and salt; mix well. Press mixture into large pan jelly-roll pan so that candy will be about ½-inch thick.

Melt chocolate over hot water; do not allow to boil. Pour chocolate on top of candy. Cool; cut in squares.
— *M.E.R. of Andover*

Million Dollar Cookies

Sept.15, 1993

4 cups sifted flour
1 teaspoon salt
1 teaspoon baking soda
2 cups shortening
1 cup white sugar

1 cup firmly packed brown sugar
2 eggs, unbeaten
2 teaspoons vanilla
1 cup nuts
Sugar, for rolling cookies

Sift dry ingredients together. Cream shortening, 1 cup white sugar, brown sugar, eggs and vanilla. Add dry ingredients and nuts.

Form in balls the size of walnuts; roll in sugar. Do not press down. Place on ungreased cookie sheet and bake at 375 degrees for 10-12 minutes. "A real crisp cookie."
— *M.L.M. of Viola*

Million Dollar Cookies

Sept. 15, 1993

1 cup brown sugar
1 cup white sugar
¾ cup oil
1 cup margarine
1 egg, beaten
1 teaspoon vanilla
3½ cups flour

1 teaspoon baking soda
1 teaspoon cream of tartar
1 teaspoon salt
3 cups Rice Krispies
1 cup uncooked oats
½ cup Grape-Nuts
1 package butterscotch chips

Mix sugars, oil and margarine; add beaten egg and vanilla. Sift flour, baking soda, cream of tartar and salt; add to first mixture. Fold in cereals and butterscotch chips.

Roll dough in balls and place on ungreased cookie sheet. Flatten with sugared glass. Bake at 350 degrees for 10-15 minutes.
— *M.L.M. of Viola*

Million-Dollar Sugar Cookies

Sept. 15, 1993

"Hope the enclosed recipe for Million-Dollar Sugar Cookies will help L.G.G. of Davenport. Have received many compliments through the years for the recipe," writes M.D.M. of Rock Island.

1 cup shortening	½ teaspoon baking soda
½ cup granulated sugar	½ teaspoon salt
½ cup brown sugar	½ cup chopped nuts
1 teaspoon vanilla	Granulated sugar, to roll cookies in
1 egg	
2 cups flour	Pecan halves or candied cherries, if desired

Cream shortening, ½ cup granulated sugar and brown sugar together; add vanilla and egg, beating well.

Sift dry ingredients together and add, along with chopped nuts, to creamed mixture. Form balls the size of walnuts and roll in granulated sugar.

Place on ungreased cookie sheets and press flat with bottom of a tumbler. Dip tumbler in sugar occasionally to keep it from sticking. Decorate with pecans and cherries if you like.

Bake at 350 degrees for 10 minutes or until edges are lightly browned. Makes about 3 dozen.

Note: D.L.M. of Moline sent in the same recipe but gives baking time as 12 to 15 minutes at 350 degrees. — *M.D.M. of Rock Island, D.L.M. of Moline*

Neopolitan Cookies

Sept. 23, 1998

- 2 cups sifted flour
- 1½ teaspoons baking powder
- ½ teaspoon salt
- 2/3 cup butter or margarine, softened
- 1 cup sugar
- 1 egg
- 1 teaspoon vanilla
- 1 square unsweetened chocolate, melted
- ¼ cup finely chopped candied red cherries
- 1 or 2 drops of red food coloring, optional
- ¼ cup finely chopped walnuts or pecans

Sift flour with baking powder and salt; set aside. In large bowl, with wooden spoon or portable electric mixer at medium speed, beat butter until light. Gradually beat in sugar. Add egg and vanilla. Continue beating until mixture is very light and fluffy.

At low speed, beat in half the flour mixture. Mix in rest with hands to form a stiff dough. Divide dough in thirds and place each in separate bowl. Add chocolate to one part, add cherries and food coloring to the second, chopped nuts to third. Blend each one well.

Turn dough separately on lightly floured surface. Divide dough in half with hands. Shape each half into a roll 7-inches long. Flatten each roll to width of 2 inches. Stack a nut layer, a chocolate and a cherry layer. Press lightly together. Wrap each in wax paper or foil. Refrigerate until firm, several hours or overnight. Preheat oven to 375 degrees.

With sharp knife cut into 1/8-inch slices as desired for baking at one time. Rewrap rest of roll and refrigerate.

Place slices 2 inches apart on ungreased cookie sheet. Bake at 375 degrees for 8 to 10 minutes until lightly browned. Remove to wire rack and cool completely. Makes about 8 dozen in all. — *E.S. of Davenport*

Pennsylvania Dutch Sugar Cakes

Oct. 28, 1998

Quad-Cities area cooks have favorite homemade sugar cookies and they're willing to share treasured recipes.

After the request for soft sugar cookies was published, we received an interesting variety of recipes. We'll share them with our readers today and next week. We'll start with L.L. of Port Byron:

L.L. has wonderful memories of her mother's sugar cookies. She shares the recipe with us to answer the request for soft sugar cookies.

"Christmas meant a batch of Mother's sugar cookies," L.L. writes. "Everyone loved them. So on the anniversary of her death, we make these cookies and ship them to her family all over the United States. Enjoy."

4 cups white sugar
4 eggs
¾ cup butter or margarine
¾ cup lard or Crisco
2 teaspoons baking powder
2 teaspoons baking soda
2 teaspoons vanilla
½ teaspoon salt
2 cups buttermilk
About 7½ cups unsifted flour, 8 cups sifted

Beat together all ingredients except the flour until smooth. This can be done with mixer.

Then, by hand, add flour in about two or three additions. Mix until smooth.

Drop by tablespoonsful on greased cookie sheet. Sprinkle with additional sugar and bake at 350 degrees for about 15 minutes or until done.

Makes about 4 dozen cookies, about 4 inches across.

— *L.L. of Port Byron*

Pumpkin Bars

Nov. 24, 1993

D.D. of Moline quickly came up with the year of the edition of our Holiday Cookbook which included an easy recipe for Pumpkin Bars. 'Twas 1989!

L.S. of Moline requested the recipe, which she had clipped from a Holiday Cookbook and then lost during a move. L.S. recalled that she used a food processor and poured the filling into a cake pan.

O.D. of East Moline also sent a recipe for Pumpkin Bars, also from the 1989 Holiday Cookbook. One of the recipes calls for mixing the filling in a blender; the other directs the cook to mix the ingredients in a large bowl and "beat well."

Curious Cook looked up a 1989 issue and found the recipe:

1 cup flour	2 eggs
½ cup oats	¾ cup white sugar
½ cup packed brown sugar	1 teaspoon cinnamon
½ cup margarine	1 teaspoon pumpkin pie spice
1 can (16 ounces) pumpkin	½ cup chopped nuts
1 can (12 ounces) evaporated milk	½ cup packed brown sugar
	2 tablespoons margarine

Mix flour, oats, ½ cup brown sugar and ½ cup margarine until crumbly. Press mixture into an ungreased 9x13x2-inch pan. Bake at 350 degrees for 15 minutes.

Place in blender: Pumpkin, evaporated milk, eggs, white sugar, cinnamon and pumpkin pie spice. Mix well. Pour mixture over crust. Bake at 350 degrees for 20 minutes.

Mix chopped nuts, ½ cup brown sugar and 2 tablespoons margarine. Sprinkle over pumpkin filling and bake at 350 degrees for 15 to 20 minutes longer, or until set. Serve with whipped topping.

Note: The recipe from O.D. of East Moline calls for 1 teaspoon ground cinnamon, ½ teaspoon ground ginger and ¼ teaspoon ground cloves instead of the pumpkin pie spice. — *1989 Holiday Cookbook*

Rosettes

Dec. 18, 1996

"Here I am to the rescue again," writes J.C. of Geneseo. "You asked for a recipe for Rosettes. I make them often and especially during the holidays.

"Where they suggest 1 tablespoon lemon extract, you can substitute other flavorings. My husband and I like anise. As he is Italian, this is a family tradition during Christmas."

2 eggs	½ teaspoon salt
2 teaspoons sugar	1 tablespoon lemon extract
1 cup milk	About 2½ quarts salad oil
1 cup all-purpose flour	Confectioners' sugar

Beat 2 eggs slightly. Add 2 teaspoons sugar; then add 1 cup milk.

Sift 1 cup all-purpose flour and ½ teaspoon salt; stir into the egg mixture and beat until smooth. Should be about the consistency of heavy cream. Add 1 tablespoon lemon extract.

Put enough salad oil — about 2½ quarts — in a 5-quart deep fryer to fill it about 2/3 full and heat to 400 degrees. Dip rosette forms into the hot oil to heat them; drain excess oil on paper towels.

Dip heated forms into the batter to not more than ¾ of their depth. If only a thin layer of batter adheres to the forms, dip them again until a smooth layer adheres.

Plunge batter-coated forms into hot oil and cook until active bubbling ceases. With fork, ease rosettes off forms and onto paper towels to drain. While still warm, dip in confectioners' sugar or sift sugar over them. Makes 6 dozen.

Note: "Where they suggest 1 tablespoon lemon extract, you can substitute other flavorings."   *— J.C. of Geneseo*

Sister Marcellina's Applesauce Bars

April 23, 1997

"Not too long ago, in one of the local papers, was a recipe from a nun for an Applesauce Cake. It was made in a jelly-roll pan and frosted with a cream cheese frosting. Thank you for your help." — *P.M. of Coal Valley*

Curious Cook's note: Our food section cover on Aug. 21, 1996, featured unfrosted cakes, including the following recipe for Sister Marcellina's Applesauce Bars.

The recipe was given to me years ago by my cousin, the late Sister Francis Clare McCarthy of the Order of St. Francis of the Immaculate Conception Convent in Peoria.

Although this recipe does not call for cream cheese frosting, it certainly would be complementary to these delicious bars.

2 cups all-purpose flour
1 teaspoon baking soda
¾ teaspoon cinnamon
¼ teaspoon nutmeg
½ cup margarine
1 cup white sugar

2 eggs
1 teaspoon vanilla
1½ cups applesauce
1 cup raisins
1 cup chopped nuts, optional

Combine flour, baking soda, cinnamon and nutmeg; mix well. Cream together the margarine and sugar; add eggs and mix well. Stir in vanilla, applesauce and raisins. Pour into greased 15x10x1-inch pan.

Bake at 350 degrees for 25 minutes or until bars test done. Cool; cut into 2½x1-inch pieces. Sprinkle with powdered sugar, if desired. Makes 56 bars.
— *From Curious Cook's files*

Soft Chocolate Chip Cookies

Jan. 25, 1995

1 cup all-purpose flour
½ cup cake flour
½ teaspoon baking powder
¼ teaspoon salt
½ cup (1 stick) unsalted butter, softened
½ cup packed dark brown sugar
½ cup granulated sugar
1 large egg
2 tablespoons whole milk
1 teaspoon vanilla extract pure
1 cup semisweet morsels
½ cup chopped walnuts

Heat oven to 375 degrees. Have greased baking sheets ready. Stir together both flours, baking powder and salt; set aside.

Beat together butter and sugar with an electric mixer on high speed until light, 2 minutes. Add the egg, milk and vanilla and beat 1 minute. Stop the mixer and add dry ingredients. Mix just until combined. Fold in the semi-sweet morsels and nuts.

Using a ¼ cup measure, scoop dough onto baking sheet, spreading them 2 inches apart. Bake at 375 degrees until cookies are browned and just set, 12 to 15 minutes. Transfer to a wire rack and cool completely. Store in an air-tight container. Yield: 12 large cookies. — *J.E. of Utica*

Soft Sugar Cookies

Oct. 28, 1998

"These are delectable and soft!" promises Mrs. I.J.A. of Reynolds.

"I have a sister-in-law in a nursing home and am sorry I can't keep more of these her way. She loves them and it's our favorite too."

1¼ cups margarine
1 cup sugar
2 eggs
1 teaspoon vanilla
3 tablespoons milk
3 cups all-purpose flour
1 teaspoon cream of tartar
½ teaspoon baking soda
¼ teaspoon salt

Beat margarine and sugar together until fluffy. Beat in eggs, vanilla, milk. Beat until just mixed. Add flour, cream of tartar, baking soda and salt; beat until just mixed.

Drop dough by teaspoonful onto greased sheet. Bake at 375 degrees for 9 to 11 minutes, only until golden edges. — *Mrs. I.J.A. of Reynolds*

Soft Sugar Cookies

Oct. 28, 1998

"I read your article from Curious Cook about wanting soft sugar cookies. Hope you will enjoy this cookie recipe."

2 sticks margarine	2 teaspoons vanilla
2 cups sugar	5 cups flour
2 eggs	2 teaspoons soda
1 cup salad oil	2 teaspoons cream of tartar
¼ teaspoon salt	

Combine margarine, sugar and eggs. Add oil, salt and vanilla. Combine flour, soda and cream of tartar and add to first mixture.

Form dough into balls 2 inches in diameter. Roll in sugar and flatten on an ungreased cookie sheet. Bake at 350 degrees for 10 minutes. — *M.N. of Colona*

Sorghum Cookies

Dec. 15, 1999

B.D. of Cambridge shares a sorghum recipe for cookies to answer the request of J.R. of New Boston.

B.D. writes: "This recipe took a blue ribbon award at the Iowa State Fair 4-H Division in 1976."

1½ cups shortening	4 teaspoons baking soda
1 cup brown sugar	½ teaspoon salt
2 eggs	1 teaspoon cloves
1 cup sorghum	2 teaspoons cinnamon
5 cups flour	2 teaspoons ginger

Mix shortening, brown sugar, eggs and sorghum. Sift dry ingredients and add to sorghum mixture. Chill dough. Roll dough in balls. Bake on greased cookie sheet at 375 degrees for 9 to 10 minutes. Makes more than 100 cookies. — *B.D. of Cambridge*

Sponge or Foam Candy

March 30, 1994

"I have never answered a request in your column before but when there was a request for FOAM CANDY which is also called SPONGE CANDY AND ANGEL FOAM, which is my favorite of all candy, I just couldn't resist," admits M.S. of Rock Island in her letter to Curious Cook.

"It is so much my favorite, that I don't dare make it unless I have a place to take it. I would eat every single piece if I made a batch and didn't get it out of the house. Anyway here is my recipe."

1 cup sugar
1 cup dark corn syrup
1 tablespoon vinegar, white or cider

1 tablespoon baking soda (make sure this is fresh)
Dark Chocolate Melts

Prepare a 9x9x2-inch pan by buttering it lightly.

Combine sugar, corn syrup and vinegar in a heavy saucepan, at least 3-quart size.

Cook over medium heat, stirring until the sugar dissolves. Continue cooking without stirring, to 300 degrees on a candy thermometer or until a small amount of the mixture dropped into cold water becomes very brittle.

Remove from the heat and quickly stir in the soda, mixing well. Pour into lightly buttered 9x9x2-inch pan. DO NOT SPREAD — the candy will spread itself as it "grows." Cool and then break into pieces.

Dip pieces into the Dark Chocolate Melts that you have melted over warm not boiling water in double boiler. Place on wax paper to cool. Yield is 1 pound. — *M.S. of Rock Island*

Unbaked Chocolate Macaroons

Sept. 27, 1995

M.M. of Moline sent a recipe and good advice.

"My kids call these 'Grandmother's Cookies' because she could prepare them so quickly when we came to visit her in Nevada, Iowa. I still make them occasionally and the cookies go fast when they and their children are around."

2 cups sugar	1 teaspoon vanilla
½ cup margarine	3 cups quick-cooking oats
½ cup milk	1 cup coconut, optional
6 tablespoons cocoa	½ cup nutmeats, chopped, optional
½ teaspoon salt	

Mix sugar, margarine, milk, cocoa and salt; bring to full boil and cook 2 minutes. Mix in vanilla and oats; add coconut and nutmeats and mix. "Do not mix too long, to prevent unnecessary cooling." Drop by teaspoonful on wax paper or roll into balls.

"Making the cookies — dropping by teaspoonful or forming balls — separate cookies must be done quickly. The mixture loses its gloss and becomes dry and hard to make stick together.

"Could possibly be patted down into a pan and cut with knife to form individual squares. I haven't tried that." — *M.M. of Moline*

Waffle Cookies

Aug. 20, 1997

"I have made these for years and my family loves them," J.J. of Tampico tells us. "Very easy. It calls for baking chocolate, but I always use the Choco-Bake, which doesn't have to be melted, just mixed with the shortening."

4 squares baking chocolate	1½ cups sugar
2/3 cup margarine	2 cups flour
4 eggs, beaten	1½ teaspoons vanilla

Melt chocolate in margarine and set aside. Mix eggs, sugar, flour and vanilla. Combine with chocolate mixture. Drop by teaspoons on hot waffle iron. Bake about 1 minute until done. Frost when cool.

— *J.J. of Tampico*

Waffle Iron Cookies

Aug. 20, 1997

Two Aledo cooks sent in this cookie recipe.

From H.J.M. of Aledo: "Here is a recipe for waffle iron cookies. My daughter gave me the recipe years ago, but don't know where she got it."

From K.S. of Aledo: "Here is the recipe for Waffle Iron Cookies from my recipe files. I don't know where I got the recipe but I enjoyed making these when I was a kid."

D.A.R. of Silvis sent the same recipe with this note: "I have had this recipe for many years. It can be left plain or frosted. I like to put a pale green icing on them for my Christmas trays of cookies."

M.S. of Davenport also sent a version of this recipe, adding "A good friend of mine always made these for me. They were delicious!"

1½ cups sugar	2 cups flour
1 cup butter or margarine	½ cup cocoa
4 eggs	Pinch of salt
1 to 2 teaspoons vanilla	

Cream margarine and sugar; beat in eggs and vanilla.

Sift dry ingredients and stir into creamed mixture.

Drop spoonfuls of batter on hot waffle iron. Close lid and bake 1 to 2 minutes.

These burn easily so watch. Are soft but will get crispy.

When cool, frost with powdered sugar frosting.

— *H.J.M. and K.S. of Aledo,*
D.A.R. of Silvis and M.S. of Davenport

Waffle Iron Cookies

April 12, 2000

Our readers have responded in their usual generous way and Curious Cook has received several versions of the requested Waffle Iron Cookies. We'll start today with V.M. of Moline, who sent two cookie recipes and a frosting recipe.

1/3 cup shortening
1 square (1 ounce) unsweetened chocolate
½ cup granulated sugar
1 egg, lightly beaten
½ teaspoon vanilla

¾ cup sifted all-purpose flour
½ teaspoon baking powder
¼ teaspoon salt
2 tablespoons milk
¾ cup finely chopped walnuts

Melt shortening and chocolate together over low heat; cool slightly. Add sugar, egg and vanilla; beat well. Resift flour with baking powder and salt. Add to chocolate mixture along with milk and walnuts. Stir until well mixed.

Drop by rounded teaspoonful onto preheated "low" (about 300 degrees) waffle iron, sprinkling each with a few nuts if desired. Bake 3 to 4 minutes.
— *V.M. of Moline*

Vanilla Waffle Iron Cookies

April 12, 2000

½ cup butter or margarine
2/3 cup sugar
2 eggs
1 teaspoon vanilla
1¼ cups flour

1 teaspoon baking powder
½ teaspoon salt
½ cup chopped nuts
Powdered sugar

Cream butter or margarine and sugar. Add eggs and vanilla; beat well. Stir in dry ingredients. Drop a teaspoonful on preheated waffle iron. Bake for 1½ minutes. Shake in powdered sugar. Yield: about 48 cookies.
— *V.M. of Moline*

Frosting for Double Batch Waffle Cookies

3 tablespoons margarine
3 tablespoons milk

¾ cup sugar
¼ cup chocolate chips

Combine margarine, milk and sugar in saucepan. Bring to boil and boil for ½ minute. Remove from heat and add chocolate chips.
— *V.M. of Moline*

Feb. 9, 2000
White Chocolate Macadamia Chunk Cookies

"I'd like to know if anyone has a recipe for Macadamia Nut Cookies?" asks S.J. of Hillsdale. "My kids and grandkids just love them. Hope you can help me. Thank you."

Curious Cook can recommend the following recipe from our files. These cookies were sold a number of years ago on one of the popular "Kitchens At Their Best" tours sponsored by the Rock Island County Medical Society Auxiliary.

Curious Cook hopes this is the recipe S.J. requested. However, our readers may share other versions of the Macadamia Nut Cookies.

- 1 cup shortening
- ¾ cup sugar
- ¾ cup packed brown sugar
- 3 eggs
- 1 teaspoon vanilla
- 2½ cups flour
- 1 teaspoon baking soda
- 1 teaspoon baking powder
- ½ teaspoon salt
- 1 cup flaked coconut
- ½ cup quick-cooking rolled oats
- ½ cup chopped macadamia nuts
- 4 Lindt White Chocolate Bars (3 ounces each), chopped, OR 1 white chocolate bar (12 ounces), chopped

In a large bowl, beat shortening, sugar and brown sugar until light and fluffy. Add eggs, one at a time. Add vanilla. Blend well.

Combine flour, baking soda, baking powder and salt in a bowl. Add to sugar mixture and mix thoroughly. Add coconut, oats, nuts and white chocolate and stir well.

Drop by rounded tablespoons onto ungreased cookie sheets. Bake at 350 degrees for 10 to 15 minutes, or until light golden brown. Cool 1 minute. Remove from baking sheets. Yield: about 5 dozen cookies.

— *From Curious Cook's files*

Zucchini Bars

1 stick margarine	1¼ cups flour (see note)
½ cup oil	1 teaspoon soda
1 cup brown sugar	½ teaspoon salt
2 eggs	2 cups oats
1 tablespoon water	3 cups grated zucchini
1 teaspoon vanilla	1 cup nuts or raisins, optional
½ cup whole-wheat flour (see note)	Cinnamon/sugar mixture

Combine margarine, oil and 1 cup brown sugar. Add eggs, water and vanilla until fluffy.

Sift flour, soda, salt; mix in oats, zucchini and nuts or raisins. Spread mixture in a buttered 10x15-inch pan. Sprinkle generously with cinnamon and sugar.

Bake at 350 degrees. for 25 to 30 minutes. Makes 20 to 24 bars.

Note: Or use all regular flour. — *J.B. of Bettendorf*

recipe index

A

Alma's Old-Fashioned
  Sugar Cookies 246
Applesauce Coffee Cake 73
Apricot Fruitcake 170
Aunt Mary's Potato Kugelis . .139

B

B.T.L. Soup 58
Baked Cabbage 141
Baked Caramel Corn 246
Baked Carrot Soufflé 142
Baked Potato Soup 57
Banana Bread Pudding 171
Bar-B-Q Biscuits 73
Belgian Lukken 247
Belgian Village
  Pumpkin Nut Waffles 5
Best Ever Pineapple Cake . .172
Bird's Nest Apple Pie 173
Bishop's Bread 74-75
Black Walnut Cookies 248
Black Walnut Jiffy Cake 174
Blarney Stones 176-177
Blarney Stones
  Peanut Bars 175
Blueberry Brunch Cake 178
Blueberry Strata 179
Bread Pudding 180
Broccoli Salad 57
Brunswick Stew 103
Bucket Bread 76
Burnt Sugar Cake 181
Burnt Sugar Frosting 181

Busy Day Drop Cookies 249
Butterscotch Ground
  Raisin Cookies 250
Butterscotch Pie
  from Scratch 182

C

California White Fudge 251
Can't Fail
  Five-Minute Fudge 251
Canned Beef-Biscuit
  Pinwheels (From UTHS) . . .6
Caramel Crunch Apple Pie . .183
Carrot Bread 77
Carrot Casserole 143
Carrots Supreme
  (Lutheran Hospital) 7
Cashew Chicken 104
Cherry Coke Salad
  from Ranch Supper Club . . .7
Cherry Cola Salad 58
Cherry Cookies 257
Cherry Crisp 184
Cherry Pudding 184
Chicken and
  Broccoli Curry 105
Chicken Broccoli
  Casserole 105
Chicken wings 106
Chipped Beef
  Cocktail Spread 49
Chocolate Chip Cake 185
Chocolate Kisses 258
Chocolate
  Pinwheel Cookies 259
Chocolate Turtle Cookies . . .259
Chocolate Zucchini
  Bread 78-79
Chocolate-Oatmeal
  Cookies 258

293

Chop Suey 107
Cleo Pompa's Enchiladas 9
Club Cracker Cookies 263
Coffee Can Bread 82
Coffee-Time Muffins 80
Concord Grape Pie 186
Copper Pennies 144
Corn Chowder 59
Country Life Cookies 265
Cousin Ed's
   Chicken Rosemary 108
Cranberry Cherry Salad 59
Cranberry Dessert
   with Hot Butter Sauce . . .187
Cranberry Mousse 188
Cranberry Salad 60-61
Cranberry Salad
   or Dessert 189
Cranberry-Orange
   Nut Bread 83
Cranberry-Waldorf
   Gelatin Salad 61
Cranoccoli Salad (Oh Nuts) . . .8
Cream Puffs 190
Creamy Pumpkin Pie 191
Crème de Menthe Pie 192
Crisp Duck a la Five 10
Crumb Muffins 81
Crunchy Chocolate
   Chip Cookies 268
Cucumber Dill
   Slice Salad 110
Custard-like
   Bread Pudding 192

D

D.J.'s Bread Pudding 195
Danish Puff 84
Date Nut Bread 85

Delicious No-Sugar
   Apple Pie 193
Deluxe Potato Soup 62
Devonshire Easy Cream 37
Dilled Fish 109
Dilled Salmon Bake 110
Diplomatic Cake 194
Double Chocolate
   and Pearl Cookies 269
Dried Apricot Pie 197
Dutch Baby Pancakes 111

E

Easter Egg Nests 269-270
Easy Cake 198
Easy Oil Pie Crust 199
Egg White Cookies 270
Eggnog Cake 199
Eggplant Parmesan 112-113
Eggplant Souffle 114
Enchiladas 12
Escalloped Cabbage 144
Escalloped Corn 145-147

F

Fadden for Christmas 86
Ferden 149
Ferden from
   Mother's Mother 87
Ferden or Furden 88
Fettuccine a la Romana 114
Fred Hitchcock's Goulash . . .115
French Toast 116
French Toast
   Overnight 116-117
Fresh Peach Pie 200
Fresh Pear Crumble Pie 201
Frog Eye Salad 63-64
Frosting for Double
   Batch Waffle Cookies 290
Frozen Pumpkin Pie 202

G

Galuska 137
Genesis Medical Center
   Creamy Cabbage Soup . . .13
German Potato Salad 148
Glaze for Chicken 117
Glenn Moore's
   Shrimp Salad 14-15
Golden Lasagna 121
Gooseberry Pie
   with Meringue 203
Grandma Bingman's
   Butter Pie 204
Grandma's Fudge 252
Grandma's Nut Roll 90-91
Grandmother Anoinette's
   Lithuanian Kugelis 140
Granny's Cake 205
Grasshopper Pie 205

H

Ham baked
   in bread dough 118-120
Hawaiian Meatballs 49-50
Heidi's Port Byron Chocolate
   Chip Cookies 271
Heise Weckens 89
Hoffman School
   Cherry Squares 16
Holiday Fruit Drops 272
Holst Family Furden 150
Honey Mustard Dressing 65
Hot Cocoa Mix 50
Hummingbird Cake 206
Huxley Kringla 273

I

Illini's
   Celery Seed Dressing 17
Irish Stew 122-123
Irv French's Clam Bisque
   Soup (El Rancho 1976) . . .20
Italian Beef 124
Italian Gourmet Beef 124

J

Jackie Tanner's
   Slow Cooker Stuffing 151
John Deere Junior High
   French Pastry 18-19
Junior High
   Snicker Doodles 275

K

Kringla 274
Kugelis 141

L

Lamb Cake 208, 210
Lee's Fried Fish 21
Lemon Nut Bread 92
Lemon Poppyseed
   Pound Cake 212
Lemon Whippersnappers . . .276
Lemon-Glazed
   Nectar Cake 211
Liver Pate
   (Diane DeBord) 23
Liver Pate
   (The Shamrock) 22

M

Macadamia Cookies 277
Make Ahead
   Mashed Potatoes 152
Make Ahead Potatoes 153
Mandarin Orange Cake 213
Mashed Potato Candy
   Basic Recipe 277
Mexican Salad 65
MHS Honey Dijon
   Salad Dressing 26
Michigan Cranberry Cake
   with Vanilla Sauce 213

Mildred Poppy's
  Turtle Cookies 260
Mile High
  Strawberry Pie 24-25
Million Dollar Cookies 278
Million-Dollar
  Sugar Cookies 279
Miss American Pie 214
Mock Apple Pie 214-215
Mock Shannon's
  Potato Salad 153
Mohl Buettle, Meal Ball
  (Johnny in the Sack) 156
Moline High Angel Pie 27
Mom's Date Cake 216
Mom's Gingerbread 217
Mongolian Beef (Yen Ching) . .34
Monkey Bread 93
Monkfish, haddock
  with lobster flavor . . .126-127
Mystery Apple Pie 216

N

Napa Cabbage 66
Napa Cabbage Salad 67
Nelda's Sausage and
  Rice Dressing 154-155
Neopolitan Cookies 280
Nests 270
'1932' Candy Apples 245
No Bake Cookies 265
No Bake Fudge Cookies 266
No-Bake Chocolate
  Oatmeal Cookies 266
No-Bake Club Cracker
  Cookies 263
Non-Chocolate Fudge 252
Nun's Fudge (ICA) 28-29

O

Oatmeal Pie Crust 202
Old Time Lemon Pie 220
Old-Fashioned
  Fudge 253-254
Onion, Tomato Salsa 157
Orange Raisin Scones 94
Orange Sauce (for duck) . . .129
Overnight Coffee Cake . . .95-96
Overnight Coffee Cake
  Swirl 97

P

Party Mix
  Microwave Recipe 51
Party Rye Pizza 51
Peachy Nut Bread 101
Peanut Butter Cake 220
Peanut Butter Fudge 254
Peanut Butter
  Streusel Pie 221
Pear and Apple Pie 222
Pear-Walnut Coffee Cake . . .100
Pecan Fruitcake 223
Pennsylvania Dutch
  Sugar Cakes 281
Perfect Chocolate Cake 218
Perfect Chocolate Cake
  Frosting and Filling 219
Perfect Pie Crust 224
Pippins 35
Plantation Dressing 30-31
Plantation
  Salad Dressing 32-33
Polynesian Meatballs 52
Poor Man's Lobster 125
Popcorn Charlie's
  Popcorn Salad 37
Pop-Up Bread 98-99
Pork Chops 128
Praline Sweet Potatoes 158

Prune Cake 225-226
Pumpkin Bars 282
Pumpkin Chiffon Pie 228
Pumpkin Custard Pie 229
Pumpkin Fudge 255
Pumpkin Spice
   Angel Food Cake 229

R

Raw Apple Cake 230
Real Easy Bread Pudding . . .196
Red Cabbage with Apples . . .68
Red, White, Blue
   Layered Salad 69
Rhubarb Punch 52
Rhubarb Slush 53
Rice Pudding 42-43, 230
Roast Duck a la Orange . . .129
Rosettes 283
Ruth Lucas' Fudge 256

S

Salmon Patties 130
Salsa 159
Sandwich Filling 160
Sauerkraut Cake 232
Scalloped Cabbage 161
Scalloped Corn 162
Scones 36-37
Shannon's Baked Pork Chops
   and Lima Beans 38
Sherried Wild Rice Soup 70
Sindt Goulash 40
Sister Marcellina's
   Applesauce Bars 284
Skillet Luau Meatballs 53
Soda Cracker Cookies 264
Soft Chocolate Chip
   Cookies 285
Soft Sugar Cookies 285-286

Something Different
   Sweet Rolls 102
Sorghum Cookies 286
Souffle Potatoes 163
Southern Sweet Potato
   Pie 164
Spiced Pecans 54-55
Spinach Soufflé 165-166
Spinach Soufflé
   a la Randall's 167
Sponge Cake
   for Blarney Stones 177
Sponge or Foam Candy 287
Strawberry Cake 233
Stuffed Eggplant 131
Sunshiny Carrot Bake 168
Swedish Apple Pie 233
Swedish Meatballs 132
Swedish Pancakes 132-133
Swedish Pancakes
   Platter 134
Swedish Rice Pudding 231
Sweet & Sour Pineapple
   Meatballs 56
Sweet Potato Custard Pie . . .235
Sweet Potato
   Pie 168, 234-235
Swiss Cheeseburger Soup . . .71

T

Taco Salad 71-72
Tamale Pie 134
10-Minute Fruitcake Ring . . .169
Texas Lightning
   White Chili 135
Texas Sheet Cake 236-237
Tex-Mex 135
Three Milk Cake 239
Three Milk Cake /
   Tres Leches Cake 240
Thunder Bay Grille's
   Baked Potato Soup 41

Toasty Rice Pudding 42-43
Toasty Shop Rice Pudding . . .42
Toasty's Rice Pudding 44
Tres Leche Cake
 (Three Milk Cake) 238
Trinity Medical Center
 Chocolate Chip Cookies . .45
Trinity Medical Center Double
 Chocolate Chip Cookies . .46
Trinity Medical Center Oatmeal
 Raisin Cookies 46
Trinity Medical Center
 Peanut Butter Cookies 47
Trinity Medical Center
 Sugar Cookies 47
Trio Swiss Steak 48
Turtle Cookies 261
Turtle or Waffle Cookies 262

U

Unbaked Chocolate
 Macaroons 288
Unbaked Chocolate
 Oatmeal Cookies 267

V

Val's Prune Cake 227
Vanilla Waffle Iron
 Cookies 290
Veal Hungarian
 Goulash 136-137
Very Berry
 Cheesecake Trifle 241
Vinegar Pie 241

W

Waffle Cookies 288
Waffle Iron Cookies 289-290
White Chocolate Cake 242
White Chocolate Cake
 Frosting 242
White Chocolate Macadamia
 Chunk Cookies 291
White Pizza 138
White Texas Sheet Cake 243

Z

Zucchini Bars 292
Zucchini Chocolate Cake . . .244

Cooking Tips

1. After stewing a chicken, cool in broth before cutting into chunks; it will have twice the flavor.
2. To slice meat into thin strips, as for stir-fry dishes, partially freeze it so it will slice more easily.
3. A roast with the bone in will cook faster than a boneless roast. The bone carries the heat to the inside more quickly.
4. When making a roast, place dry onion soup mix in the bottom of your roaster pan. After removing the roast, add 1 can of mushroom soup and you will have a good brown gravy.
5. For a juicier hamburger, add cold water to the beef before grilling (½ cup to 1 pound of meat).
6. To freeze meatballs, place them on a cookie sheet until frozen. Place in plastic bags. They will stay separated so that you may remove as many as you want.
7. To keep cauliflower white while cooking, add a little milk to the water.
8. When boiling corn, add sugar to the water instead of salt. Salt will toughen the corn.
9. To ripen tomatoes, put them in a brown paper bag in a dark pantry, and they will ripen.
10. To keep celery crisp, stand it upright in a pitcher of cold, salted water and refrigerate.
11. When cooking cabbage, place a small tin cup or can half full of vinegar on the stove near the cabbage. It will absorb the odor.
12. Potatoes soaked in salt water for 20 minutes before baking will bake more rapidly.
13. Let raw potatoes stand in cold water for at least a half-hour before frying in order to improve the crispness of French-fried potatoes. Dry potatoes thoroughly before adding to oil.
14. Use greased muffin tins as molds when baking stuffed green peppers.
15. A few drops of lemon juice in the water will whiten boiled potatoes.
16. Buy mushrooms before they "open." When stems and caps are attached firmly, mushrooms are truly fresh.
17. Do not use metal bowls when mixing salads. Use wood, glass or china.
18. Lettuce keeps better if you store it in the refrigerator without washing it. Keep the leaves dry. Wash lettuce the day you are going to use it.
19. Do not use soda to keep vegetables green. It destroys Vitamin C.
20. Do not despair if you oversalt gravy. Stir in some instant mashed potatoes to repair the damage. Just add a little more liquid in order to offset the thickening.

Copyright © 1999
Morris Press Cookbooks

Herbs & Spices

Acquaint yourself with herbs and spices. Add in small amounts, ¼ teaspoon for every 4 servings. Crush dried herbs or snip fresh ones before using. Use 3 times more fresh herbs if substituting fresh for dried.

Basil	Sweet, warm flavor with an aromatic odor. Use whole or ground. Good with lamb, fish, roast, stews, ground beef, vegetables, dressing and omelets.
Bay Leaves	Pungent flavor. Use whole leaf but remove before serving. Good in vegetable dishes, seafood, stews and pickles.
Caraway	Spicy taste and aromatic smell. Use in cakes, breads, soups, cheese and sauerkraut.
Chives	Sweet, mild flavor like that of onion. Excellent in salads, fish, soups and potatoes.
Cilantro	Use fresh. Excellent in salads, fish, chicken, rice, beans and Mexican dishes.
Curry Powder	Spices are combined to proper proportions to give a distinct flavor to meat, poultry, fish and vegetables.
Dill	Both seeds and leaves are flavorful. Leaves may be used as a garnish or cooked with fish, soup, dressings, potatoes and beans. Leaves or the whole plant may be used to flavor pickles.
Fennel	Sweet, hot flavor. Both seeds and leaves are used. Use in small quantities in pies and baked goods. Leaves can be boiled with fish.
Ginger	A pungent root, this aromatic spice is sold fresh, dried or ground. Use in pickles, preserves, cakes, cookies, soups and meat dishes.

Herbs & Spices

Marjoram	May be used both dried or green. Use to flavor fish, poultry, omelets, lamb, stew, stuffing and tomato juice.
Mint	Aromatic with a cool flavor. Excellent in beverages, fish, lamb, cheese, soup, peas, carrots, and fruit desserts.
Oregano	Strong, aromatic odor. Use whole or ground in tomato juice, fish, eggs, pizza, omelets, chili, stew, gravy, poultry and vegetables.
Paprika	A bright red pepper, this spice is used in meat, vegetables and soups or as a garnish for potatoes, salads or eggs.
Parsley	Best when used fresh, but can be used dried as a garnish or as a seasoning. Try in fish, omelets, soup, meat, stuffing and mixed greens.
Rosemary	Very aromatic. Can be used fresh or dried. Season fish, stuffing, beef, lamb, poultry, onions, eggs, bread and potatoes. Great in dressings.
Saffron	Orange-yellow in color, this spice flavors or colors foods. Use in soup, chicken, rice and breads.
Sage	Use fresh or dried. The flowers are sometimes used in salads. May be used in tomato juice, fish, omelets, beef, poultry, stuffing, cheese spreads and breads.
Tarragon	Leaves have a pungent, hot taste. Use to flavor sauces, salads, fish, poultry, tomatoes, eggs, green beans, carrots and dressings.
Thyme	Sprinkle leaves on fish or poultry before broiling or baking. Throw a few sprigs directly on coals shortly before meat is finished grilling.

Baking Breads

Hints for Baking Breads

1. Kneading dough for 30 seconds after mixing improves the texture of baking powder biscuits.
2. Instead of shortening, use cooking or salad oil in waffles and hot cakes.
3. When bread is baking, a small dish of water in the oven will help keep the crust from hardening.
4. Dip a spoon in hot water to measure shortening, butter, etc., and the fat will slip out more easily.
5. Small amounts of leftover corn may be added to pancake batter for variety.
6. To make bread crumbs, use the fine cutter of a food grinder and tie a large paper bag over the spout in order to prevent flying crumbs.
7. When you are doing any sort of baking, you got better results if you remember to preheat your cookie sheet, muffin tins or cake pans.

Rules for Use of Leavening Agents

1. In simple flour mixtures, use 2 teaspoons baking powder to leaven 1 cup flour. Reduce this amount ½ teaspoon for each egg used.
2. To 1 teaspoon soda use 2¼ teaspoons cream of tartar, 2 cups freshly soured milk, or 1 cup molasses.
3. To substitute soda and an acid for baking powder, divide the amount of baking powder by 4. Take that as your measure and add acid according to rule 2.

Proportions of Baking Powder to Flour

biscuits ....to 1 cup flour use 1¼ tsp. baking powder
cake with oil..........................to 1 cup flour use 1 tsp. baking powder
muffins ....to 1 cup flour use 1½ tsp. baking powder
popovers..............................to 1 cup flour use 1¼ tsp. baking powder
waffles ....to 1 cup flour use 1¼ tsp. baking powder

Proportions of Liquid to Flour

drop batter ....to 1 cup liquid use 2 to 2½ cups flour
pour batter ....to 1 cup liquid use 1 cup flour
soft dough ....to 1 cup liquid use 3 to 3½ cups flour
stiff dough................................to 1 cup liquid use 4 cups flour

Time and Temperature Chart

Breads	Minutes	Temperature
biscuits	12-15	400°-450°
cornbread	25-30	400°-425°
gingerbread	40-50	350°-370°
loaf	50-60	350°-400°
nut bread	50-75	350°
popovers	30-40	425°-450°
rolls	20-30	400°-450°

Baking Desserts

Perfect Cookies

Cookie dough that is to be rolled is much easier to handle after it has been refrigerated for 10 to 30 minutes. This keeps the dough from sticking, even though it may be soft. If not done, the soft dough may require more flour and too much flour makes cookies hard and brittle. Place on a floured board only as much dough as can be easily managed.

Flour the rolling pin slightly and roll lightly to desired thickness. Cut shapes close together and add trimmings to dough that needs to be rolled. Place pans or sheets in upper third of oven. Watch cookies carefully while baking in order to avoid burned edges. When sprinkling sugar on cookies, try putting it into a salt shaker in order to save time.

Perfect Pies

1. Pie crust will be better and easier to make if all the ingredients are cool.
2. The lower crust should be placed in the pan so that it covers the surface smoothly. Air pockets beneath the surface will push the crust out of shape while baking.
3. Folding the top crust over the lower crust before crimping will keep juices in the pie.
4. In making custard pie, bake at a high temperature for about ten minutes to prevent a soggy crust. Then finish baking at a low temperature.
5. When making cream pie, sprinkle crust with powdered sugar in order to prevent it from becoming soggy.

Perfect Cakes

1. Fill cake pans two-thirds full and spread batter into corners and sides, leaving a slight hollow in the center.
2. Cake is done when it shrinks from the sides of the pan or if it springs back when touched lightly with the finger.
3. After removing a cake from the oven, place it on a rack for about five minutes. Then, the sides should be loosened and the cake turned out on a rack in order to finish cooling.
4. Do not frost cakes until thoroughly cool.
5. Icing will remain where you put it if you sprinkle cake with powdered sugar first.

Time and Temperature Chart

Dessert	Time	Temperature
butter cake, layer	20-40 min.	380°-400°
butter cake, loaf	40-60 min.	360°-400°
cake, angel	50-60 min.	300°-360°
cake, fruit	3-4 hrs.	275°-325°
cake, sponge	18-20 min.	350°-375°
cookies, molasses	18-20 min.	350°-375°
cookies, thin	10-12 min.	380°-390°
cream puffs	45-60 min.	300°-350°
meringue	40-60 min.	250°-300°
pie crust	20-40 min.	400°-500°

Vegetables & Fruits

Vegetable	Cooking Method	Time
artichokes	boiled	40 min.
	steamed	45-60 min.
asparagus tips	boiled	10-15 min.
beans, lima	boiled	20-40 min.
	steamed	60 min.
beans, string	boiled	15-35 min.
	steamed	60 min.
beets, old	boiled or steamed	1-2 hours
beets, young with skin	boiled	30 min.
	steamed	60 min.
	baked	70-90 min.
broccoli, flowerets	boiled	5-10 min.
broccoli, stems	boiled	20-30 min.
brussels sprouts	boiled	20-30 min.
cabbage, chopped	boiled	10-20 min.
	steamed	25 min.
carrots, cut across	boiled	8-10 min.
	steamed	40 min.
cauliflower, flowerets	boiled	8-10 min.
cauliflower, stem down	boiled	20-30 min.
corn, green, tender	boiled	5-10 min.
	steamed	15 min.
	baked	20 min.
corn on the cob	boiled	8-10 min.
	steamed	15 min.
eggplant, whole	boiled	30 min.
	steamed	40 min.
	baked	45 min.
parsnips	boiled	25-40 min.
	steamed	60 min.
	baked	60-75 min.
peas, green	boiled or steamed	5-15 min.
potatoes	boiled	20-40 min.
	steamed	60 min.
	baked	45-60 min.
pumpkin or squash	boiled	20-40 min.
	steamed	45 min.
	baked	60 min.
tomatoes	boiled	5-15 min.
turnips	boiled	25-40 min.

Drying Time Table

Fruit	Sugar or Honey	Cooking Time
apricots	¼ c. for each cup of fruit	about 40 min.
figs	1 T. for each cup of fruit	about 30 min.
peaches	¼ c. for each cup of fruit	about 45 min.
prunes	2 T. for each cup of fruit	about 45 min.

Vegetables & Fruits

Buying Fresh Vegetables

Artichokes: Look for compact, tightly closed heads with green, clean-looking leaves. Avoid those with leaves that are brown or separated.

Asparagus: Stalks should be tender and firm; tips should be close and compact. Choose the stalks with very little white; they are more tender. Use asparagus soon because it toughens rapidly.

Beans, Snap: Those with small seeds inside the pods are best. Avoid beans with dry-looking pods.

Broccoli, Brussels Sprouts and Cauliflower: Flower clusters on broccoli and cauliflower should be tight and close together. Brussels sprouts should be firm and compact. Smudgy, dirty spots may indicate pests or disease.

Cabbage and Head Lettuce: Choose heads that are heavy for their size. Avoid cabbage with worm holes and lettuce with discoloration or soft rot.

Cucumbers: Choose long, slender cucumbers for best quality. May be dark or medium green, but yellow ones are undesirable.

Mushrooms: Caps should be closed around the stems. Avoid black or brown gills.

Peas and Lima Beans: Select pods that are well-filled but not bulging. Avoid dried, spotted, yellow or flabby pods.

Buying Fresh Fruits

Bananas: Skin should be free of bruises and black or brown spots. Purchase them green and allow them to ripen at home at room temperature.

Berries: Select plump, solid berries with good color. Avoid stained containers, which indicate wet or leaky berries. Berries with clinging caps, such as blackberries and raspberries, may be unripe. Strawberries without caps may be overripe.

Melons: In cantaloupes, thick, close netting on the rind indicates best quality. Cantaloupes are ripe when the stem scar is smooth and the space between the netting is yellow or yellow-green. They are best when fully ripe with fruity odor.

Honeydews are ripe when rind has creamy to yellowish color and velvety texture. Immature honeydews are whitish-green.

Ripe watermelons have some yellow color on one side. If melons are white or pale green on one side, they are not ripe.

Oranges, Grapefruits and Lemons: Choose those heavy for their size. Smoother, thinner skins usually indicate more juice. Most skin markings do not affect quality. Oranges with a slight greenish tinge may be just as ripe as fully colored ones. Light or greenish-yellow lemons are more tart than deep yellow ones. Avoid citrus fruits showing withered, sunken or soft areas.

Measurements & Substitutions

Measurements

a pinch	1/8 teaspoon or less
3 teaspoons	1 tablespoon
4 tablespoons	¼ cup
8 tablespoons	½ cup
12 tablespoons	¾ cup
16 tablespoons	1 cup
2 cups	1 pint
4 cups	1 quart
4 quarts	1 gallon
8 quarts	1 peck
4 pecks	1 bushel
16 ounces	1 pound
32 ounces	1 quart
1 ounce liquid	2 tablespoons
8 ounces liquid	1 cup

Use standard measuring spoons and cups. All measurements are level.

Substitutions

Ingredient	Quantity	Substitute
baking powder	1 teaspoon	¼ tsp. baking soda plus ½ tsp. cream of tartar
catsup or chili sauce (for use in cooking)	1 cup	1 c. tomato sauce plus ½ c. sugar and 2 T. vinegar
chocolate	1 square (1 oz.)	3 or 4 T. cocoa plus 1 T. butter
cornstarch	1 tablespoon	2 T. flour or 2 tsp. quick-cooking tapioca
cracker crumbs	¾ cup	1 c. bread crumbs
dates	1 lb.	1½ c. dates, pitted and cut
dry mustard	1 teaspoon	1 T. prepared mustard
flour, self-rising	1 cup	1 c. all-purpose flour, ½ tsp. salt, and 1 tsp. baking powder
herbs, fresh	1 tablespoon	1 tsp. dried herbs
milk, sour	1 cup	1 T. lemon juice or vinegar plus sweet milk to make 1 c. (let stand 5 minutes)
whole	1 cup	½ c. evaporated milk plus ½ c. water
min. marshmallows	10	1 lg. marshmallow
onion, fresh	1 small	1 T. instant minced onion, rehydrated
sugar, brown	½ cup	2 T. molasses in ½ c. granulated sugar
powdered	1 cup	1 c. granulated sugar plus 1 tsp. cornstarch
tomato juice	1 cup	½ c. tomato sauce plus ½ c. water

When substituting cocoa for chocolate in cakes, the amount of flour must be reduced. Brown and white sugars usually can be interchanged.

Equivalency Chart

Food	Quantity	Yield
apple	1 medium	1 cup
banana, mashed	1 medium	1/3 cup
bread	1½ slices	1 cup soft crumbs
bread	1 slice	¼ cup fine, dry crumbs
butter	1 stick or ¼ pound	2 2/3 cups
cheese, American, cubed	1 pound	2 2/3 cups
American, grated	1 pound	5 cups
cream cheese	3-ounce package	6 2/3 tablespoons
chocolate, bitter	1 square	1 ounce
cocoa	1 pound	4 cups
coconut	1½ pound package	2 2/3 cups
coffee, ground	1 pound	5 cups
cornmeal	1 pound	3 cups
cornstarch	1 pound	3 cups
crackers, graham	14 squares	1 cup fine crumbs
saltine	28 crackers	1 cup fine crumbs
egg	4-5 whole	1 cup
whites	8-10	1 cup
yolks	10-12	1 cup
evaporated milk	1 cup	3 cups whipped
flour, cake, sifted	1 pound	4½ cups
rye	1 pound	5 cups
white, sifted	1 pound	4 cups
white, unsifted	1 pound	3¾ cups
gelatin, flavored	3¼ ounces	½ cup
unflavored	¼ ounce	1 tables
lemon	1 medium	3 tablespoon juice
marshmallows	16	¼ pound
noodles, cooked	8-ounce package	7 cups
uncooked	4 ounces (1½ cups)	2-3 cups cooked
macaroni, cooked	8-ounce package	6 cups
macaroni, uncooked	4 ounces (1¼ cups)	2¼ cups cooked
spaghetti, uncooked	7 ounces	4 cups cooked
nuts, chopped	¼ pound	1 cup
almonds	1 pound	3½ cups
walnuts, broken	1 pound	3 cups
walnuts, unshelled	1 pound	1½ to 1¾ cups
onion	1 medium	½ cup
orange	3-4 medium	1 cup juice
raisins	1 pound	3½ cups
rice, brown	1 cup	4 cups cooked
converted	1 cup	4 cups cooked
regular	1 cup	3 cups cooked
wild	1 cup	4 cups cooked
sugar, brown	1 pound	2½ cups
powdered	1 pound	3½ cups
white	1 pound	2 cups
vanilla waters	22	1 cup fine crumbs
zwieback, crumbled	4	1 cup

Food Quantities for Large Servings

	25 Servings	50 Servings	100 Servings

Beverages:
coffee ....½ pound & ....1 pound & ....2 pounds &
　　　　　　1½ gallons water　3 gallons water　6 gallons water
lemonade ....10-15 lemons & ....20-30 lemons &......40-60 lemons &
　　　　　　1½ gallons water　3 gallons water　6 gallons water
tea ....1/12 pound & ....1/6 pound & ....1/3 pound &
　　　　　　1½ gallons water　3 gallons water　6 gallons water

Desserts:
layered
　cake ....1 12" cake ....3 10" cakes ....6 10" cakes
sheet cake....1 10" x 12" cake ....1 12" x 20" cake ....2 12" x 20" cake
watermelon ..37½ pounds ....75 pounds ....150 pounds
whipping
　cream ......¾ pint ....1½ to 2 pints ....3-4 pints

Ice cream:
brick..............3¼ quarts ....6½ quarts .... 13 quarts
bulk ....2¼ quarts ....4½ quarts or .... 9 quarts or
　　　　　　　　　　　　　　　1¼ gallons　　　　2½ gallons

Meat, poultry or fish:
fish ....13 pounds ....25 pounds ....50 pounds
fish, fillets
　or steak....7½ pounds ....15 pounds ....30 pounds
hamburger....9 pounds ....18 pounds ....35 pounds
turkey or
　chicken ....13 pounds ....25 to 35 pounds ....50 to 75 pounds
wieners
　(beef) ......6½ pounds ....13 pounds ....25 pounds

Salads, casseroles:
baked
　beans ......¾ gallon ....1¼ gallons..............2½ gallons
jello salad ....¾ gallon ....1¼ gallons..............2½ gallons
potato
　salad........4 ¼ quarts ....2¼ gallons..............4½ gallons
scalloped
　potatoes....4½ quarts or ....9 quarts or ....18 quarts
　　　　　　1 12" x 20" pan　　2¼ gallons　　　　4½ gallons
spaghetti ......1¼ gallons ....2½ gallons..............5 gallons

Sandwiches:
bread............50 slices or............100 slices or ....200 slices or
　　　　　　　3 1-pound loaves　6 1-pound loaves　12 1-lb loaves
butter............½ pound ....1 pound ....2 pounds
lettuce ....1 ½ heads ....3 heads ....6 heads
mayonnaise....1 cup ....2 cups ....4 cups
mixed filling
　meat,
　eggs, fish....1½ quarts ....3 quarts ....6 quarts
　jam, jelly....1 quart......................2 quarts ....4 quarts

Dear Curious Cook

Microwave Hints

1. Place an open box of hardened brown sugar in the microwave oven with 1 cup hot water. Microwave on high for 1½ to 2 minutes for ½ pound or 2 to 3 minutes for 1 pound.
2. Soften hard ice cream by microwaving at 30% power. One pint will take 15 to 30 seconds; one quart, 30-45 seconds; and one-half gallon, 45-60 seconds.
3. To melt chocolate, place ½ pound in glass bowl or measuring cup. Melt uncovered at 50% power for 3-4 minutes; stir after 2 minutes.
4. Soften one 8-ounce package of cream cheese by microwave at 30% power for 2 to 2½ minutes. One 3-ounce package of cream cheese will soften in 1½ to 2 minutes.
5. A 4½-ounce carton of whipped topping will thaw in 1 minute on the defrost setting. Whipped topping should be slightly firm in the center, but it will blend well when stirred. Do not over thaw!
6. Soften jello that has set up too hard — perhaps you were to chill it until slightly thickened and forgot it. Heat on a low power setting for a very short time.
7. Heat hot packs. A wet fingertip towel will take about 25 seconds. It depends on the temperature of the water used to wet the towel.
8. To scald milk, cook 1 cup for 2 to 2½ minutes, stirring once each minute.
9. To make dry bread crumbs, cut 6 slices of bread into ½-inch cubes. Microwave in 3-quart casserole 6-7 minutes, or until dry, stirring after 3 minutes. Crush in blender.
10. Refresh stale potato chips, crackers or other snacks of such type by putting a plateful in the microwave for 30-45 seconds. Let stand for 1 minute to crisp. Cereals can also be crisped.
11. Nuts will be easier to shell if you place 2 cups of nuts in a 1-quart casserole with 1 cup of water. Cook for 4 to 5 minutes and the nutmeats will slip out whole after cracking the shell.
12. Stamps collectors can place a few drops of water on a stamp to remove it from an envelope. Heat in the microwave for 20 seconds, and the stamp will come off.
13. Using a round dish instead of a square one eliminates overcooked corners in baking cakes.
14. Sprinkle a layer of medium, finely chopped walnuts evenly onto the bottom and side of a ring pan or bundt cake pan to enhance the looks and eating quality. Pour in batter and microwave as recipe directs.
15. Do not salt foods on the surface as it causes dehydration and toughens food. Salt after you remove from the oven unless the recipe calls for using salt in the mixture.
16. Heat leftover custard and use it as frosting for a cake.
17. Melt marshmallow crème. Half of a 7-ounce jar will melt in 35-40 seconds on high. Stir to blend.
18. To toast coconut, spread ½ cup coconut in a pie plate and cook for 3-4 minutes, stirring every 30 seconds after 2 minutes. Watch closely, as it quickly browns.
19. To melt crystallized honey; heat uncovered jar on high for 30-45 seconds. If jar is large, repeat.
20. One stick of butter or margarine will soften in 1 minute when microwaved at 20% power.

Calorie Counter

Beverages

apple juice, 6 oz 90
coffee (black) 0
cola type, 12 oz 115
cranberry juice, 6 oz 115
ginger ale, 12 oz 115
grape juice,
    (prepared from frozen
    concentrate), 6 oz 142
lemonade,
    (prepared from frozen
    concentrate), 6 oz 85
milk, protein fortified, 1 c. 105
    skim, 1 c. 90
    whole, 1 c. 160
orange juice, 6 oz 85
pineapple juice,
    unsweetened, 6 oz..............95
root beer, 12 oz 150
tonic (quinine water) 12 oz 132

Breads

cornbread, 1 sm. square........130
dumpling, 1 med 70
French toast, 1 slice 135
melba toast, 1 slice 25
muffins, blueberry, 1 muffin ..110
    bran, 1 muffin.....................106
    corn, 1 muffin......................125
    English, 1 muffin 280
pancakes, 1 (4-in.) 60
pumpernickel, 1 slice 75
rye, 1 slice 60
waffle, 1 216
white, 1 slice 60-70
whole wheat, 1 slice 55-65

Cereals

cornflakes, 1 c. 105
cream of wheat, 1 c. 120
oatmeal, 1 c. 148
rice flakes, 1 c. 105
shredded wheat, 1 biscuit......100
sugar krisps, ¾ c. 110

Crackers

graham, 1 cracker 15-30
rye crisp, 1 cracker 35
saltine, 1 cracker 17-20
wheat thins, 1 cracker................9

Dairy Products

butter or margarine, 1 T 100
cheese, American, 1 oz 100
    camembert, 1 oz 85
    cheddar, 1 oz.....................115
    cottage cheese, 1 oz 30
    mozzarella, 1 oz 90
    parmesan, 1 oz 130
    ricotta, 1 oz 50
    roquefort, 1 oz 105
    Swiss, 1 oz.........................105
cream, light, 1 T 30
    heavy, 1 T 55
    sour, 1 T...............................45
hot chocolate,
    with milk, 1 c. 277
milk chocolate, 1 oz........145-155
yogurt
    made w/ whole milk,
    1 c. 150-165
    made w/ skimmed milk,
    1 c. 125

Eggs

fried, 1 lg................................100
poached or boiled, 1 lg 75-80
scrambled or
    in omelet, 1 lg 110-130

Fish and Seafood

bass, 4 oz 105
salmon, broiled or
    baked, 3 oz 155
sardines,
    canned in oil, 3 oz 170
trout, fried, 3 ½ oz 220
tuna, in oil, 3 oz 170
    in water, 3 oz 110

Calorie Counter

Fruits
apple, 1 med 80-100
applesauce,
    sweetened, ½ c. 90-115
    unsweetened, ½ c...............50
banana, 1 med 85
blueberries, ½ c. 45
cantaloupe, ½ c. 24
cherries (pitted), raw, ½ c. 40
grapefruit, ½ med 55
grapes, ½ c...........................35-55
honeydew, ½ c........................55
mango, 1 med 90
orange, 1 med 65-75
peach, 1 med 35
pear, 1 med 60-100
pineapple, fresh, ½ c. 40
    canned in syrup, ½ c. 95
plum, 1 med 30
strawberries, fresh, ½ c. 30
    frozen and
      sweetened, ½ c. 120-140
tangerine, 1 lg...........................39
watermelon, ½ c. 42

Meat and Poultry
beef, ground (lean), 3 oz 185
    roast, 3 oz 185
chicken, broiled, 3 oz 115
lamb chop (lean), 3 oz 175-200
steak, sirloin, 3 oz..................175
    tenderloin, 3 oz 174
    top round, 3 oz.................162
turkey, dark meat, 3 oz 175
    white meat, 3 oz 150
veal, cutlet, 3 oz 156
    roast, 3 oz 76

Nuts
almond, 2 T...........................105
cashews, 2 T.........................100
peanuts, 2 T 105
peanut butter, 1 T 95
pecans, 2 T 95
pistachios, 2 T.........................92
walnuts, 2 T 80

Pasta
macaroni or
    spaghetti, cooked, ¾ c. 115

Salad Dressings
blue cheese, 1 T 70
French, 1 T 65
Italian, 1 T................................80
mayonnaise, 1 T 100
olive oil, 1 T 124
Russian, 1 T 70
salad oil, 1 T 120

Soups
bean, 1 c. 130-180
beef noodle, 1 c........................70
bouillon and
    consommé, 1 c. 30
chicken noodle, 1 c. 65
chicken with rice, 1 c. 50
minestrone, 1 c.................80-150
split pea, 1 c. 145-170
tomato with milk, 1 c. 170
vegetable, 1 c. 80-100

Vegetables
asparagus, 1 c. 35
broccoli, cooked, ½ c...............25
cabbage, cooked, ½ c. 15-20
carrots, cooked, ½ c. 25-30
cauliflower, ½ c. 10-15
corn (kernels), ½ c. 70
green beans, 1 c. 30
lettuce, shredded, ½ c. 5
mushrooms, canned, ½ c. 20
onions, cooked, ½ c................30
peas, cooked, ½ c. 60
potato, baked, 1 med 90
    chips, 8-10 100
    mashed, w/milk &
      butter, 1 c................200-300
spinach, 1 c. 40
tomato, raw, 1 med 25
    cooked, ½ c. 30

Cooking Terms

Au gratin: Topped with crumbs and/or cheese and browned in oven or under broiler.
Au jus: Served in its own juices.
Baste: To moisten foods during cooking with pan drippings or special sauce in order to add flavor and prevent drying.
Bisque: A thick cream soup.
Blanch: To immerse in rapidly boiling water and allow to cook slightly.
Cream: To soften a fat, especially butter, by beating it at room temperature. Butter and sugar are often creamed together, making a smooth, soft paste.
Crimp: To seal the edges of a two-crust pie either by pinching them at intervals with the fingers or by pressing them together with the tines of a fork.
Crudites: An assortment of raw vegetables (i.e. carrots, broccoli, celery, mushrooms) that is served as an hors d'oeuvre, often accompanied by a dip.
Degrease: To remove fat from the surface of stews, soups, or stock. Usually cooled in the refrigerator so that fat hardens and is easily removed.
Dredge: To coat lightly with flour, cornmeal, etc.
Entrée: The main course.
Fold: To incorporate a delicate substance, such as whipped cream or beaten egg whites, into another substance without releasing air bubbles. A spatula is used to gently bring part of the mixture from the bottom of the bowl to the top. The process is repeated, while slowly rotating the bowl, until the ingredients are thoroughly blended.
Glaze: To cover with a glossy coating, such as a melted and somewhat diluted jelly for fruit desserts.
Julienne: To cut vegetables, fruits or cheese into match-shaped slivers.
Marinate: To allow food to stand in a liquid in order to tenderize or to add flavor.
Meuniéré: Dredged with flour and sautéed in butter.
Mince: To chop food into very small pieces.
Parboil: To boil until partially cooked; to blanch. Usually final cooking in a seasoned sauce follows this procedure.
Pare: To remove the outermost skin of a fruit or vegetable.
Poach: To cook gently in hot liquid kept just below the boiling point.
Puree: To mash foods by hand by rubbing through a sieve or food mill, or by whirling in a blender or food processor until perfectly smooth.
Refresh: To run cold water over food that has been parboiled in order to stop the cooking process quickly.
Sauté: To cook and/or brown food in a small quantity of hot shortening.
Scald: To heat to just below the boiling point, when tiny bubbles appear at the edge of the saucepan.
Simmer: To cook in liquid just below the boiling point. The surface of the liquid should be barely moving, broken from time to time by slowly rising bubbles.
Steep: To let food stand in hot liquid in order to extract or to enhance flavor, like tea in hot water or poached fruit in sugar syrup.
Toss: To combine ingredients with a repeated lifting motion.
Whip: To beat rapidly in order to incorporate air and produce expansion, as in heavy cream or egg whites.

You supply the recipes and we'll do the rest!™

Publish Your Own Cookbook

Churches, schools, organizations, and families can preserve their favorite recipes by publishing a custom cookbook. Cookbooks make a great **fundraiser** because they are easy to sell and highly profitable. Our low prices make cookbooks the perfect affordable **keepsake**. Morris Press Cookbooks is the nation's leading publisher of community cookbooks. We offer:

- Low prices, high quality, and prompt service.
- Many options and styles to suit your needs.
- 90 days to pay and a written no-risk guarantee.

Order our FREE Cookbook Kit for all the details:

- Call us at 800-445-6621, ext. CB
- Visit our web site at **www.morriscookbooks.com**
- Mail the **postage-paid reply card** below.

Discover the right ingredients for a really great cookbook.

Order our **FREE** Cookbook Kit. Please print neatly.

Name _____

Organization _____

Address _____

City _____ State _____ Zip _____

Email _____

Phone (_____) _____

Back Card 6-06

P. O. Box 2110 • Kearney, NE 68848

Morris Press Cookbooks has all the right ingredients to make a really great cookbook. Your group can raise $500–$50,000 or create a cookbook as a lasting keepsake, preserving favorite family recipes.

3 ways to order our **FREE** Cookbook Kit:
- Call us at **800-445-6621, ext. CB**.
- Visit our web site at **www.morriscookbooks.com**.
- Complete and mail the **postage-paid reply card** below.

BUSINESS REPLY MAIL
FIRST-CLASS MAIL   PERMIT NO. 36   KEARNEY, NE

POSTAGE WILL BE PAID BY ADDRESSEE

Morris Press Cookbooks
P.O. Box 2110
Kearney, NE 68848-9985